BATTLE
ANGEL ALITA
CHRONICLE **8**
by YUKITO KISHIRO

BATTLE ANGEL ALITA MARS CHRONICLE
PRESENTED by YUKITO KISHIRO

CONTENTS

ADDITIONAL STAFF:
TSUTOMU KISHIRO / EMIYA KINARI

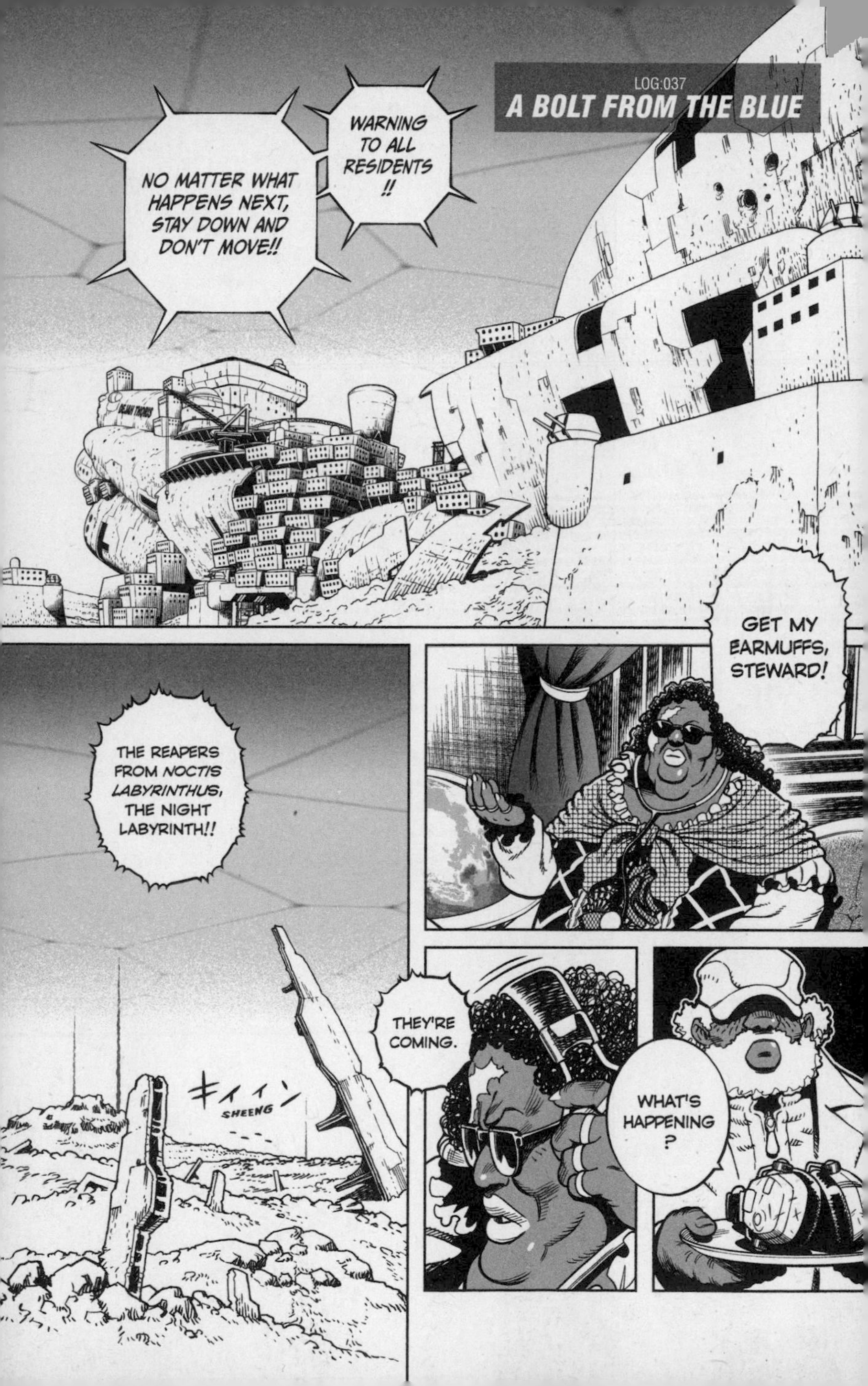
LOG:037
A BOLT FROM THE BLUE
WARNING TO ALL RESIDENTS !!
NO MATTER WHAT HAPPENS NEXT, STAY DOWN AND DON'T MOVE!!
GET MY EARMUFFS, STEWARD!
WHAT'S HAPPENING ?
THEY'RE COMING.
THE REAPERS FROM *NOCTIS LABYRINTHUS*, THE NIGHT LABYRINTH!!
キイン
SHEENG

LOG:037

A BOLT FROM THE BLUE

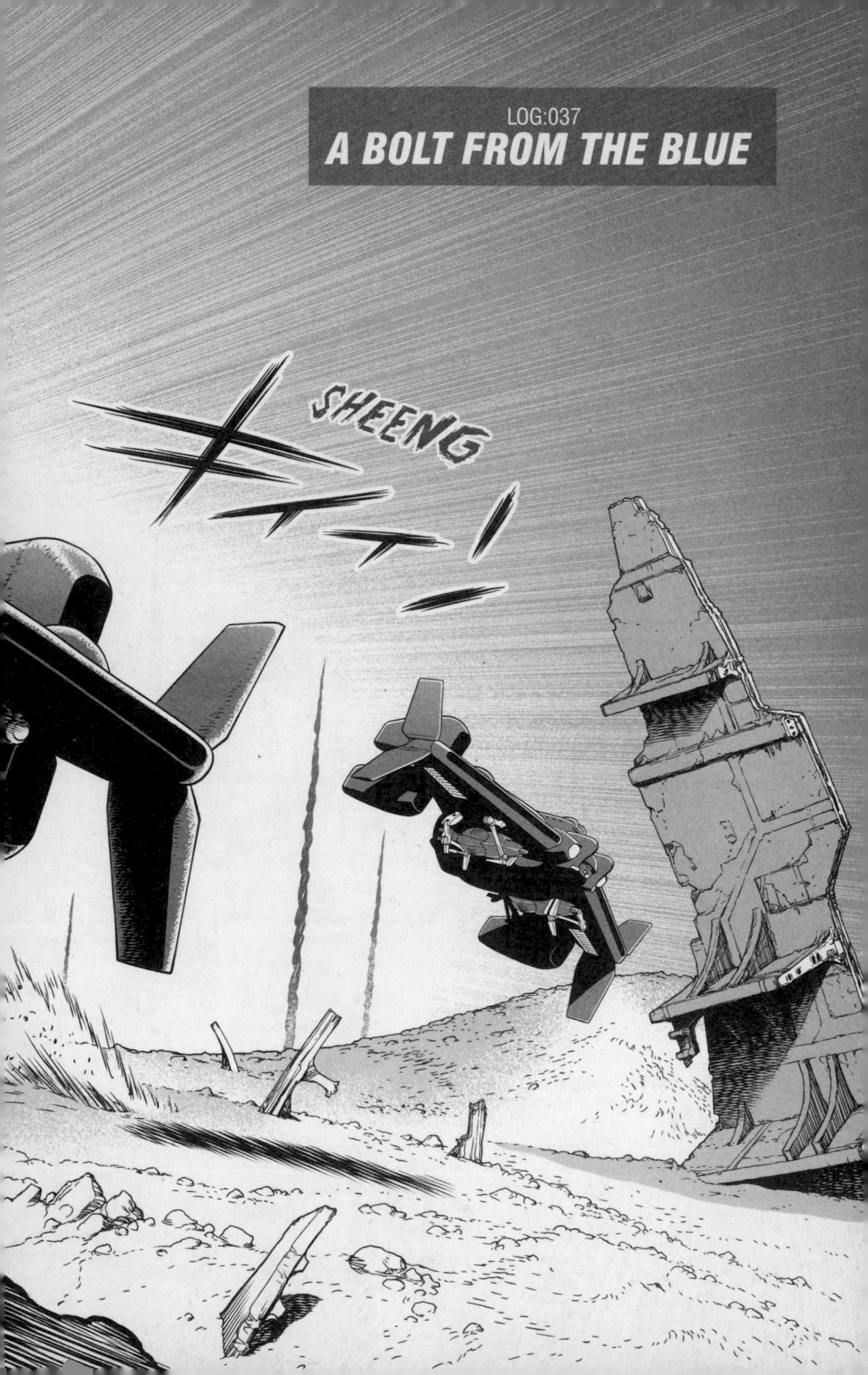
SHEENG

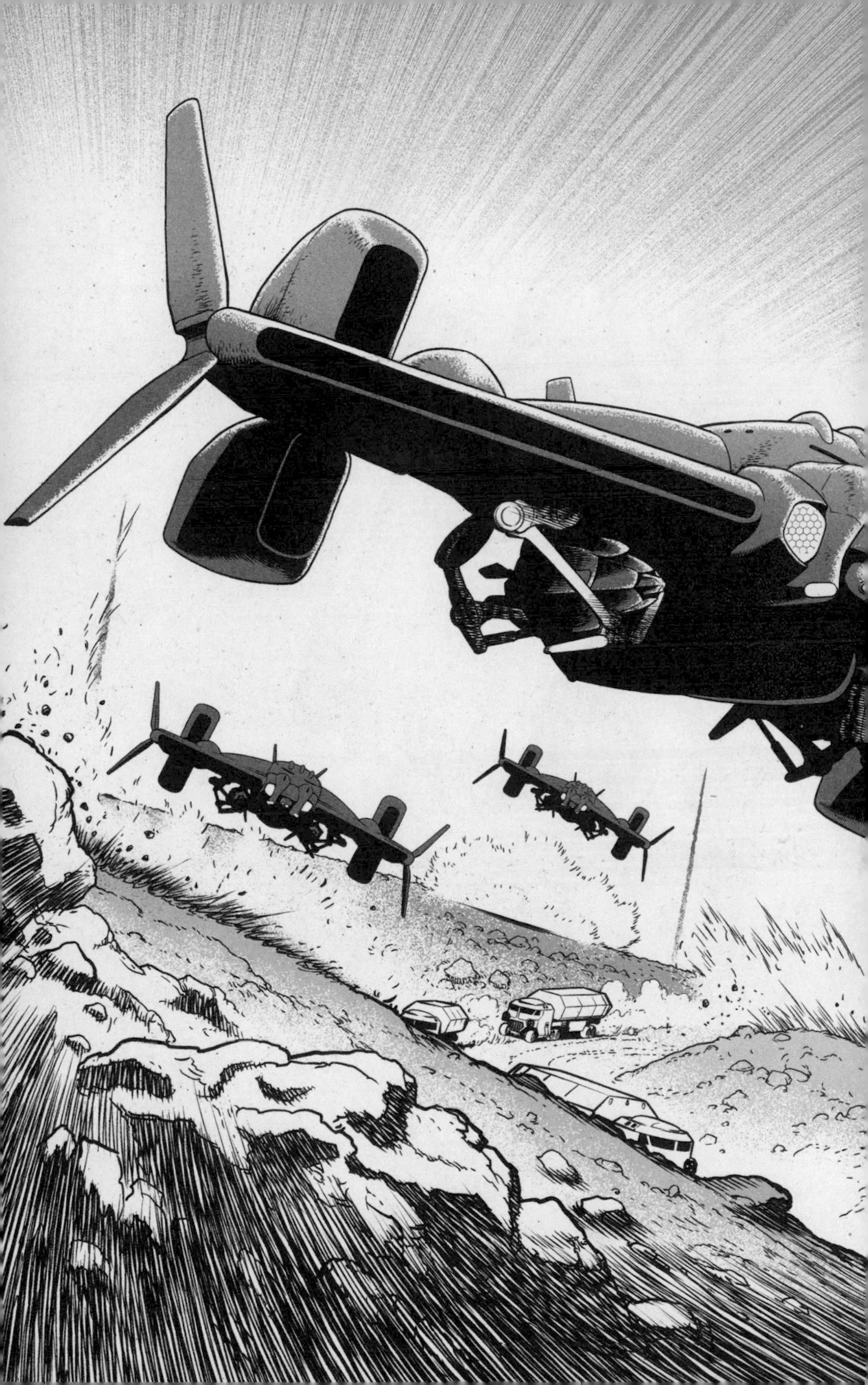

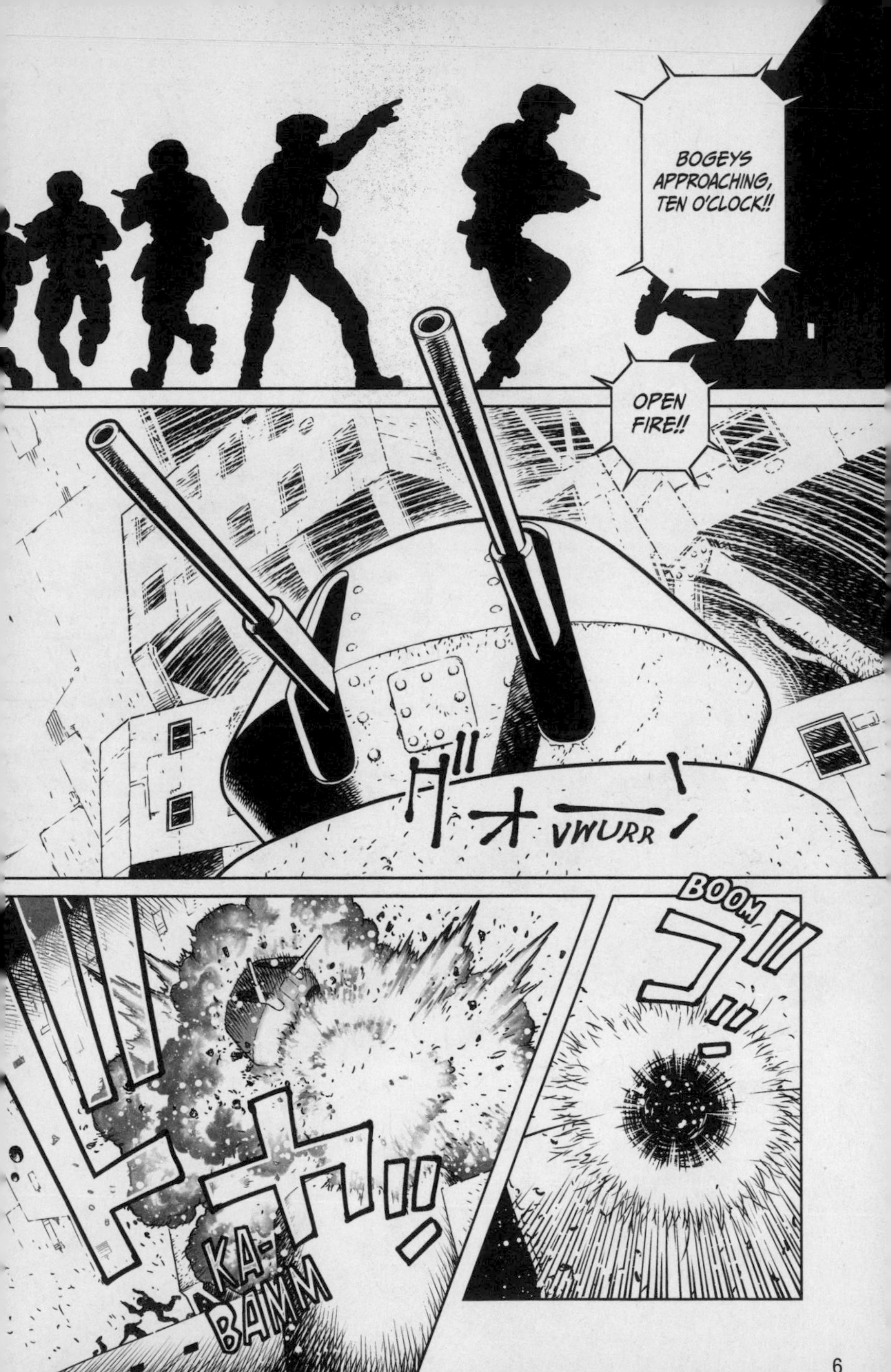
BOGEYS APPROACHING, TEN O'CLOCK!!
OPEN FIRE!!
VWURR
BOOM
KA-BAMM

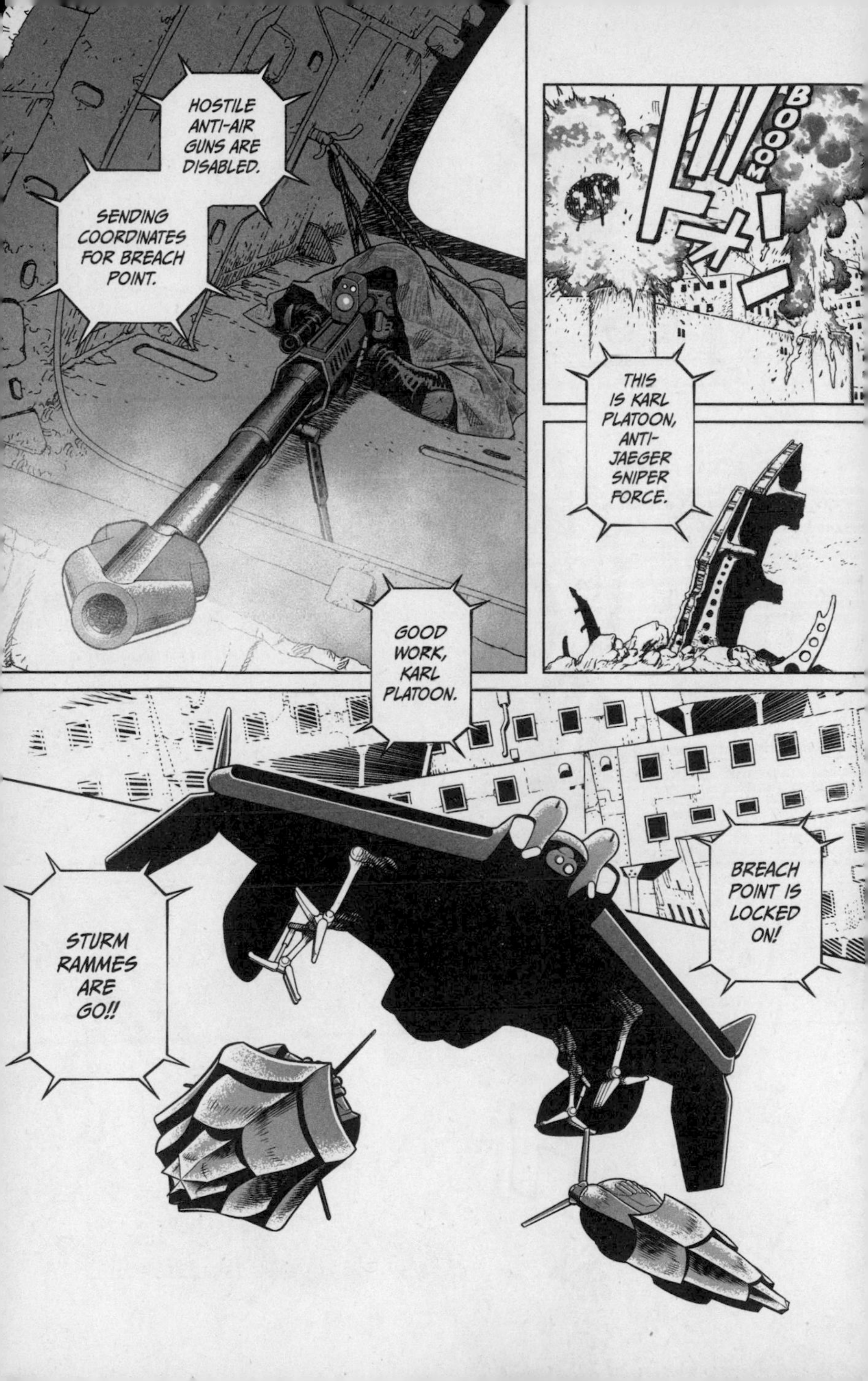
BOOOOM
THIS IS KARL PLATOON, ANTI-JAEGER SNIPER FORCE.
HOSTILE ANTI-AIR GUNS ARE DISABLED.
SENDING COORDINATES FOR BREACH POINT.
GOOD WORK, KARL PLATOON.
BREACH POINT IS LOCKED ON!
STURM RAMMES ARE GO!!

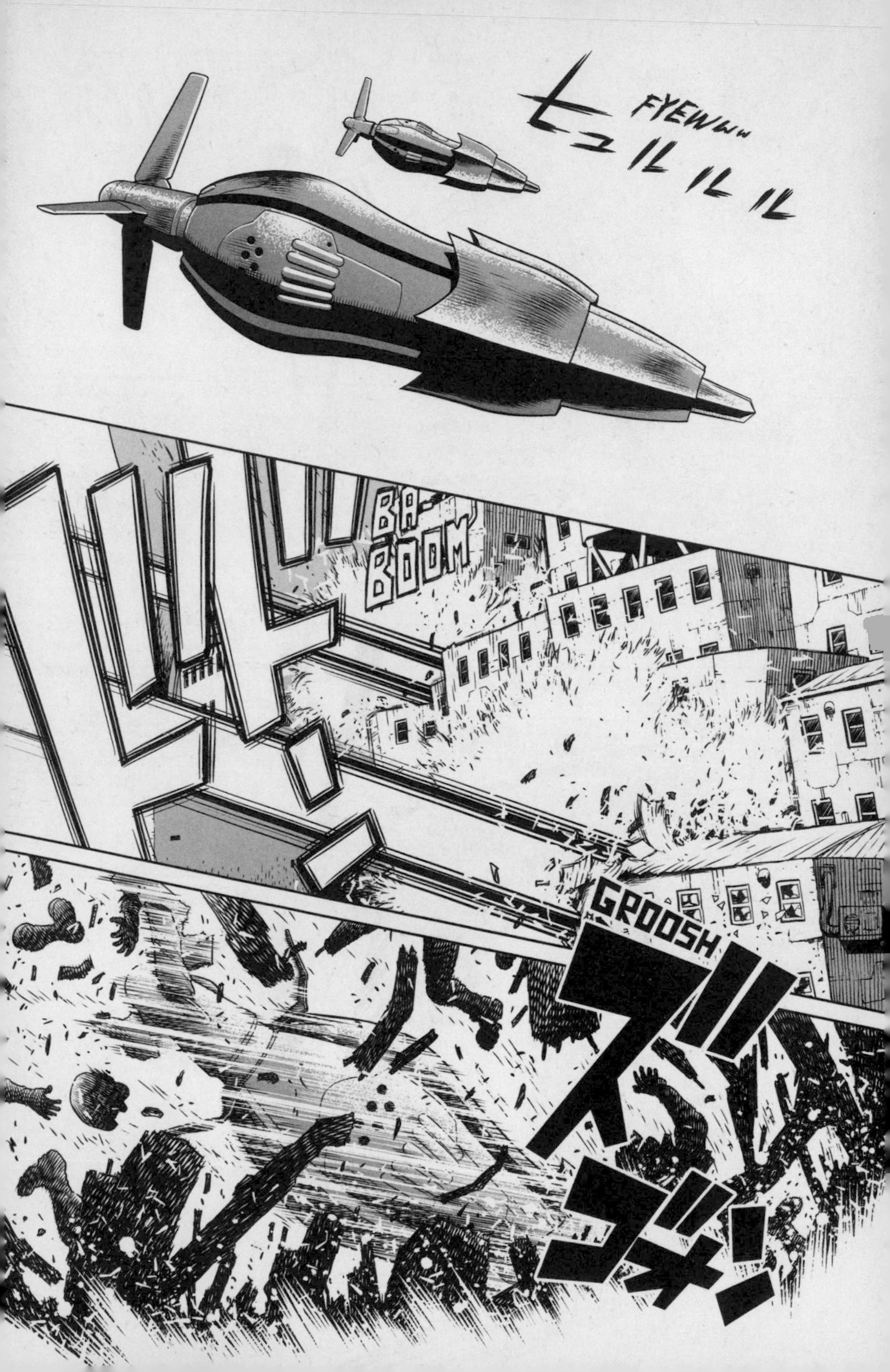
FYEWww
ヒュルルル
BA-BOOM
GROOSH

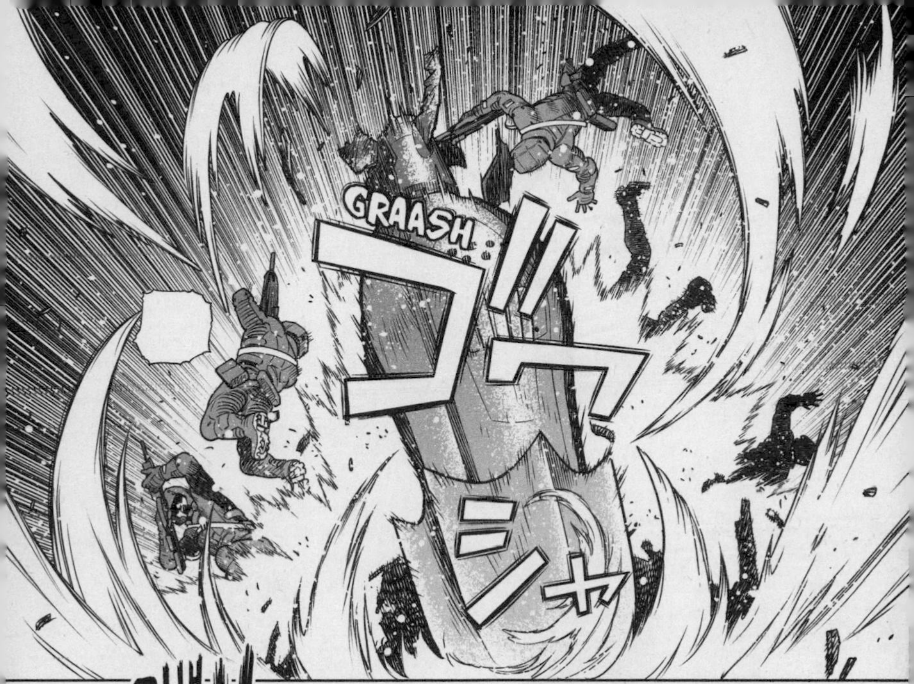
GRAASH
ゴワシャ
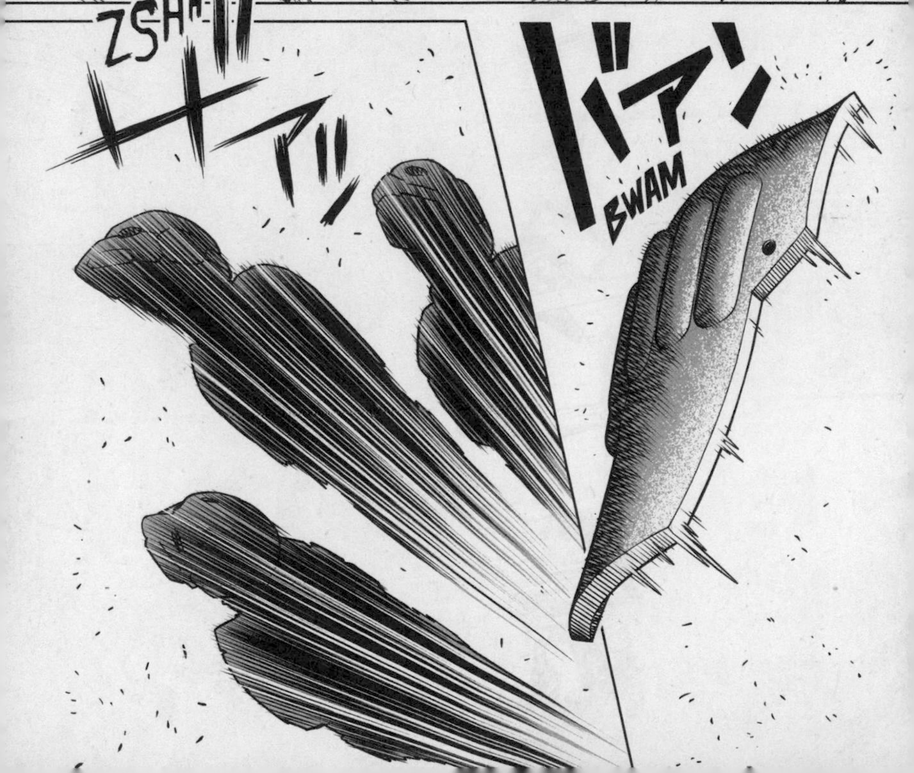
バアン
BWAM
ZSHH
ザアッ

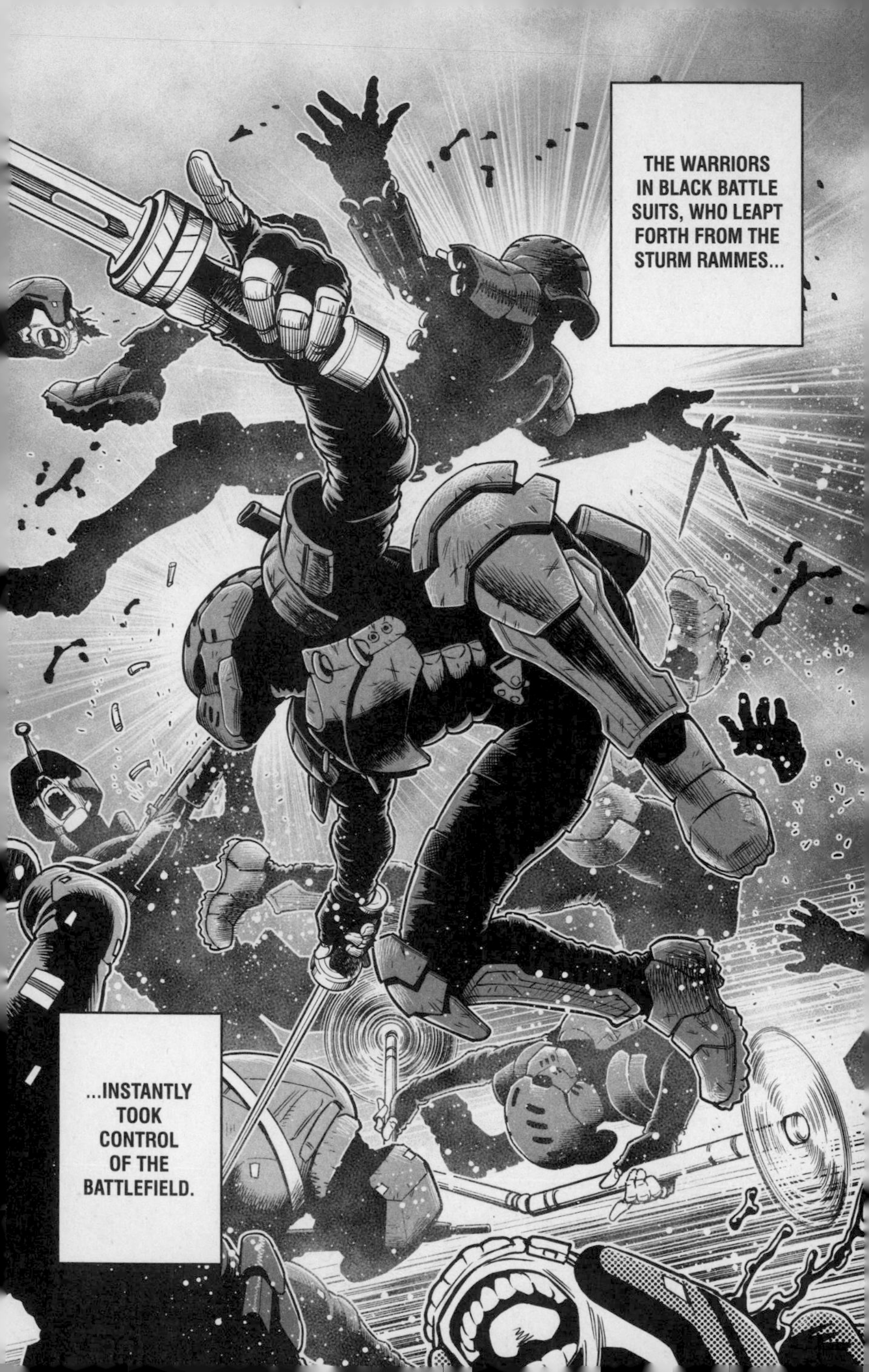
THE WARRIORS IN BLACK BATTLE SUITS, WHO LEAPT FORTH FROM THE STURM RAMMES...
...INSTANTLY TOOK CONTROL OF THE BATTLEFIELD.

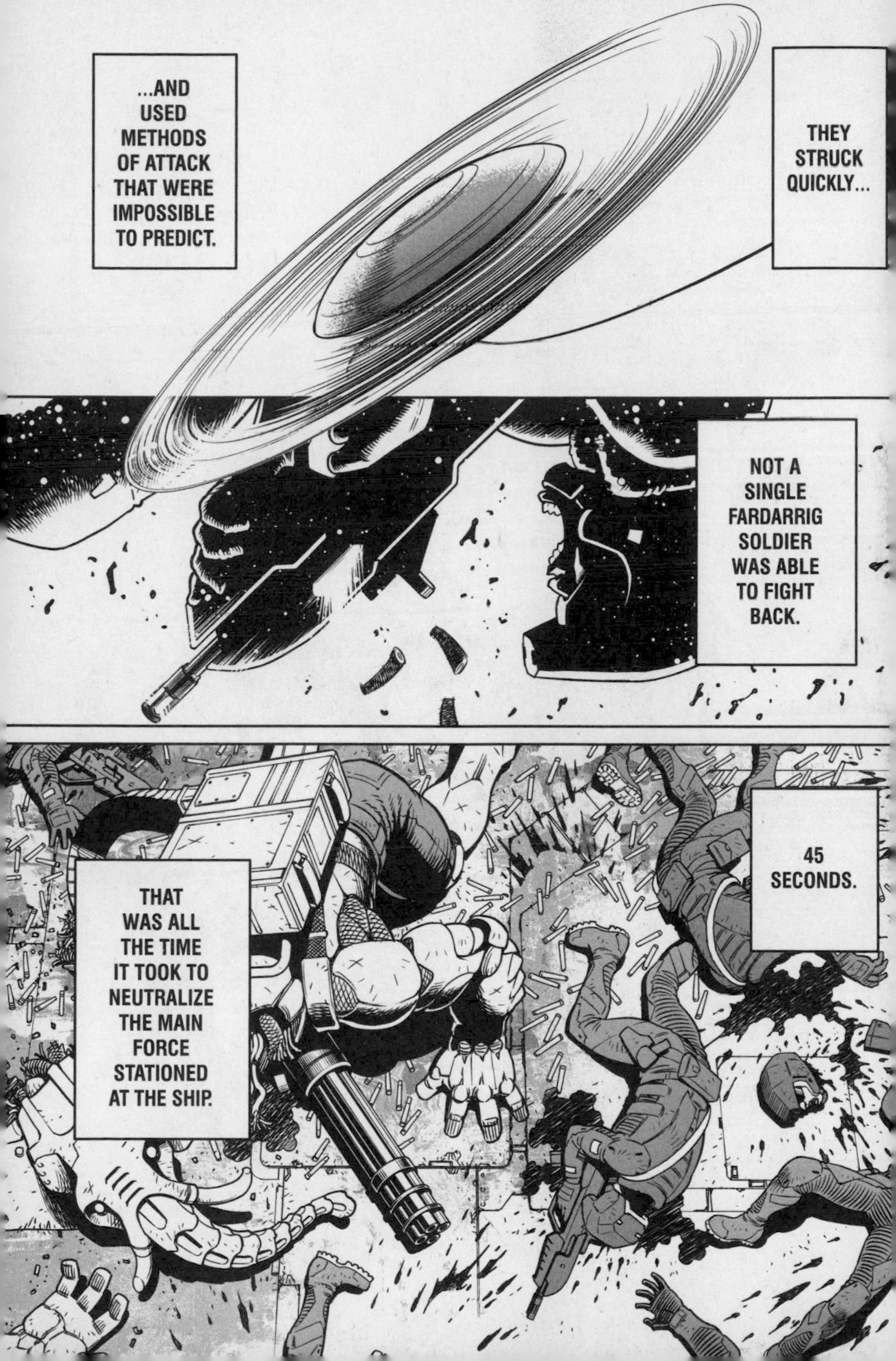
THEY STRUCK QUICKLY...
...AND USED METHODS OF ATTACK THAT WERE IMPOSSIBLE TO PREDICT.
NOT A SINGLE FARDARRIG SOLDIER WAS ABLE TO FIGHT BACK.
45 SECONDS.
THAT WAS ALL THE TIME IT TOOK TO NEUTRALIZE THE MAIN FORCE STATIONED AT THE SHIP.

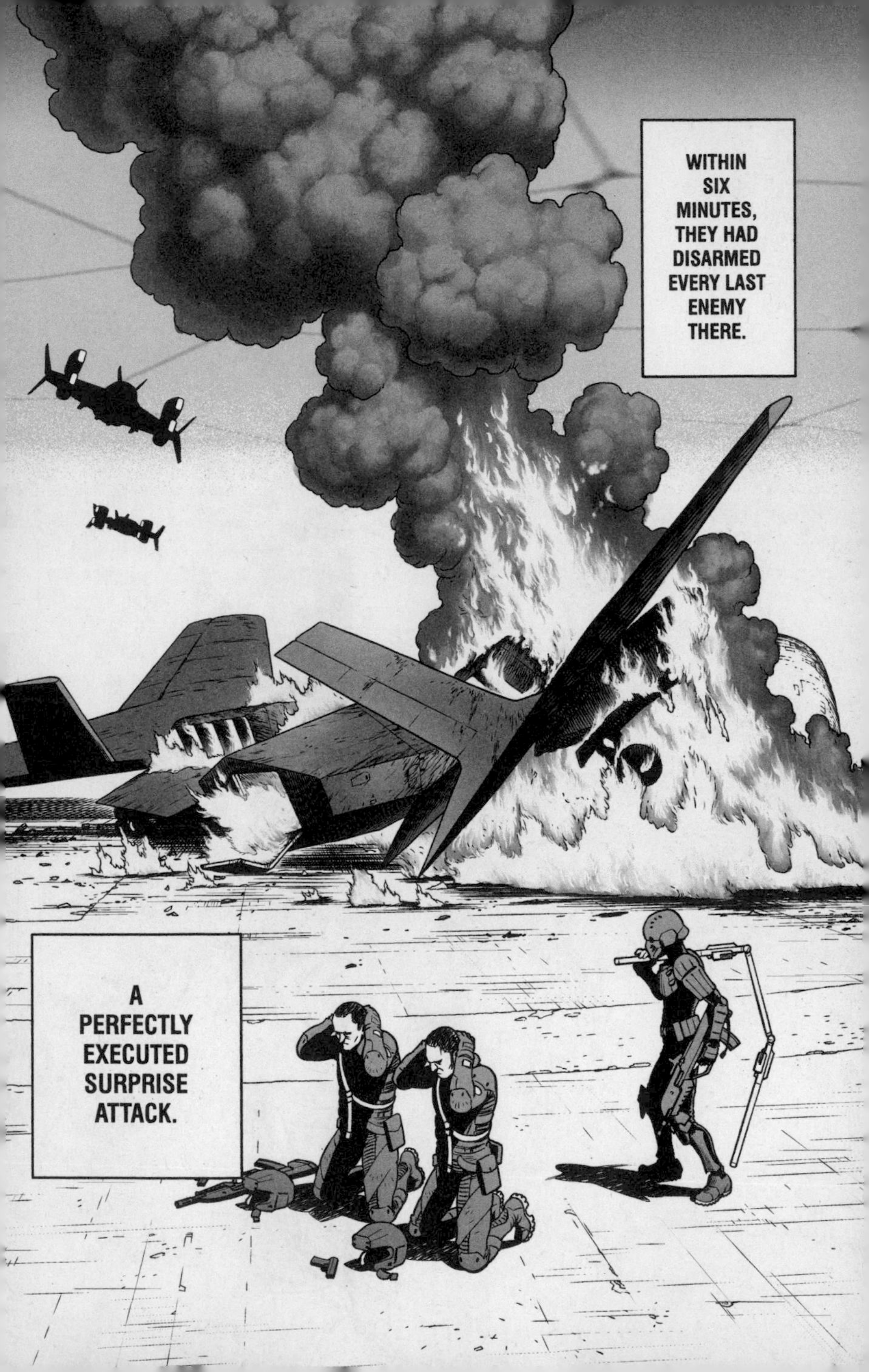
WITHIN SIX MINUTES, THEY HAD DISARMED EVERY LAST ENEMY THERE.
A PERFECTLY EXECUTED SURPRISE ATTACK.

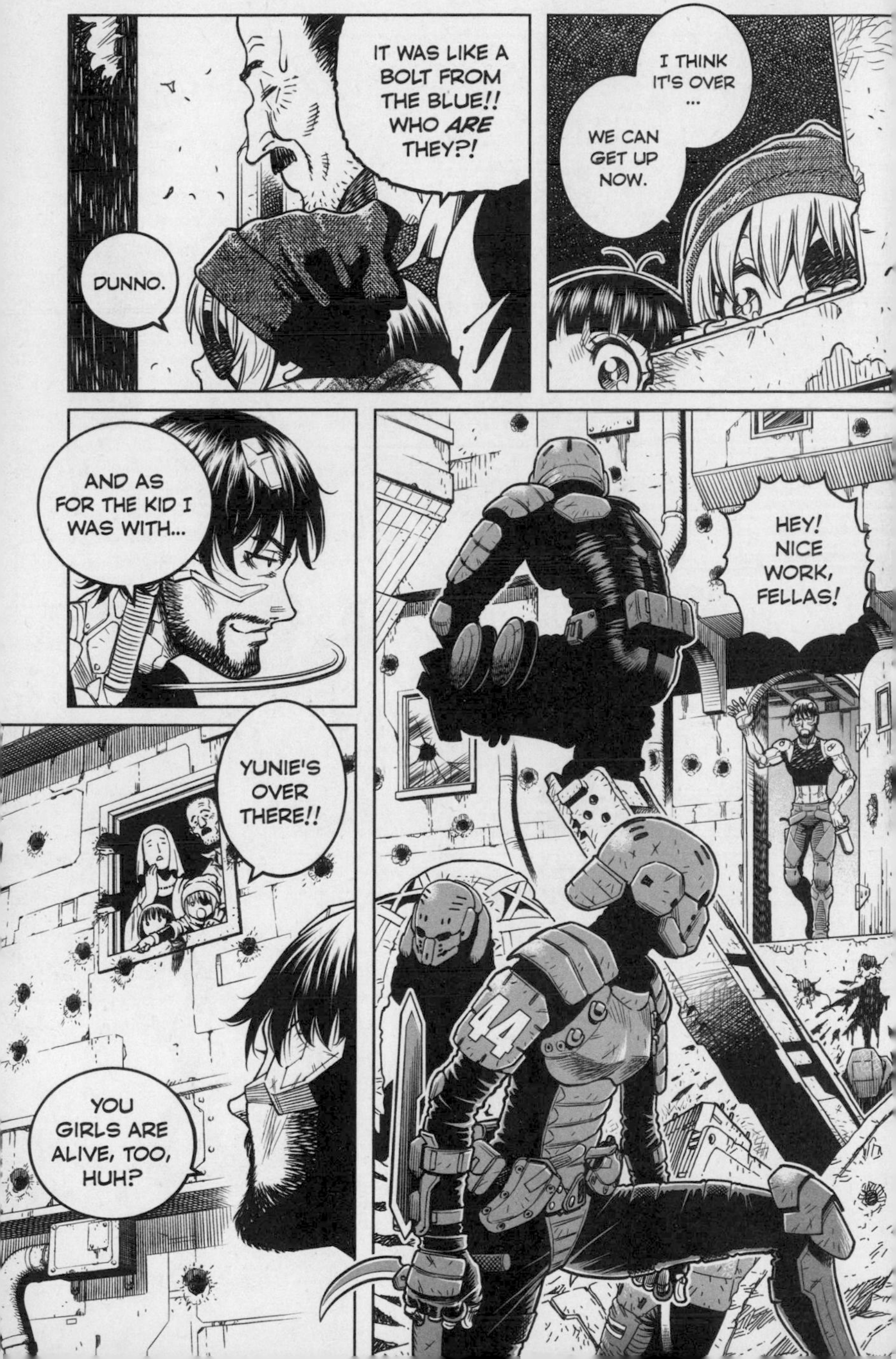
I THINK IT'S OVER ...
WE CAN GET UP NOW.
IT WAS LIKE A BOLT FROM THE BLUE!! WHO *ARE* THEY?!
DUNNO.
HEY! NICE WORK, FELLAS!
AND AS FOR THE KID I WAS WITH...
YUNIE'S OVER THERE!!
YOU GIRLS ARE ALIVE, TOO, HUH?

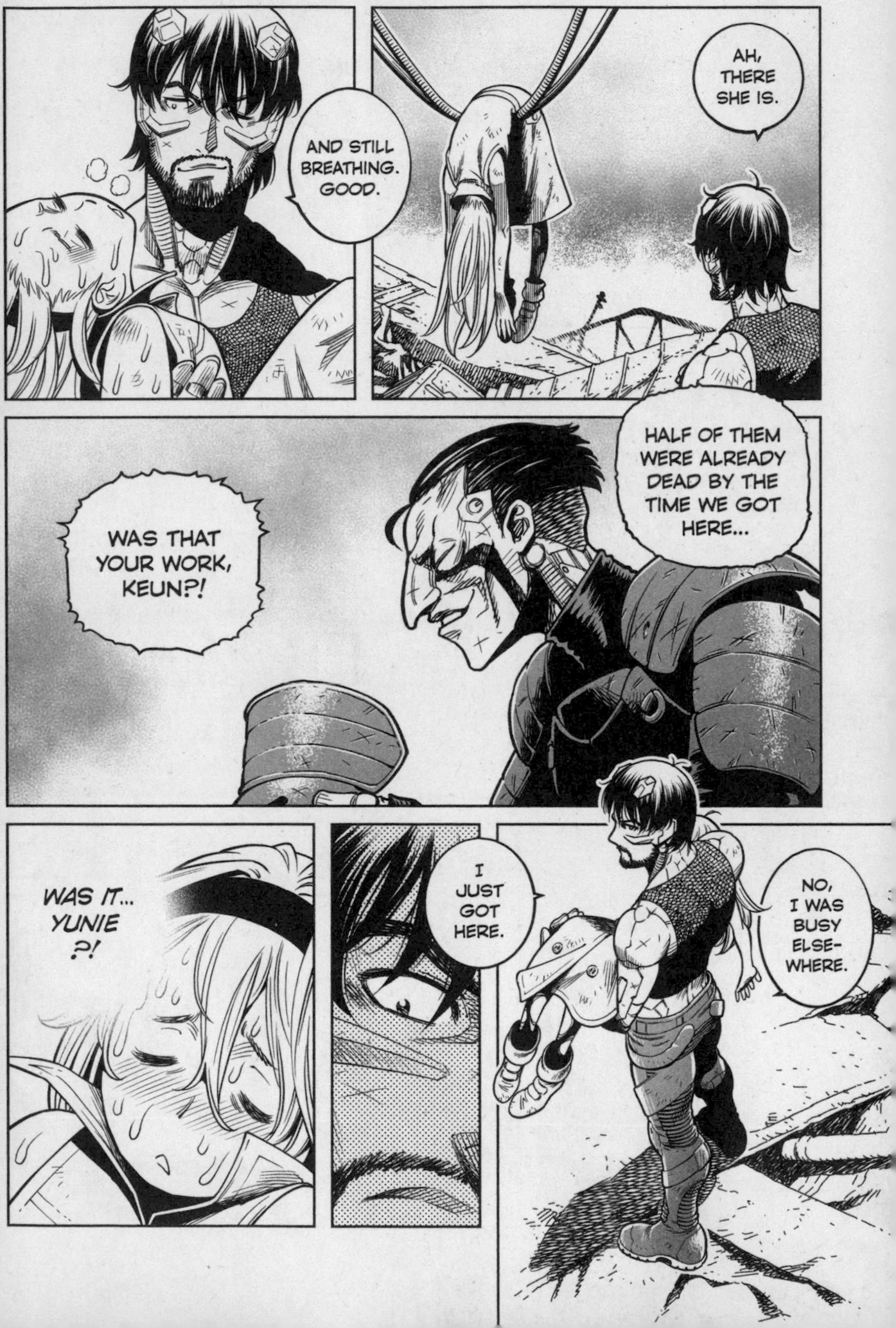
AH, THERE SHE IS.
AND STILL BREATHING. GOOD.
HALF OF THEM WERE ALREADY DEAD BY THE TIME WE GOT HERE...
WAS THAT YOUR WORK, KEUN?!
NO, I WAS BUSY ELSE-WHERE.
I JUST GOT HERE.
WAS IT... YUNIE ?!

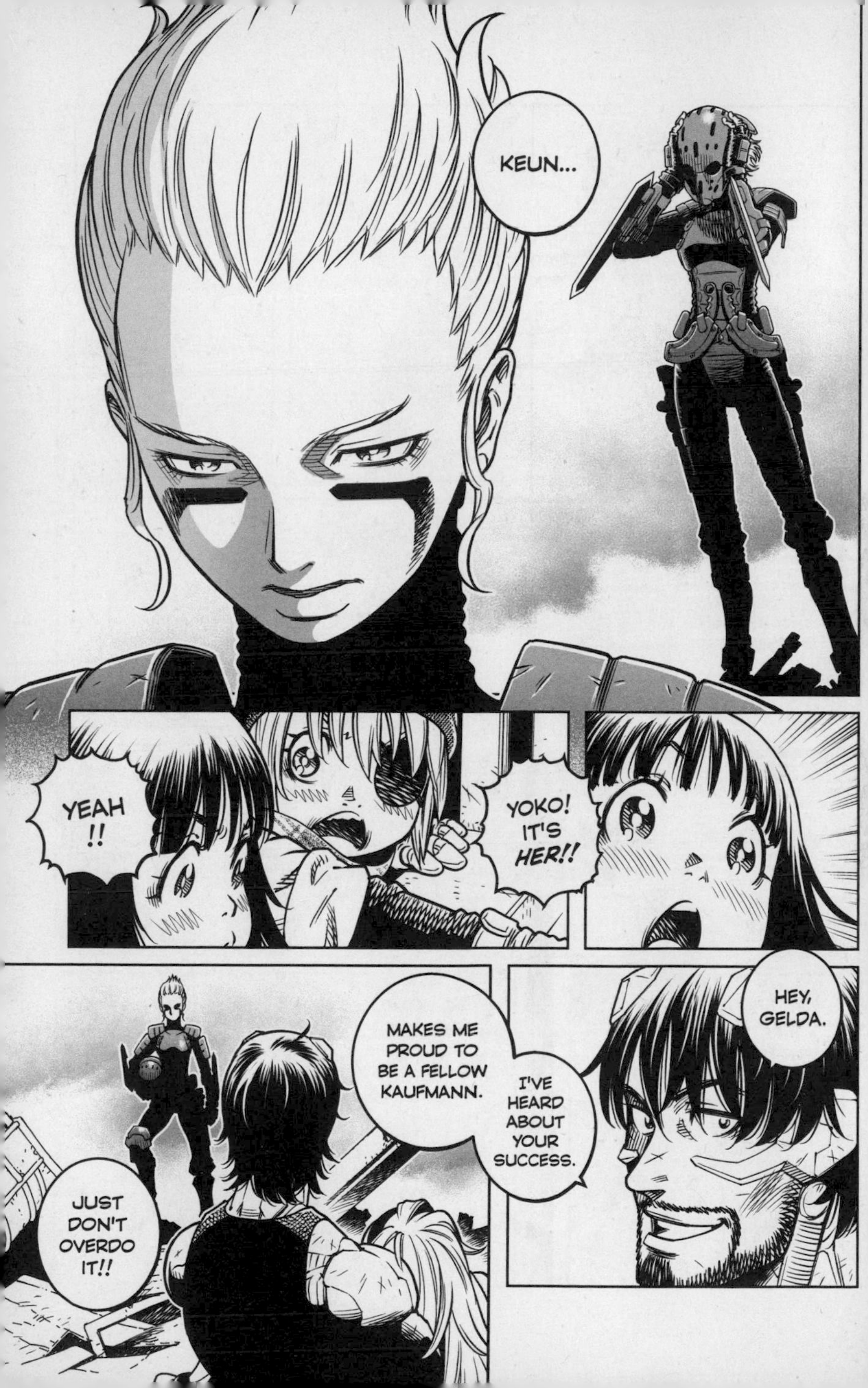
KEUN...
YOKO! IT'S HER!!
YEAH !!
HEY, GELDA.
I'VE HEARD ABOUT YOUR SUCCESS.
MAKES ME PROUD TO BE A FELLOW KAUFMANN.
JUST DON'T OVERDO IT!!

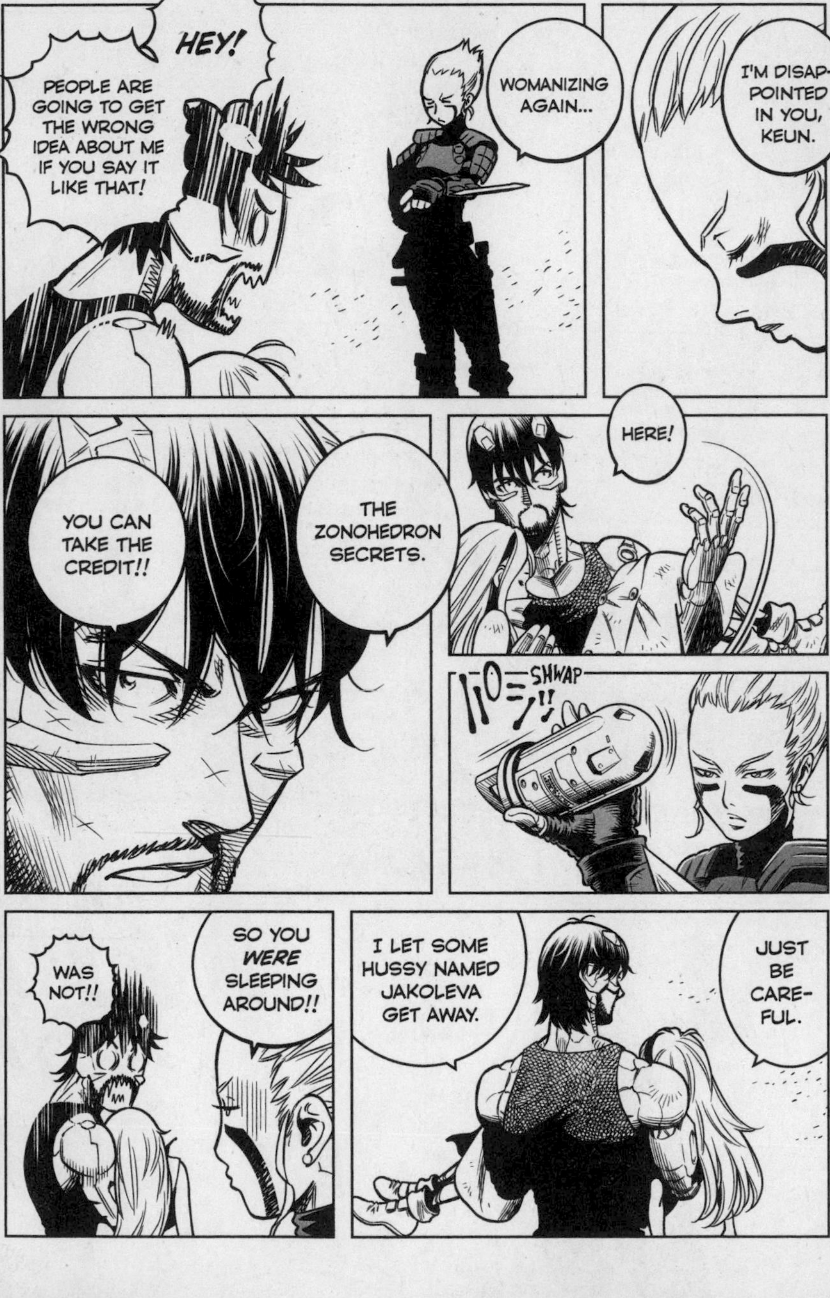
I'M DISAPPOINTED IN YOU, KEUN.
WOMANIZING AGAIN...
HEY!
PEOPLE ARE GOING TO GET THE WRONG IDEA ABOUT ME IF YOU SAY IT LIKE THAT!
HERE!
SHWAP !!
THE ZONOHEDRON SECRETS.
YOU CAN TAKE THE CREDIT!!
JUST BE CAREFUL.
I LET SOME HUSSY NAMED JAKOLEVA GET AWAY.
SO YOU *WERE* SLEEPING AROUND!!
WAS NOT!!

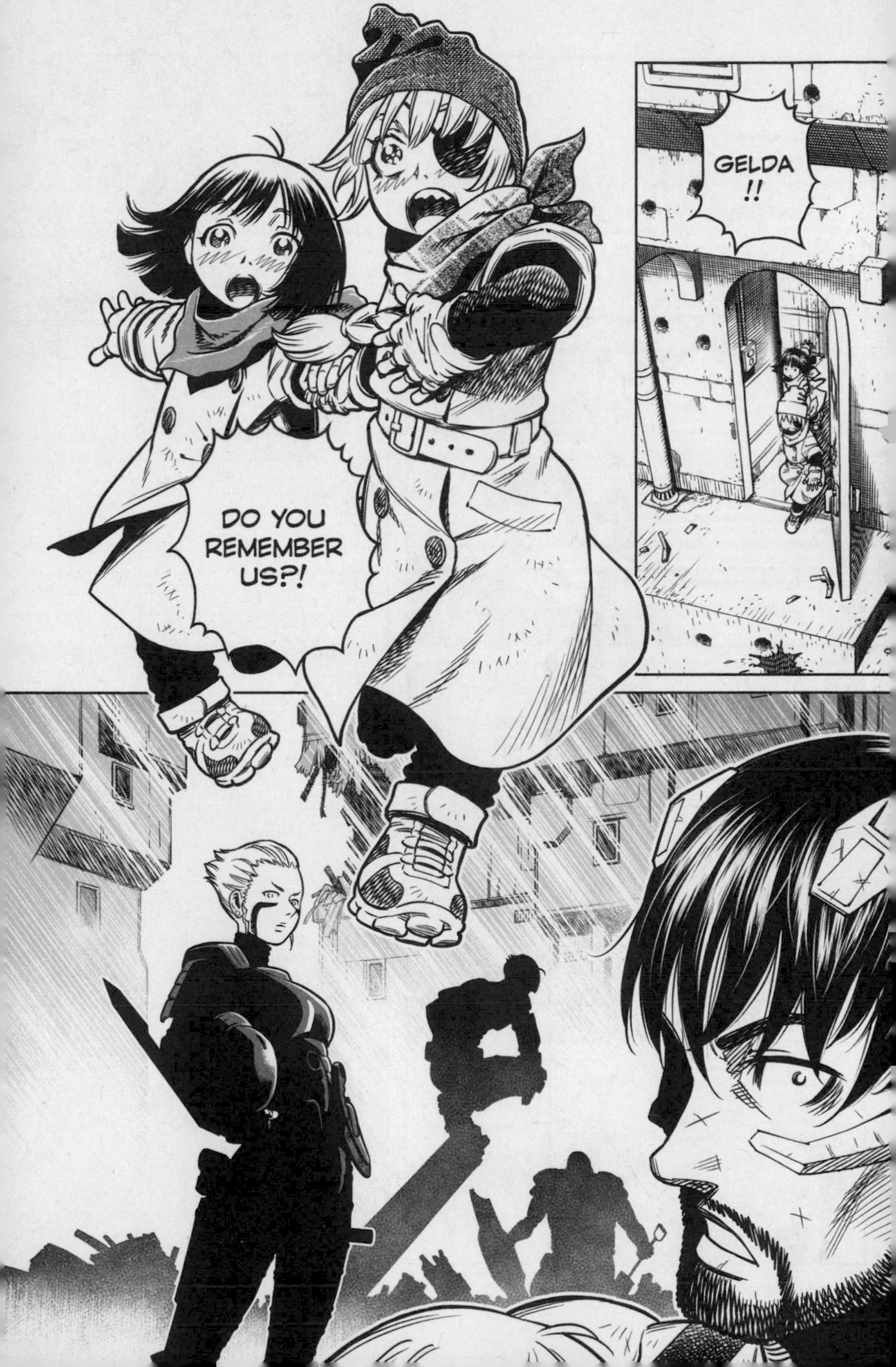
GELDA !!
DO YOU REMEMBER US?!

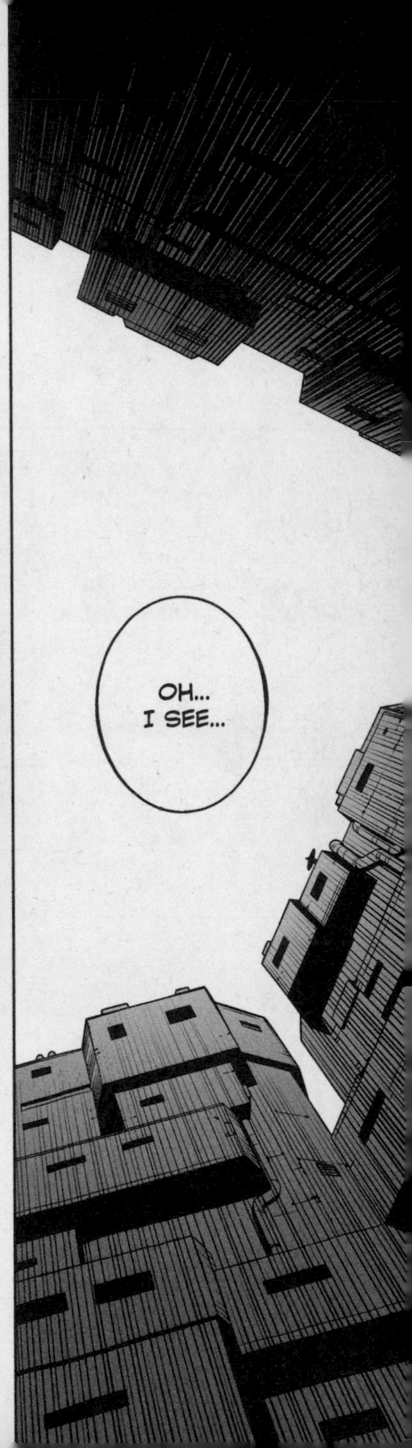
OH... I SEE...

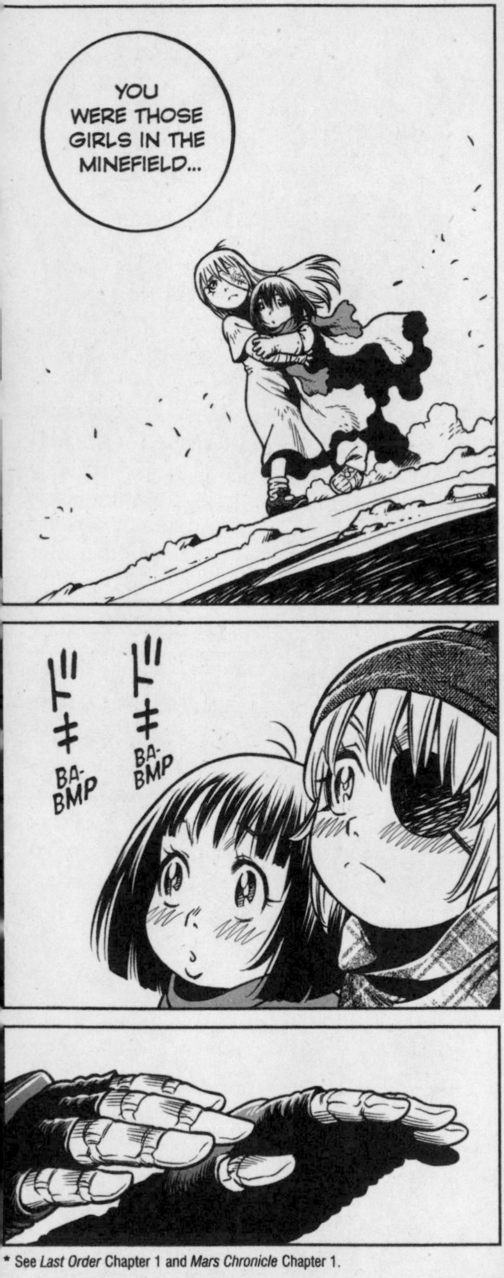
YOU WERE THOSE GIRLS IN THE MINEFIELD...
ドキ BA-BMP
ドキ BA-BMP

* See *Last Order* Chapter 1 and *Mars Chronicle* Chapter 1.

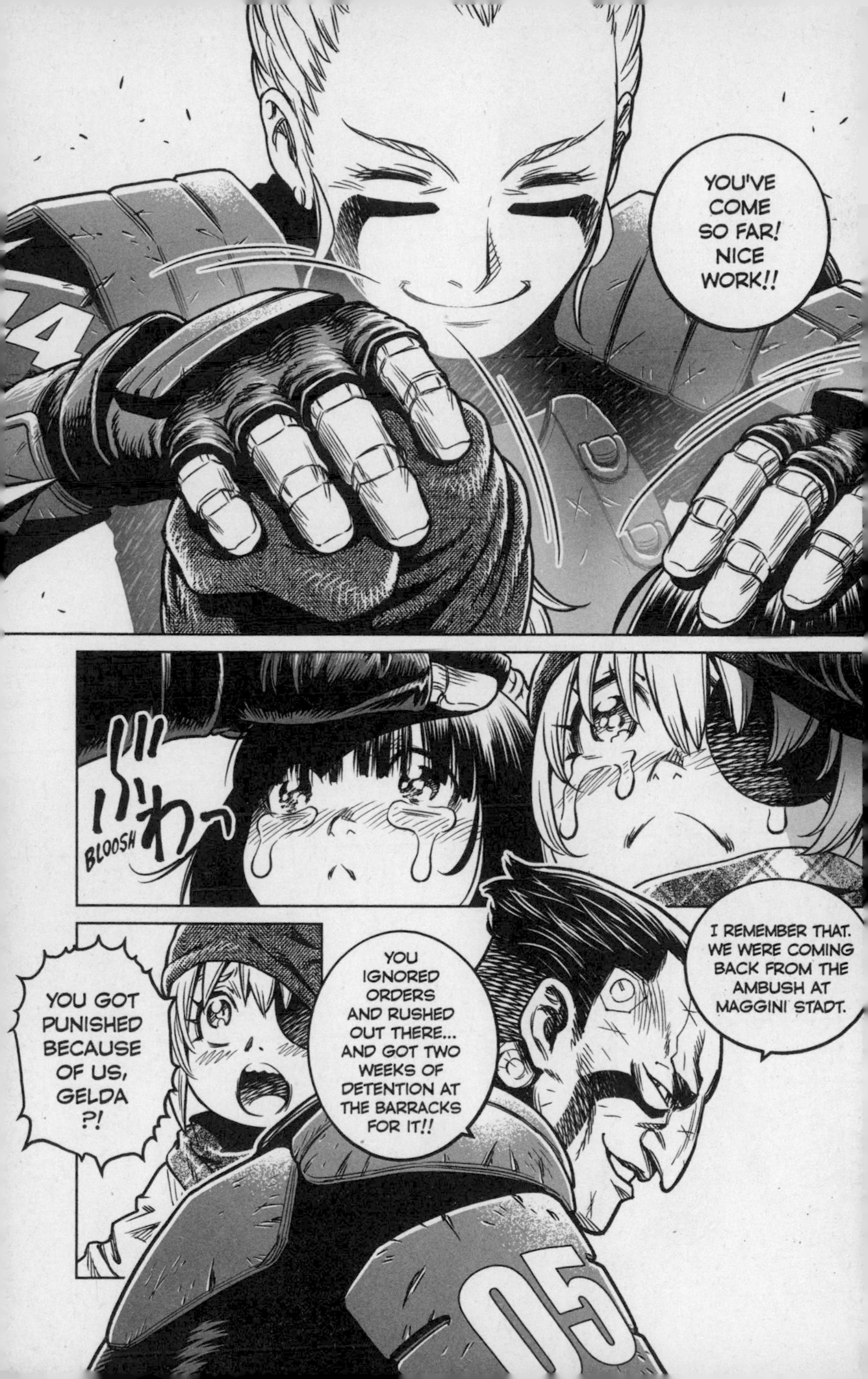
YOU'VE COME SO FAR! NICE WORK!!
ぶわっ
BLOOSH
I REMEMBER THAT. WE WERE COMING BACK FROM THE AMBUSH AT MAGGINI STADT.
YOU IGNORED ORDERS AND RUSHED OUT THERE... AND GOT TWO WEEKS OF DETENTION AT THE BARRACKS FOR IT!!
YOU GOT PUNISHED BECAUSE OF US, GELDA ?!

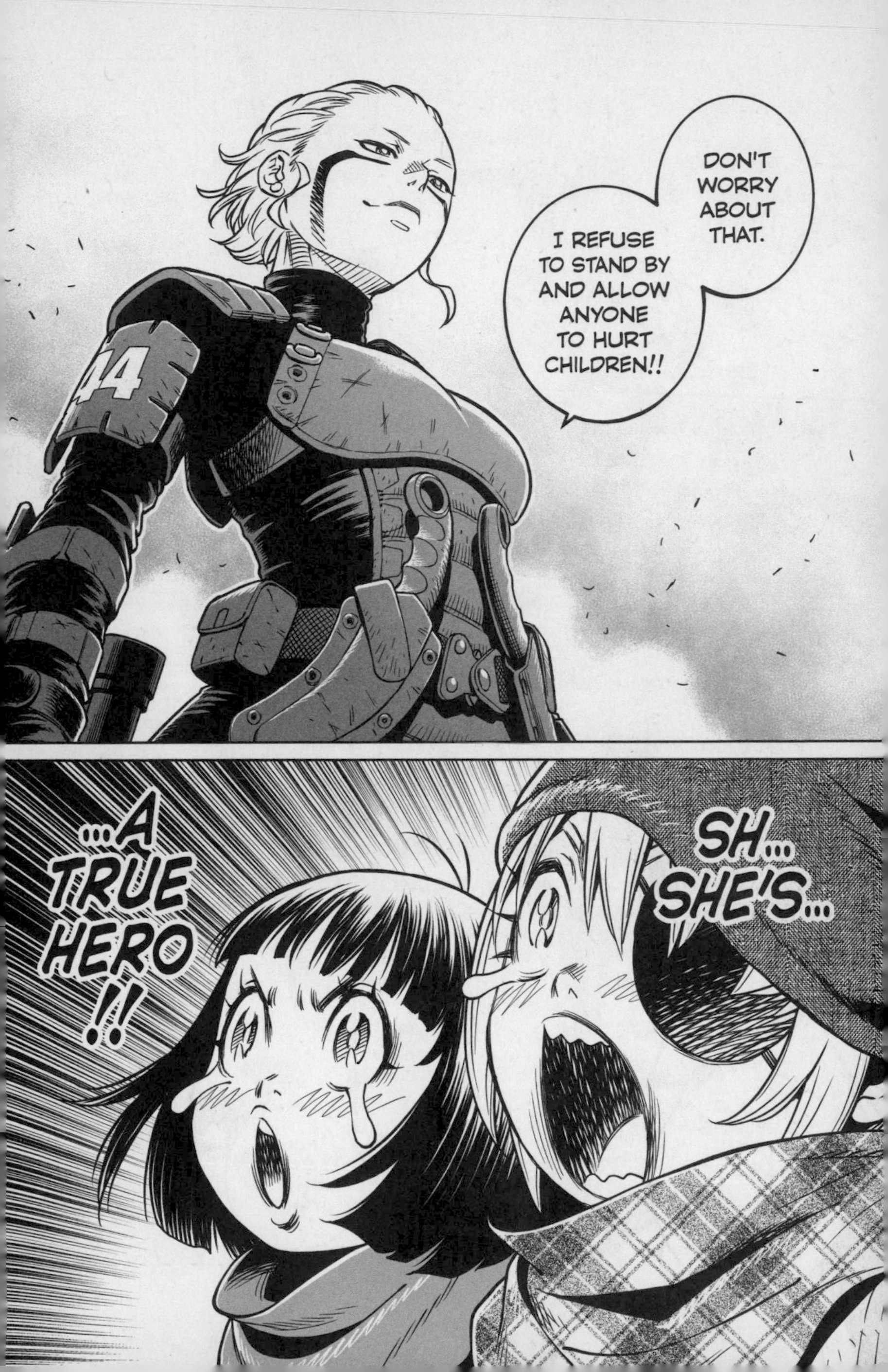
DON'T WORRY ABOUT THAT.
I REFUSE TO STAND BY AND ALLOW ANYONE TO HURT CHILDREN!!
SH... SHE'S...
...A TRUE HERO!!

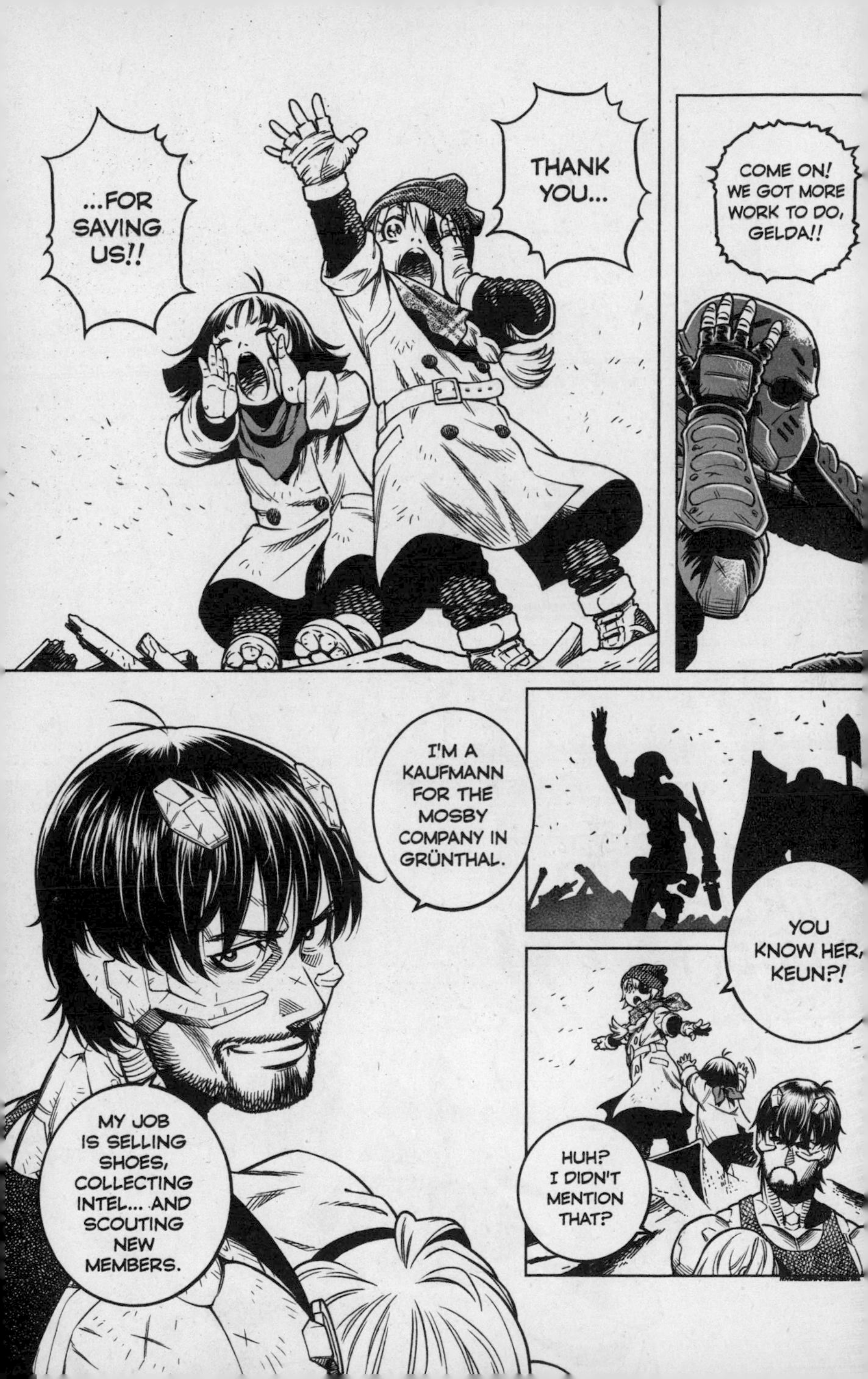
COME ON! WE GOT MORE WORK TO DO, GELDA!!
THANK YOU...
...FOR SAVING US!!
YOU KNOW HER, KEUN?!
HUH? I DIDN'T MENTION THAT?
I'M A KAUFMANN FOR THE MOSBY COMPANY IN GRÜNTHAL.
MY JOB IS SELLING SHOES, COLLECTING INTEL... AND SCOUTING NEW MEMBERS.

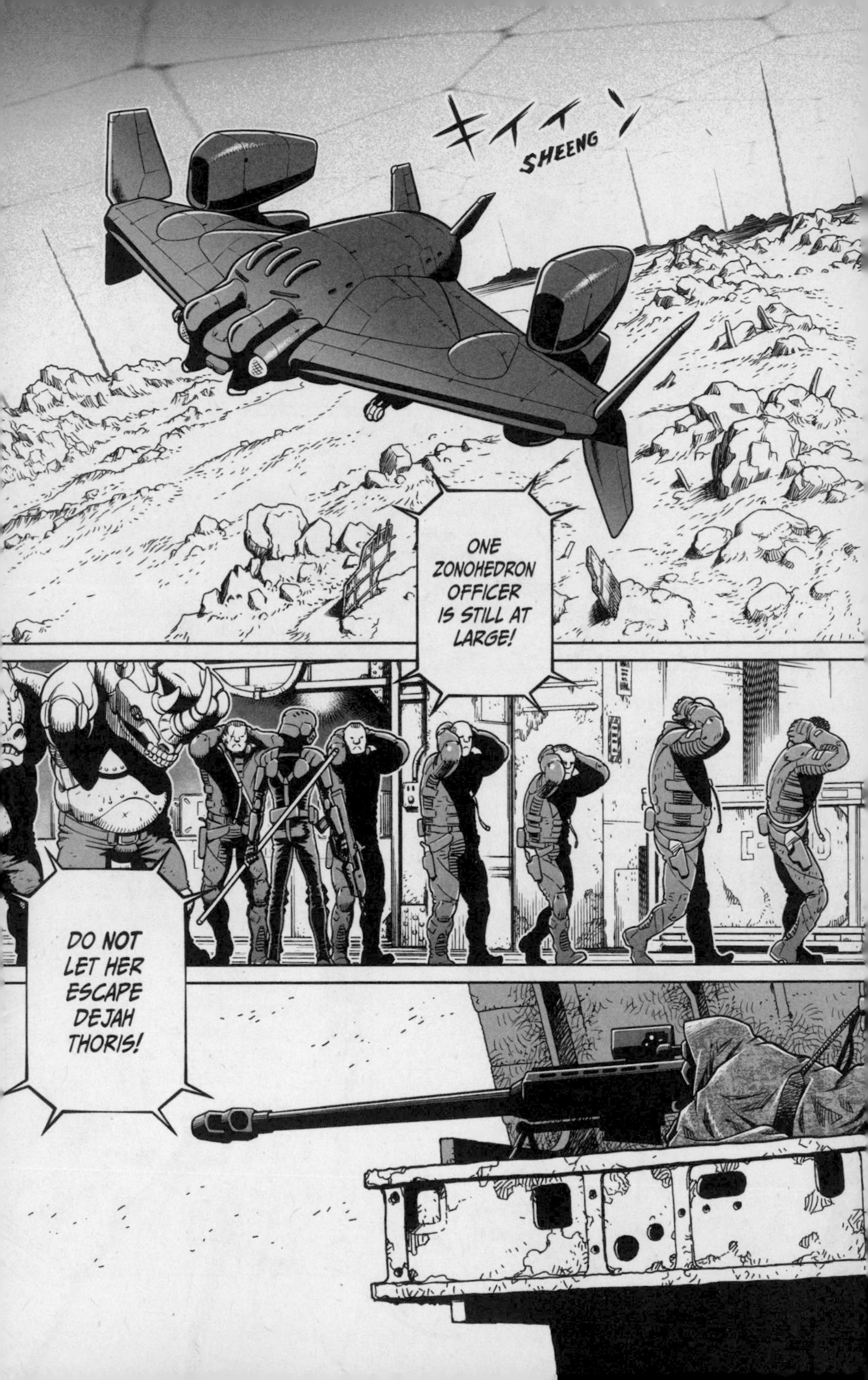
キイイン
SHEENG
ONE ZONOHEDRON OFFICER IS STILL AT LARGE!
DO NOT LET HER ESCAPE DEJAH THORIS!

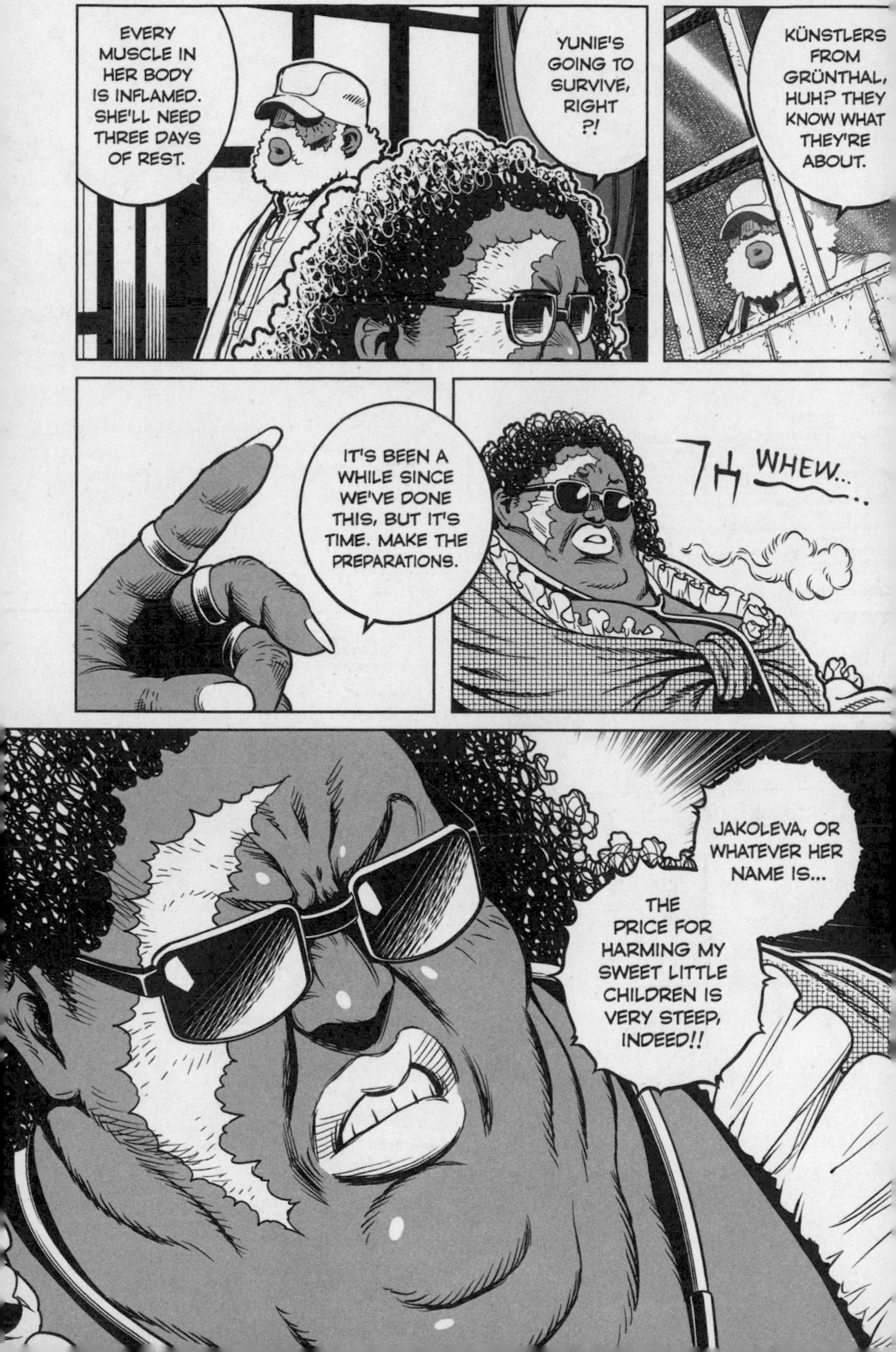
KÜNSTLERS FROM GRÜNTHAL, HUH? THEY KNOW WHAT THEY'RE ABOUT.
YUNIE'S GOING TO SURVIVE, RIGHT ?!
EVERY MUSCLE IN HER BODY IS INFLAMED. SHE'LL NEED THREE DAYS OF REST.
WHEW...
IT'S BEEN A WHILE SINCE WE'VE DONE THIS, BUT IT'S TIME. MAKE THE PREPARATIONS.
JAKOLEVA, OR WHATEVER HER NAME IS...
THE PRICE FOR HARMING MY SWEET LITTLE CHILDREN IS VERY STEEP, INDEED!!

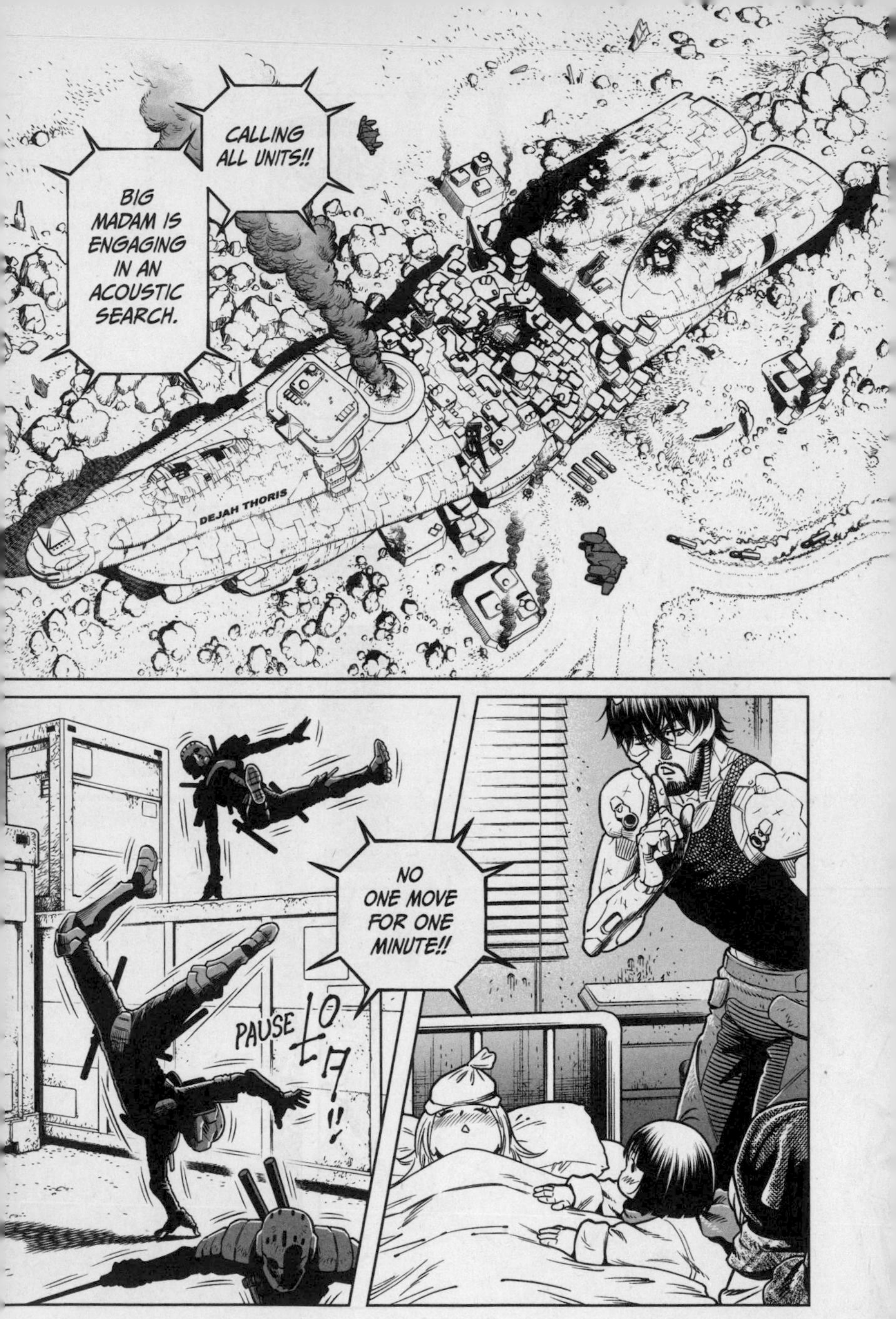
CALLING ALL UNITS!!
BIG MADAM IS ENGAGING IN AN ACOUSTIC SEARCH.
DEJAH THORIS
NO ONE MOVE FOR ONE MINUTE!!
PAUSE

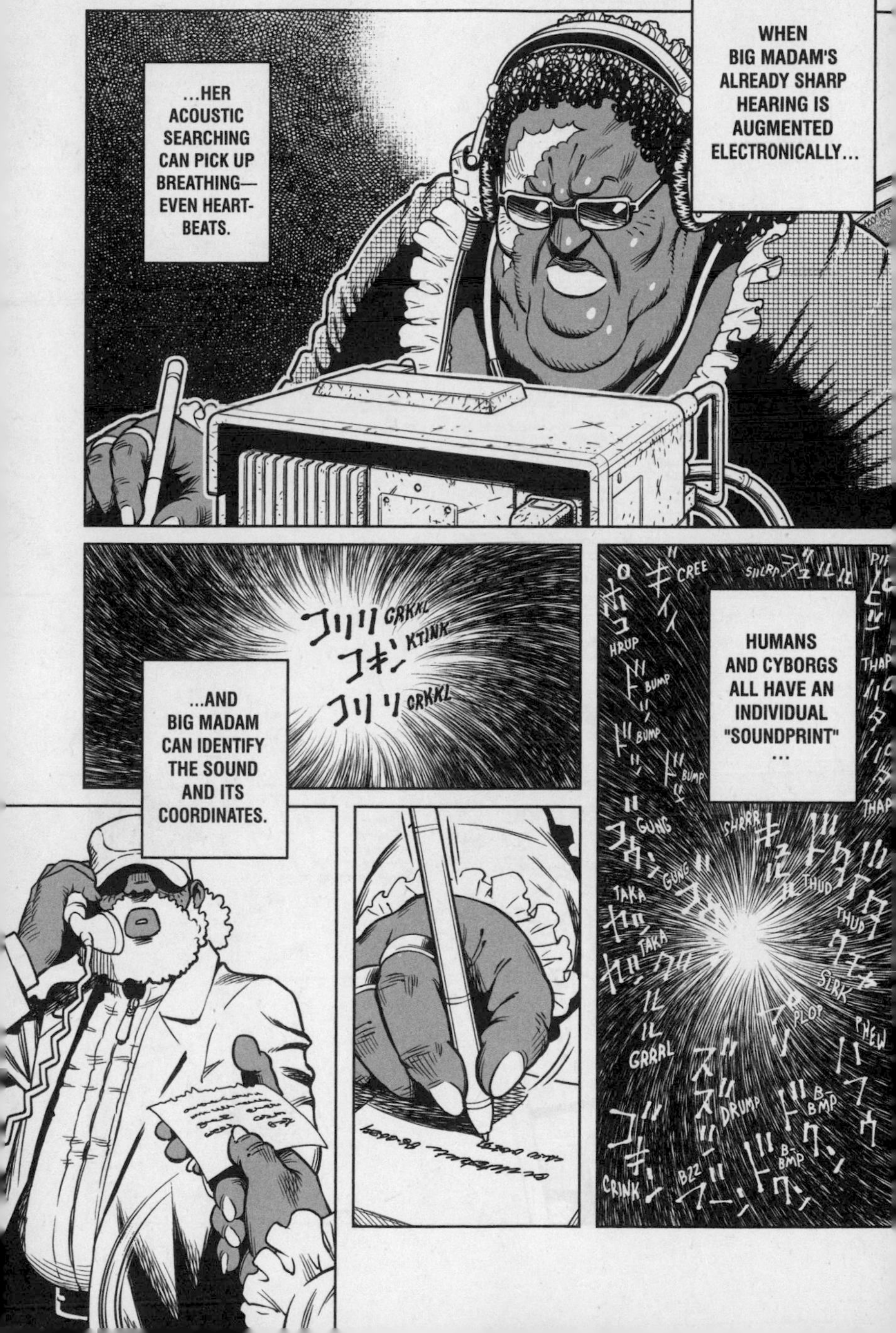
WHEN BIG MADAM'S ALREADY SHARP HEARING IS AUGMENTED ELECTRONICALLY...
...HER ACOUSTIC SEARCHING CAN PICK UP BREATHING—EVEN HEART-BEATS.
HUMANS AND CYBORGS ALL HAVE AN INDIVIDUAL "SOUNDPRINT" ...
CREE
SHLRP
HRUP
BUMP
BUMP
BUMP
THAP
THAP
GUNG
GUNG
SHRRR
THUD
THUD
TAKA
TAKA
SLRK
PLOP
PHEW
GRRRL
DRUMP
B-BMP
B-BMP
CRINK
BZZ
コリリ CRKKL
コキン KTINK
コリリ CRKKL
...AND BIG MADAM CAN IDENTIFY THE SOUND AND ITS COORDINATES.

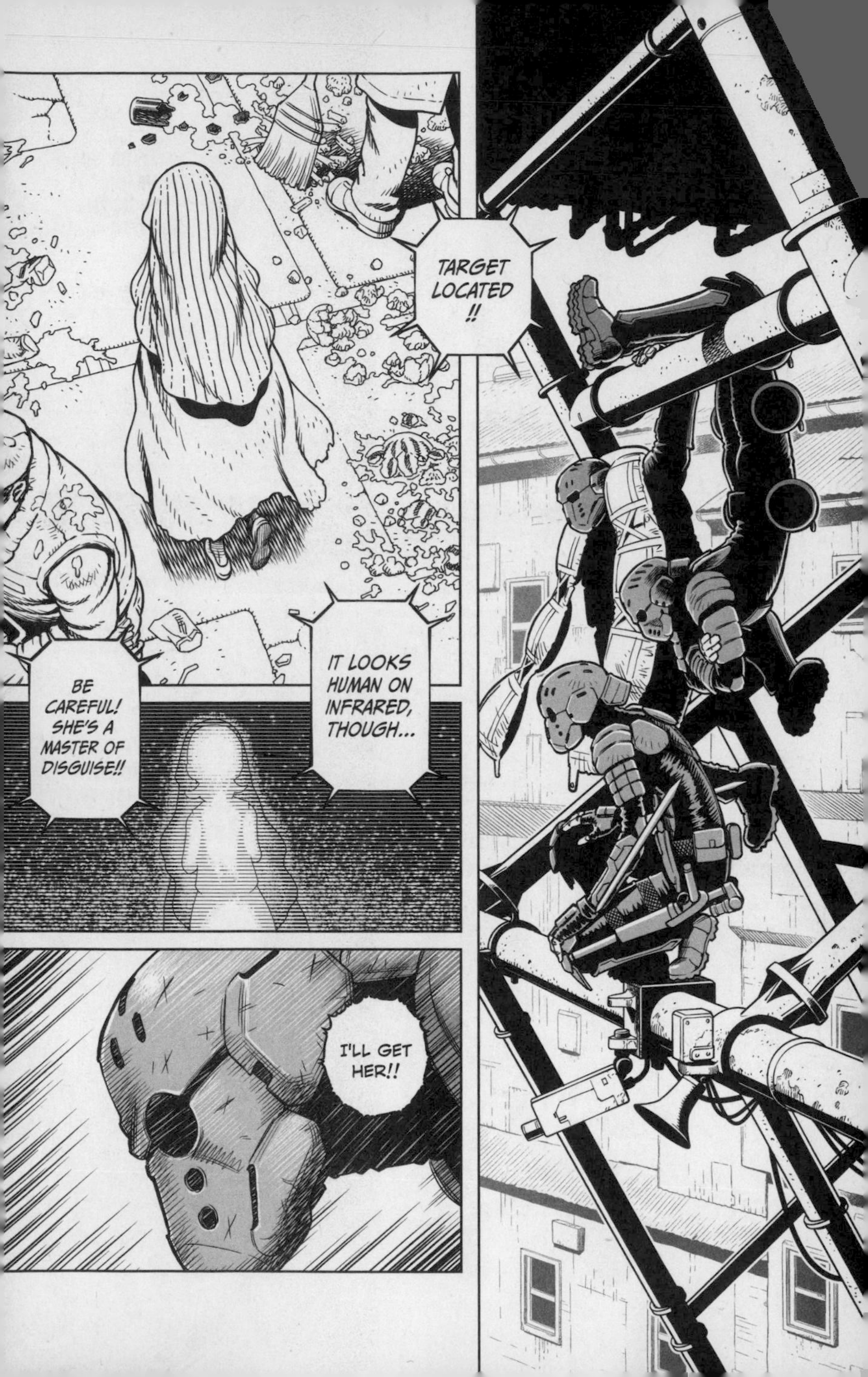
TARGET LOCATED !!
IT LOOKS HUMAN ON INFRARED, THOUGH...
BE CAREFUL! SHE'S A MASTER OF DISGUISE!!
I'LL GET HER!!

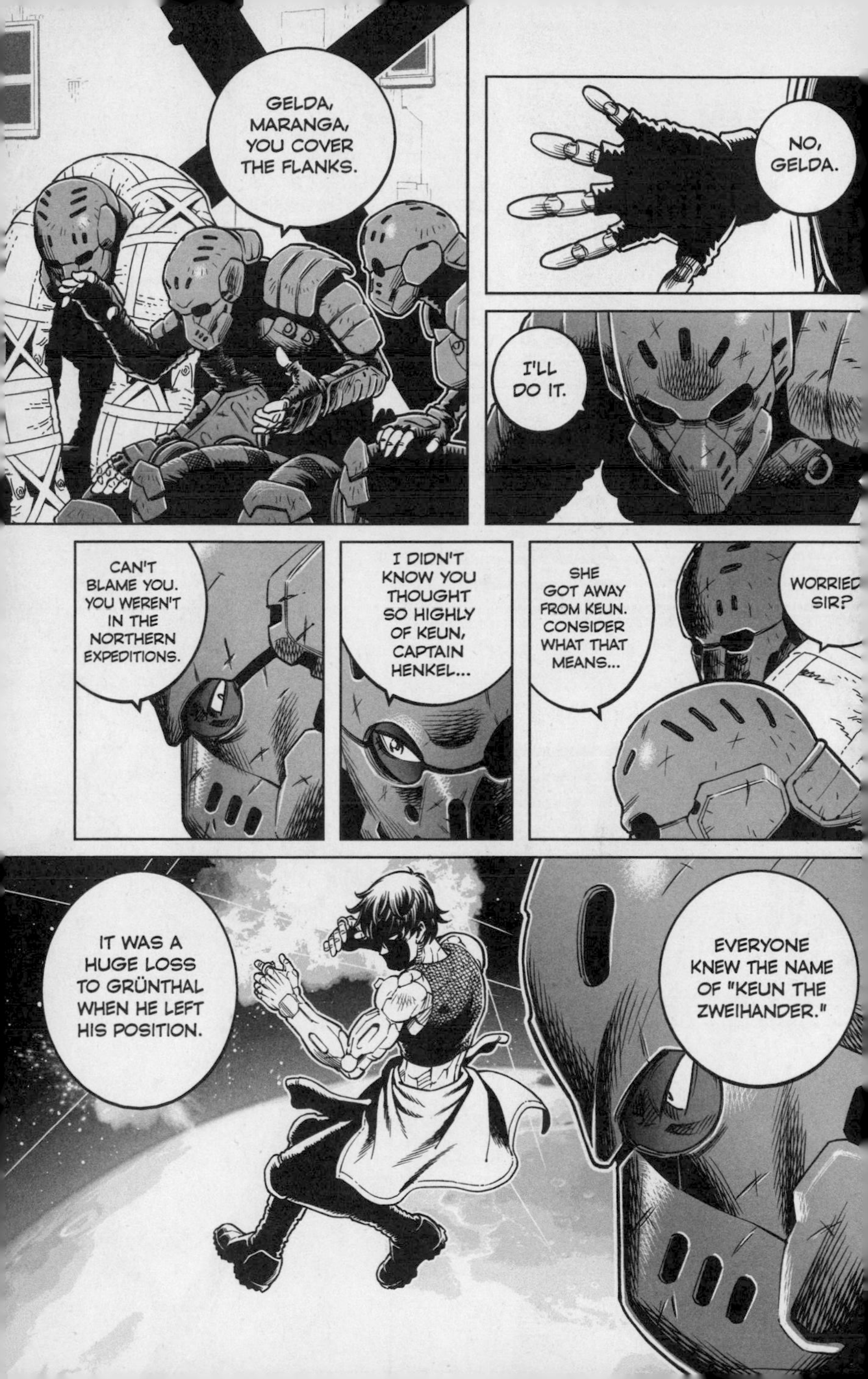
NO, GELDA.
I'LL DO IT.
GELDA, MARANGA, YOU COVER THE FLANKS.
WORRIED SIR?
SHE GOT AWAY FROM KEUN. CONSIDER WHAT THAT MEANS...
I DIDN'T KNOW YOU THOUGHT SO HIGHLY OF KEUN, CAPTAIN HENKEL...
CAN'T BLAME YOU. YOU WEREN'T IN THE NORTHERN EXPEDITIONS.
EVERYONE KNEW THE NAME OF "KEUN THE ZWEIHANDER."
IT WAS A HUGE LOSS TO GRÜNTHAL WHEN HE LEFT HIS POSITION.

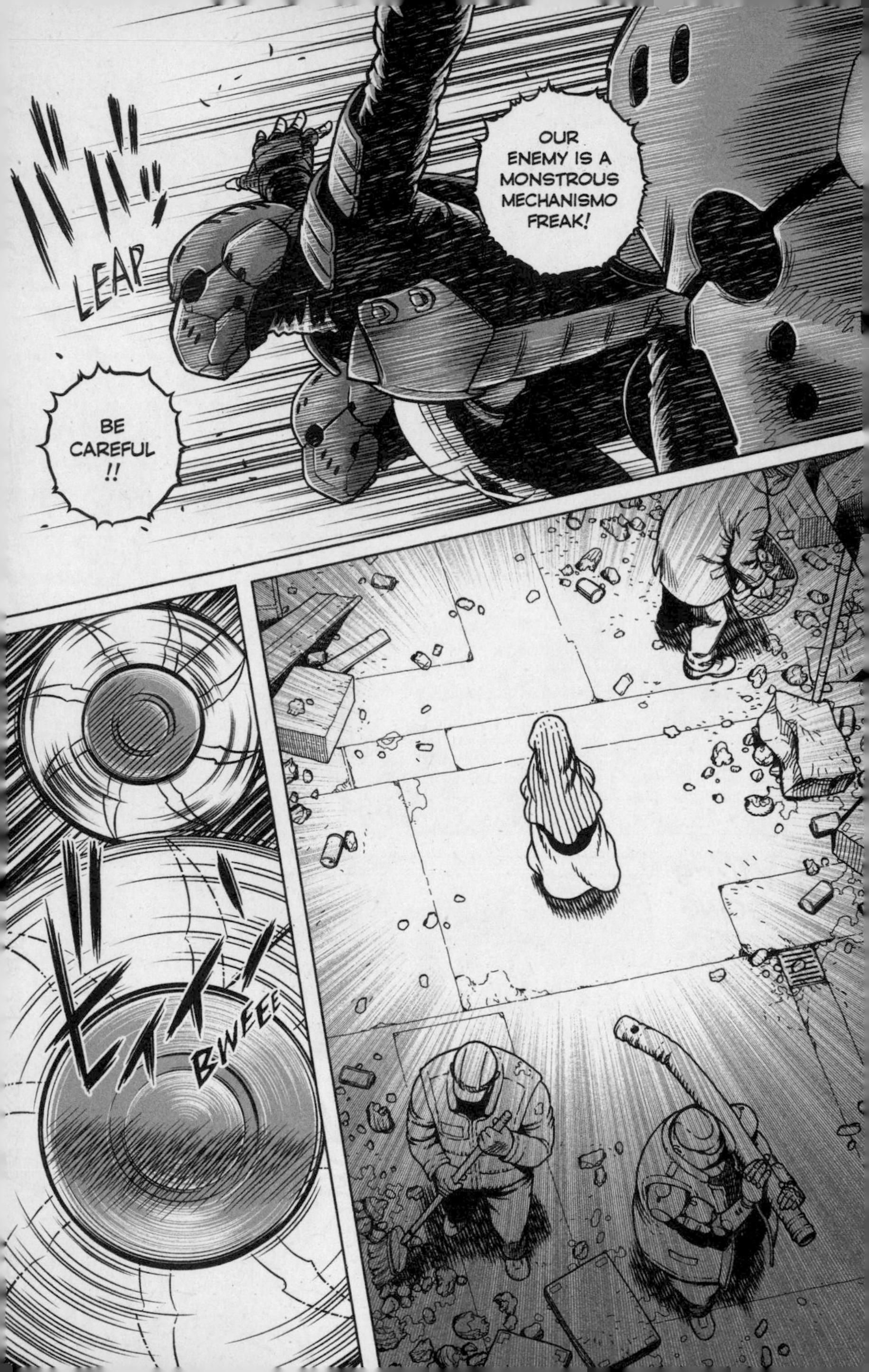
OUR ENEMY IS A MONSTROUS MECHANISMO FREAK!
LEAP
BE CAREFUL !!
BWEEE

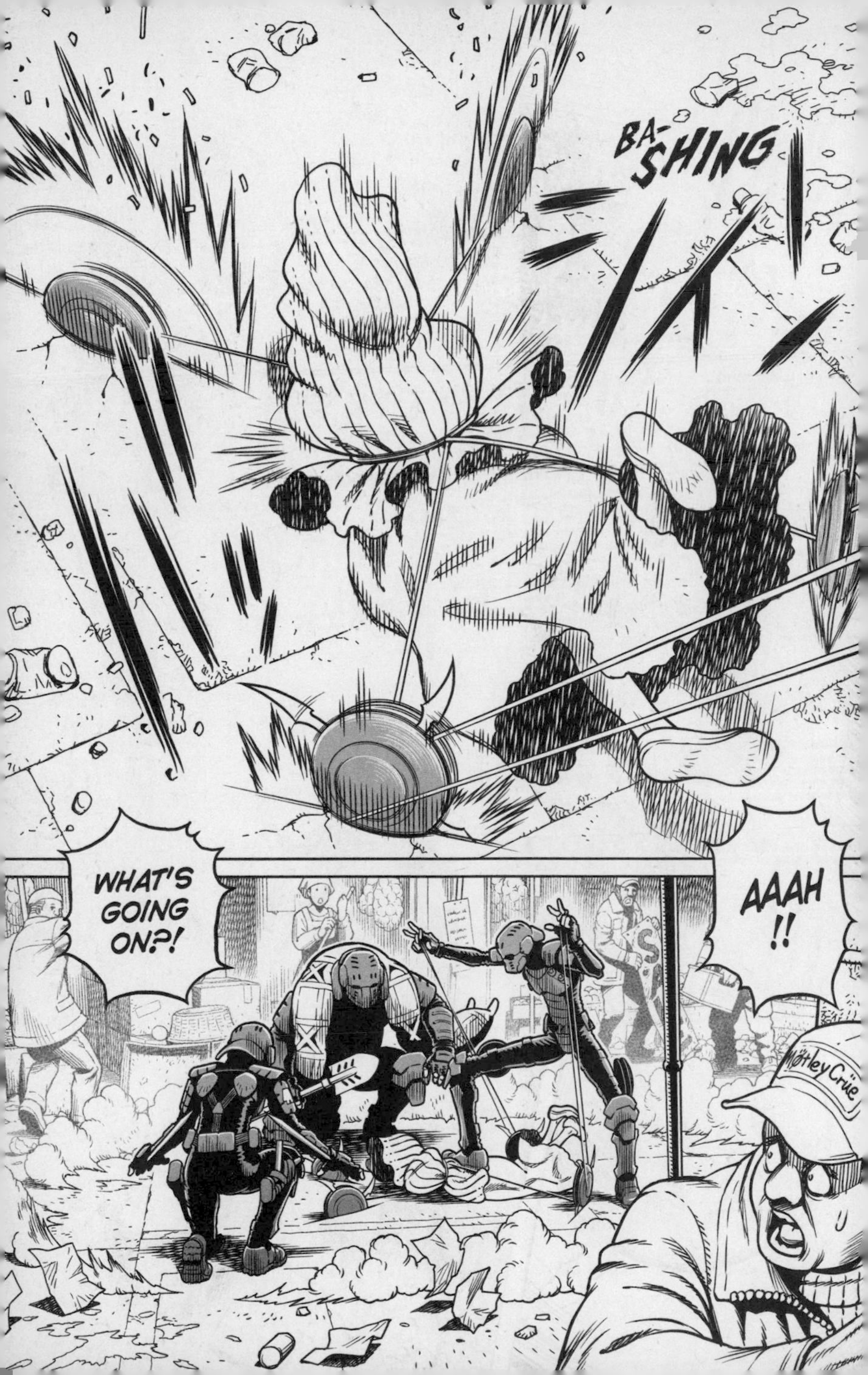
BA-SHING
AAAH !!
WHAT'S GOING ON?!
Mötley Crüe

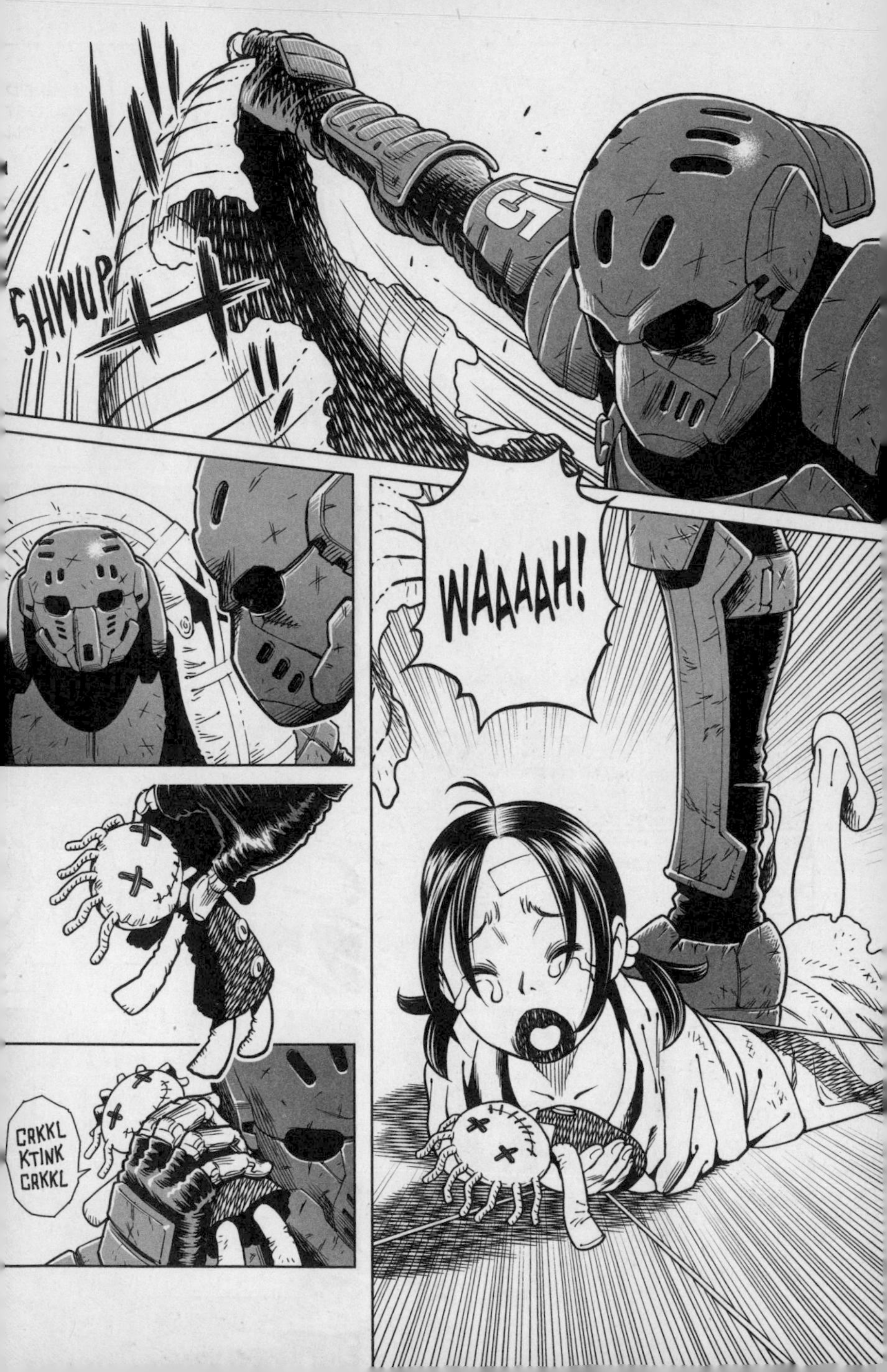
SHWUP
WAAAAH!
CRKKL
KTINK
CRKKL

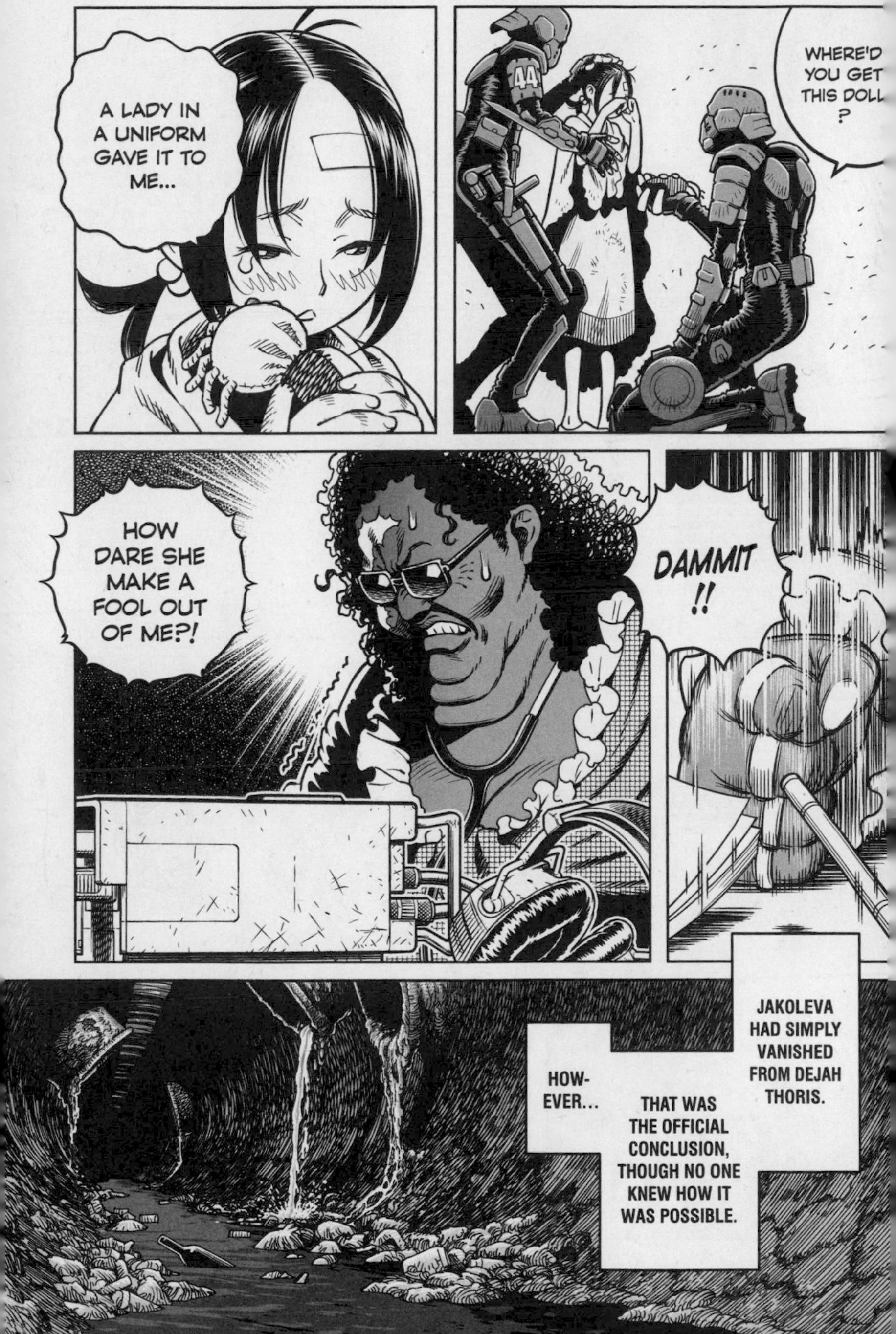
WHERE'D YOU GET THIS DOLL ?
A LADY IN A UNIFORM GAVE IT TO ME...
DAMMIT !!
HOW DARE SHE MAKE A FOOL OUT OF ME?!
JAKOLEVA HAD SIMPLY VANISHED FROM DEJAH THORIS.
THAT WAS THE OFFICIAL CONCLUSION, THOUGH NO ONE KNEW HOW IT WAS POSSIBLE.
HOW-EVER...

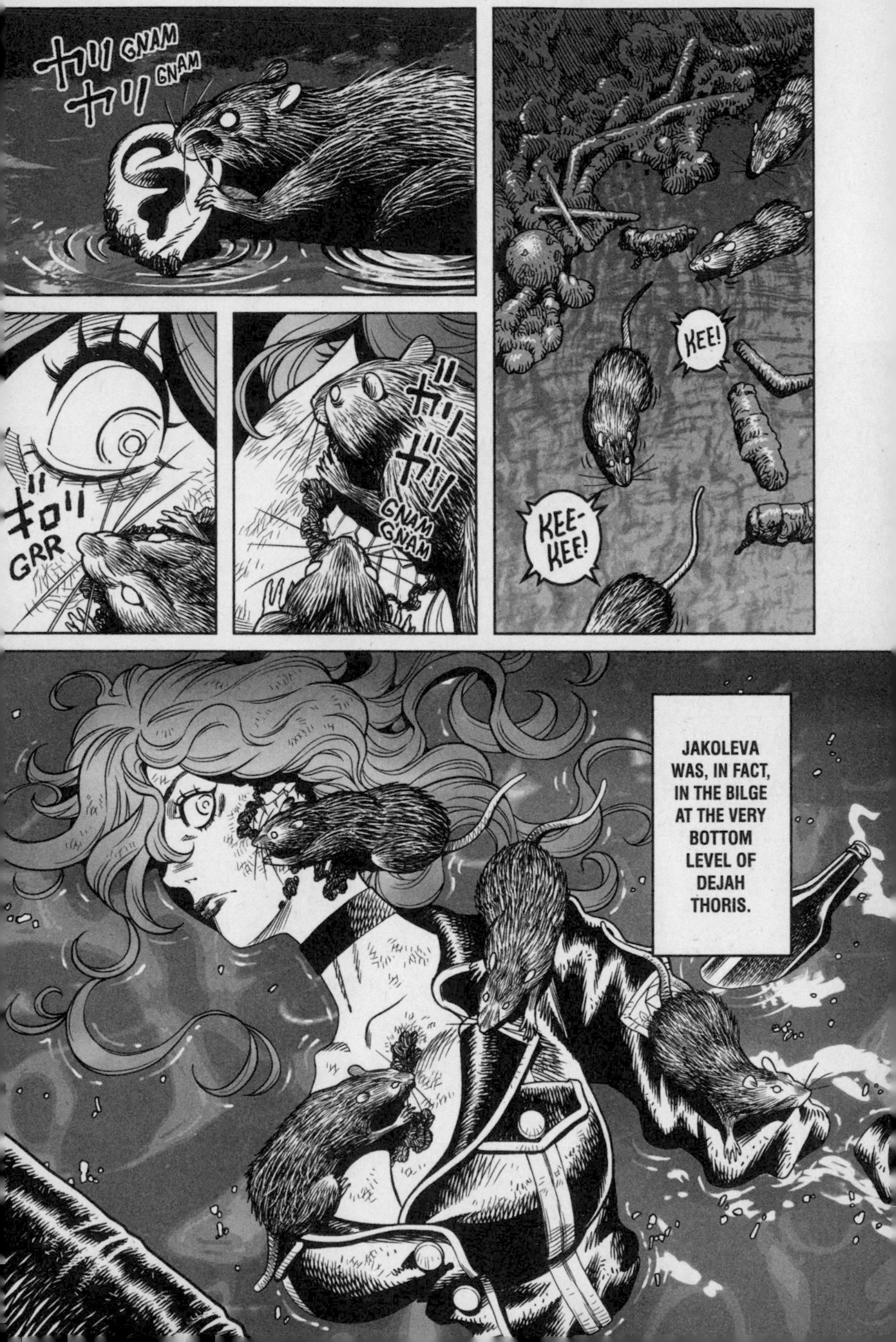
KEE!
KEE-KEE!
カリ GNAM
カリ GNAM
ガリ ガリ
GNAM GNAM
ギロリ
GRR
JAKOLEVA WAS, IN FACT, IN THE BILGE AT THE VERY BOTTOM LEVEL OF DEJAH THORIS.

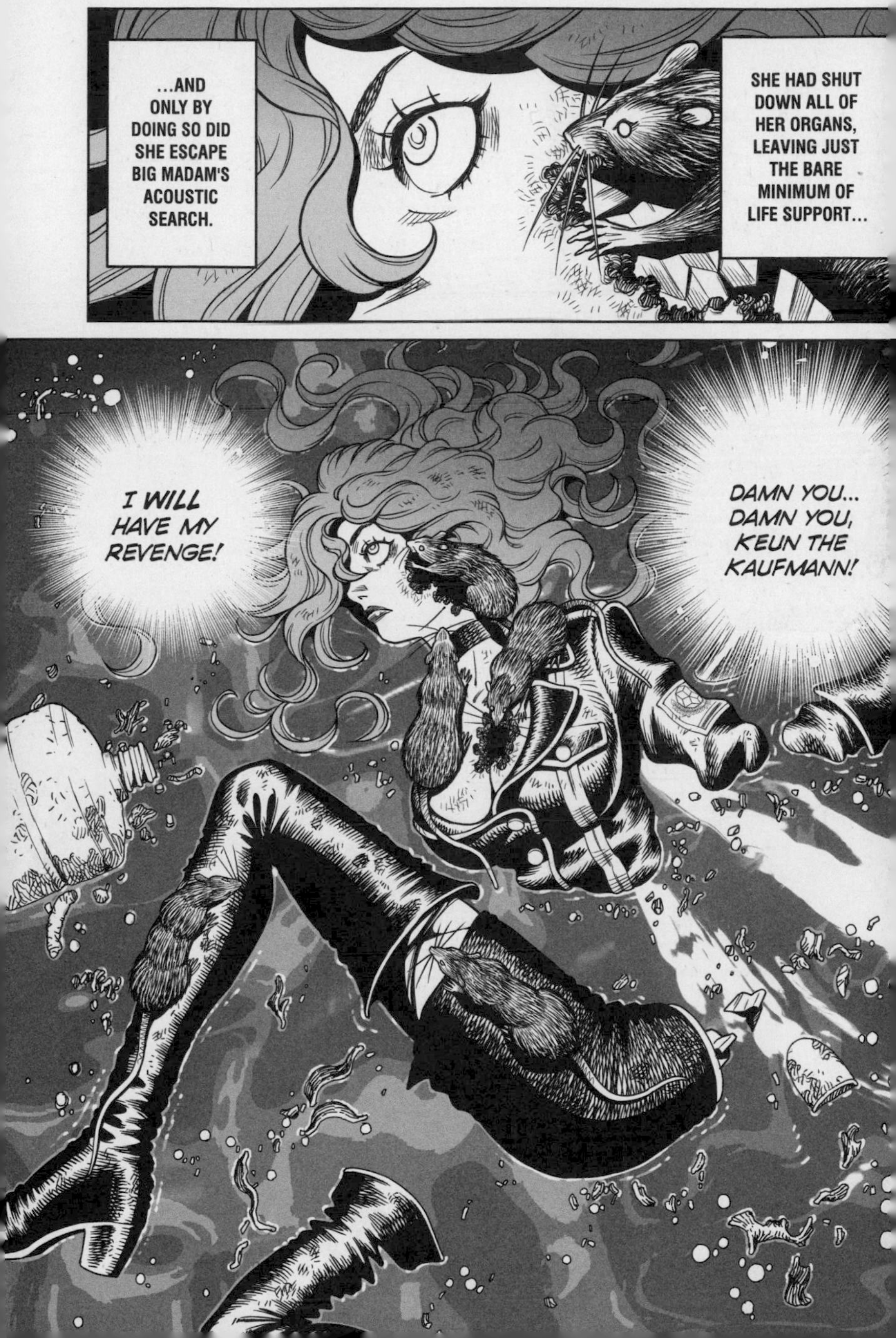
SHE HAD SHUT DOWN ALL OF HER ORGANS, LEAVING JUST THE BARE MINIMUM OF LIFE SUPPORT...
...AND ONLY BY DOING SO DID SHE ESCAPE BIG MADAM'S ACOUSTIC SEARCH.
DAMN YOU... DAMN YOU, KEUN THE KAUFMANN!
I WILL HAVE MY REVENGE!

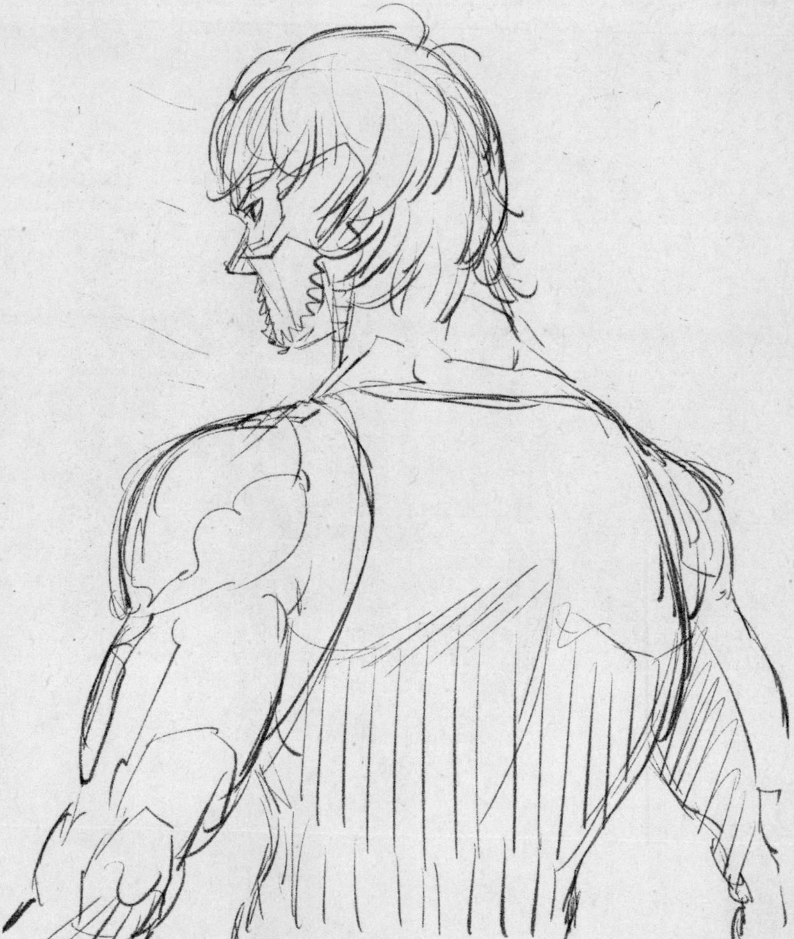

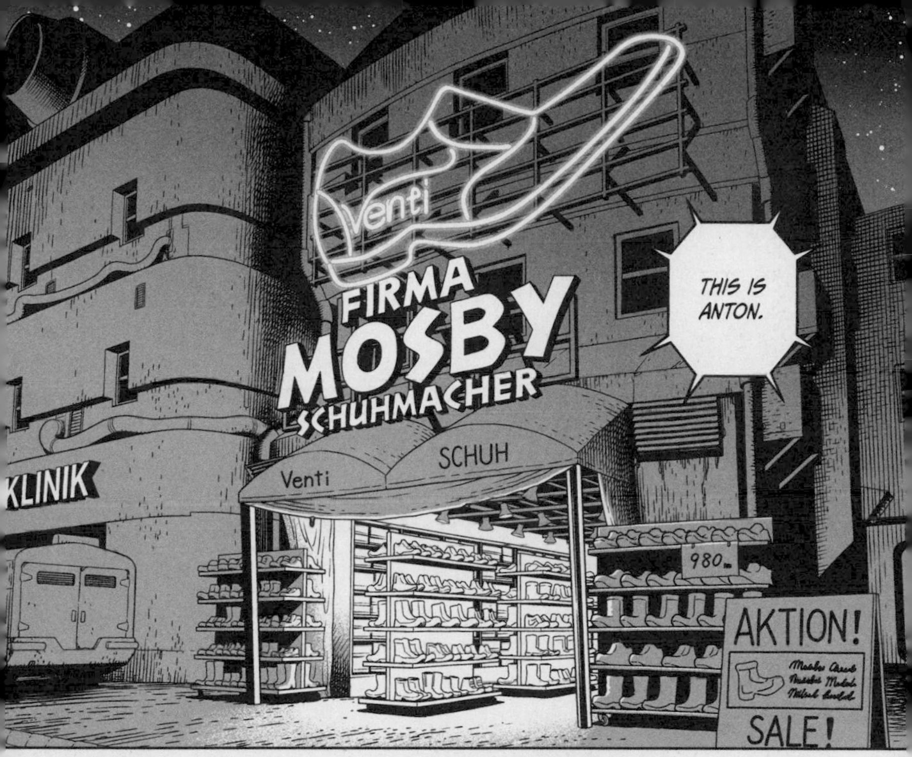
Venti
FIRMA
MOSBY
SCHUHMACHER
THIS IS ANTON.
KLINIK
Venti
SCHUH
980
AKTION!
SALE!

LOG:038
THIS IS HOW YOU STRIKE A DEAL!!

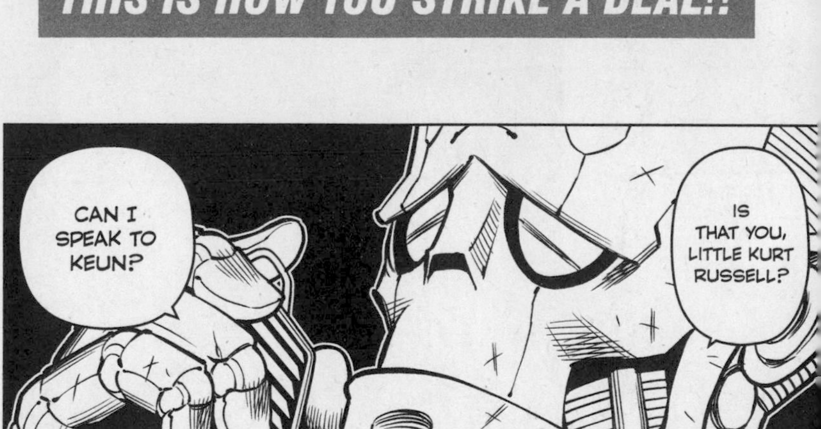
IS THAT YOU, LITTLE KURT RUSSELL?
CAN I SPEAK TO KEUN?

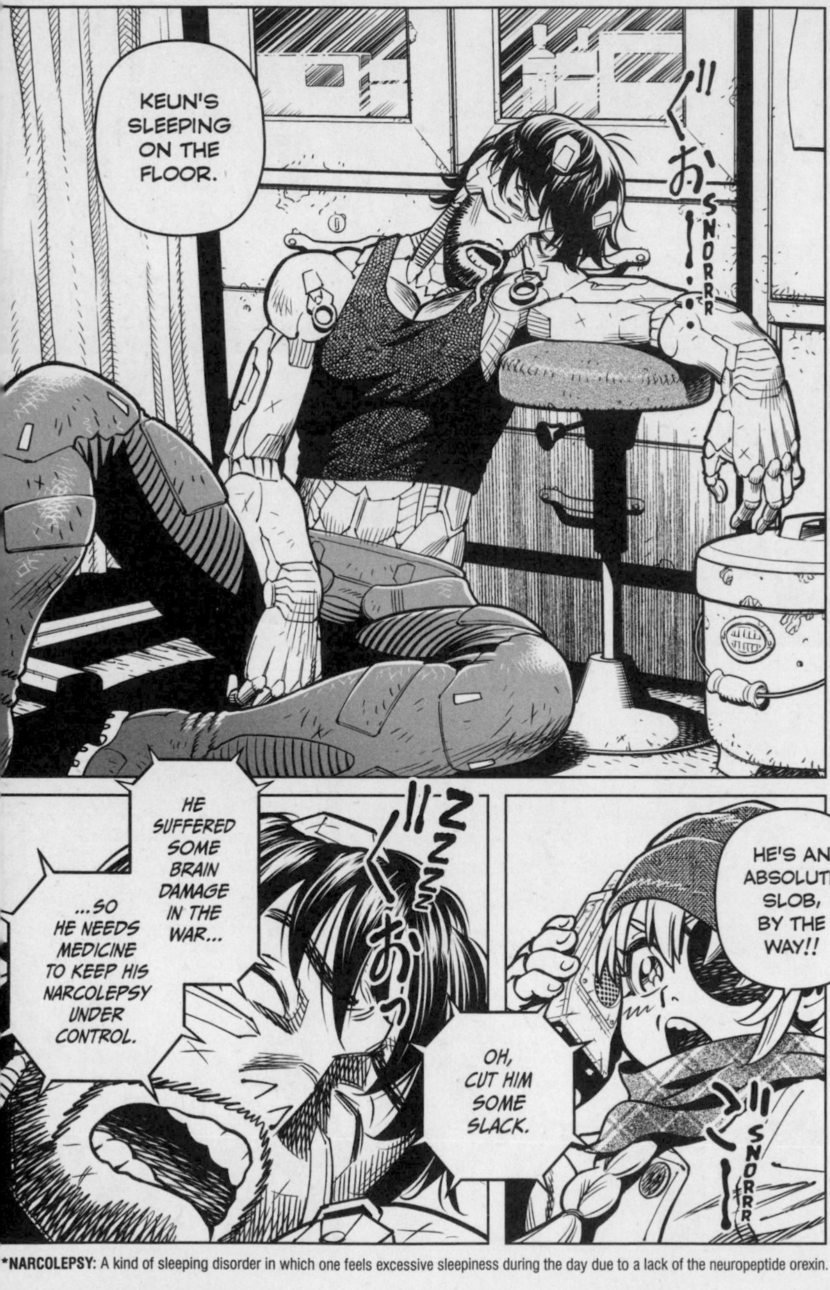
KEUN'S SLEEPING ON THE FLOOR.
SNORRR
HE'S AN ABSOLUTE SLOB, BY THE WAY!!
OH, CUT HIM SOME SLACK.
SNORRR
HE SUFFERED SOME BRAIN DAMAGE IN THE WAR...
...SO HE NEEDS MEDICINE TO KEEP HIS NARCOLEPSY UNDER CONTROL.
ZZZ

***NARCOLEPSY:** A kind of sleeping disorder in which one feels excessive sleepiness during the day due to a lack of the neuropeptide orexin.

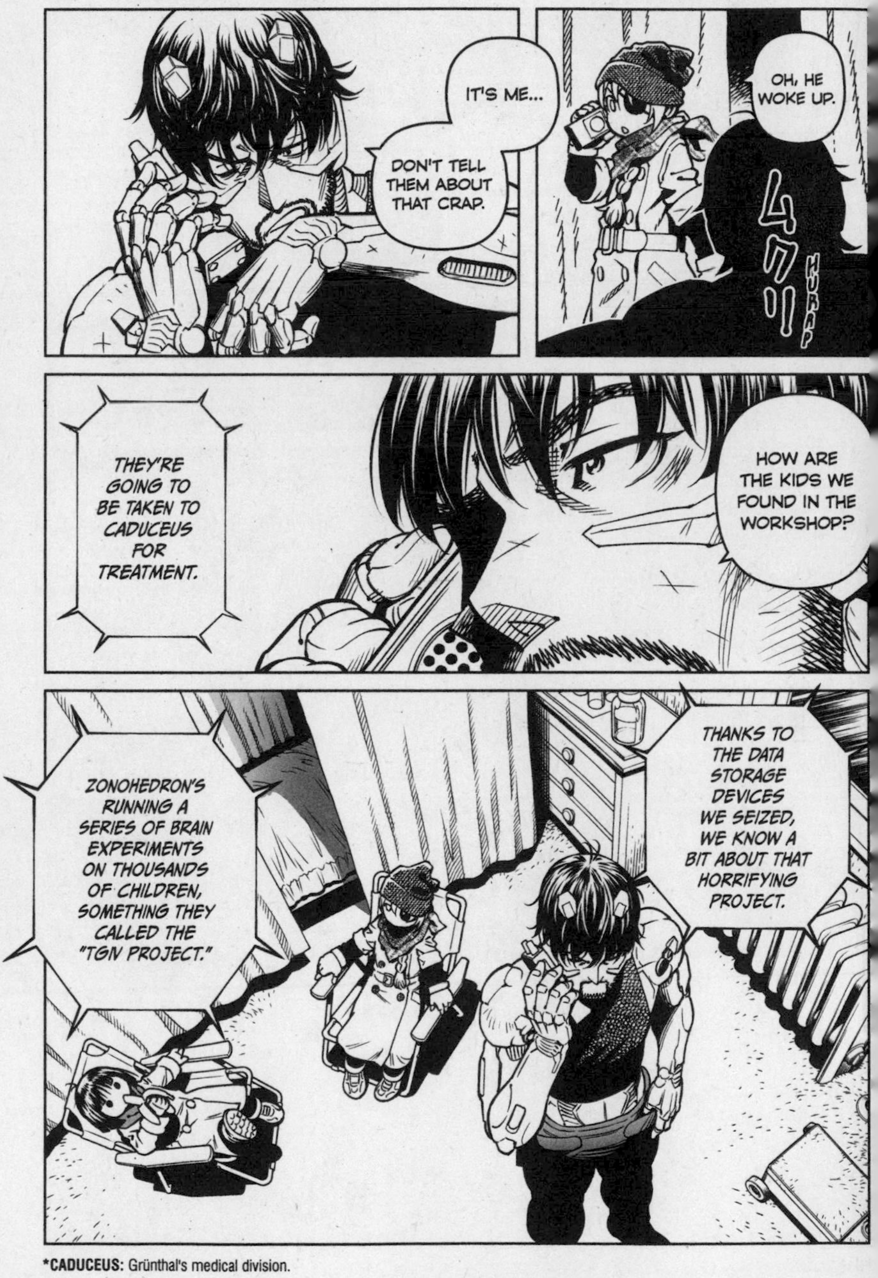
OH, HE WOKE UP.
ムクリ
HURAP
IT'S ME...
DON'T TELL THEM ABOUT THAT CRAP.
HOW ARE THE KIDS WE FOUND IN THE WORKSHOP?
THEY'RE GOING TO BE TAKEN TO CADUCEUS FOR TREATMENT.
THANKS TO THE DATA STORAGE DEVICES WE SEIZED, WE KNOW A BIT ABOUT THAT HORRIFYING PROJECT.
ZONOHEDRON'S RUNNING A SERIES OF BRAIN EXPERIMENTS ON THOUSANDS OF CHILDREN, SOMETHING THEY CALLED THE "TGIV PROJECT."

***CADUCEUS:** Grünthal's medical division.

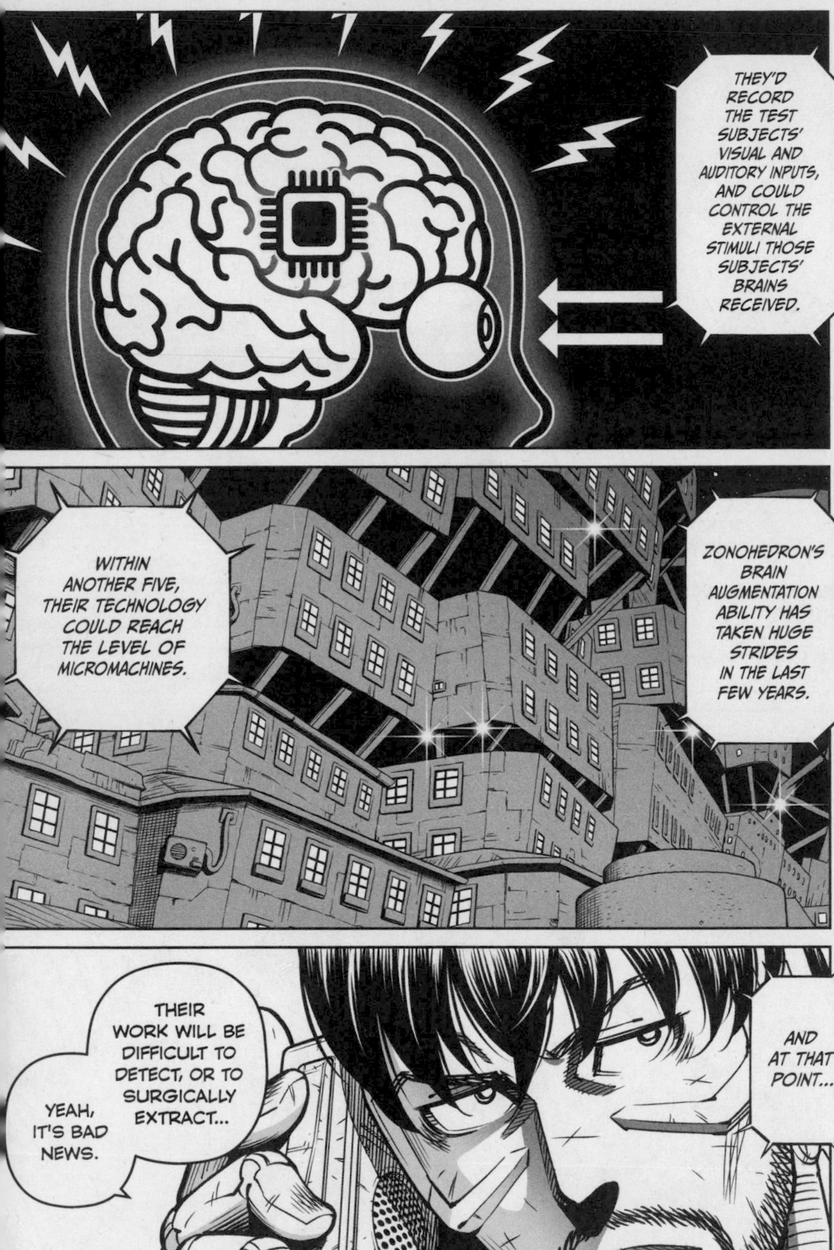
THEY'D RECORD THE TEST SUBJECTS' VISUAL AND AUDITORY INPUTS, AND COULD CONTROL THE EXTERNAL STIMULI THOSE SUBJECTS' BRAINS RECEIVED.
ZONOHEDRON'S BRAIN AUGMENTATION ABILITY HAS TAKEN HUGE STRIDES IN THE LAST FEW YEARS.
WITHIN ANOTHER FIVE, THEIR TECHNOLOGY COULD REACH THE LEVEL OF MICROMACHINES.
AND AT THAT POINT...
THEIR WORK WILL BE DIFFICULT TO DETECT, OR TO SURGICALLY EXTRACT...
YEAH, IT'S BAD NEWS.

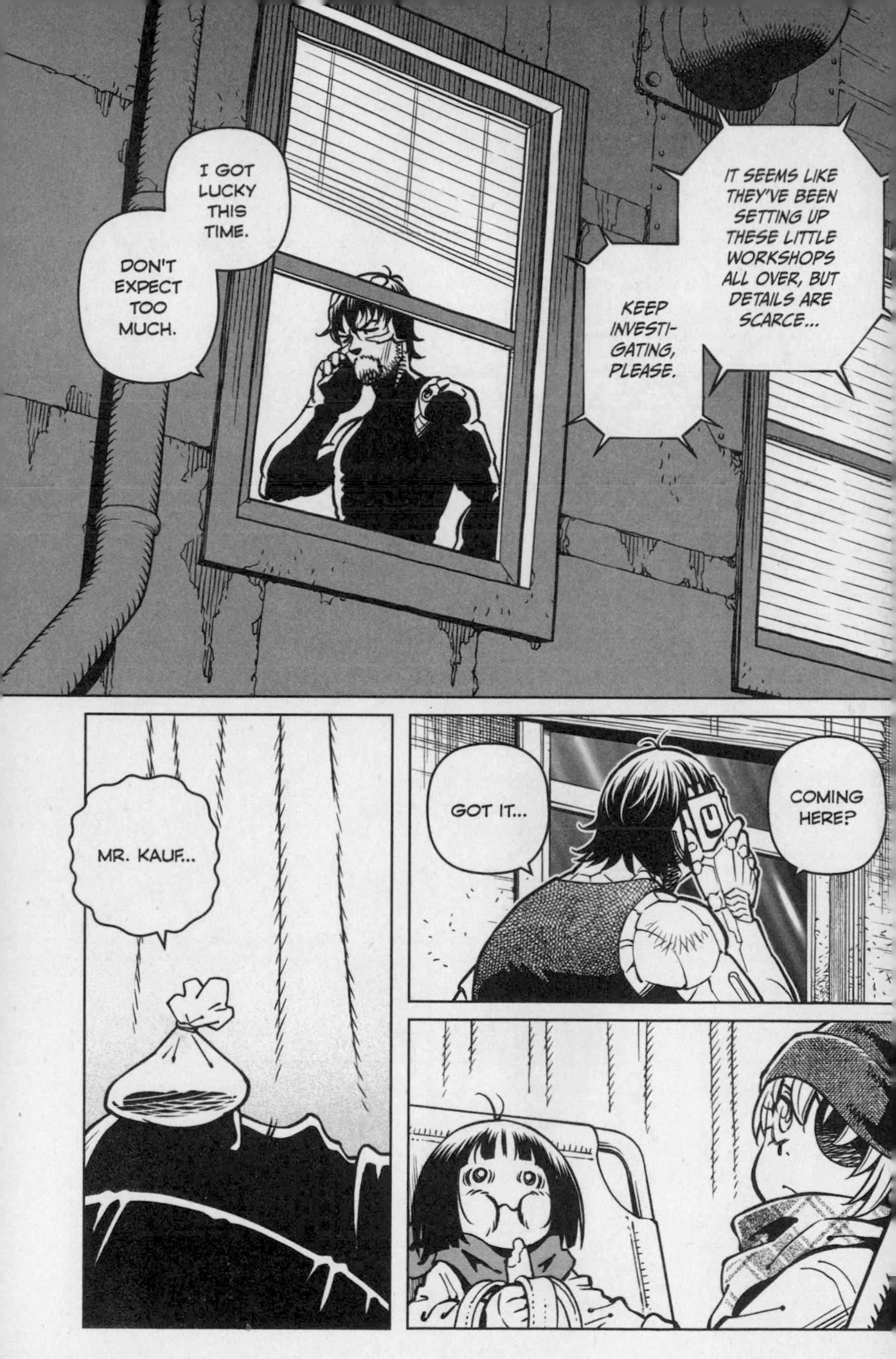
IT SEEMS LIKE THEY'VE BEEN SETTING UP THESE LITTLE WORKSHOPS ALL OVER, BUT DETAILS ARE SCARCE...
KEEP INVESTI-GATING, PLEASE.
I GOT LUCKY THIS TIME.
DON'T EXPECT TOO MUCH.
COMING HERE?
GOT IT...
MR. KAUF...

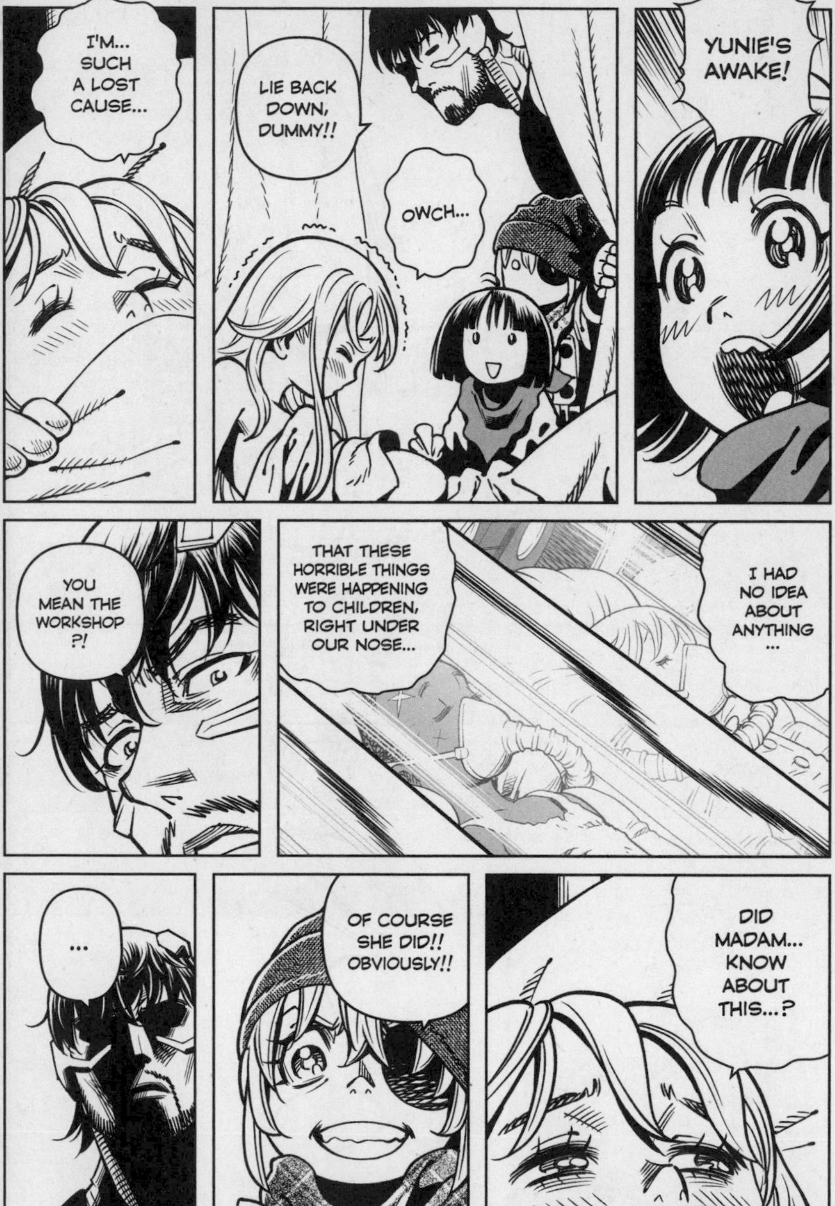
YUNIE'S AWAKE!
LIE BACK DOWN, DUMMY!!
OWCH...
I'M... SUCH A LOST CAUSE...
I HAD NO IDEA ABOUT ANYTHING ...
THAT THESE HORRIBLE THINGS WERE HAPPENING TO CHILDREN, RIGHT UNDER OUR NOSE...
YOU MEAN THE WORKSHOP ?!
DID MADAM... KNOW ABOUT THIS...?
OF COURSE SHE DID!! OBVIOUSLY!!
...

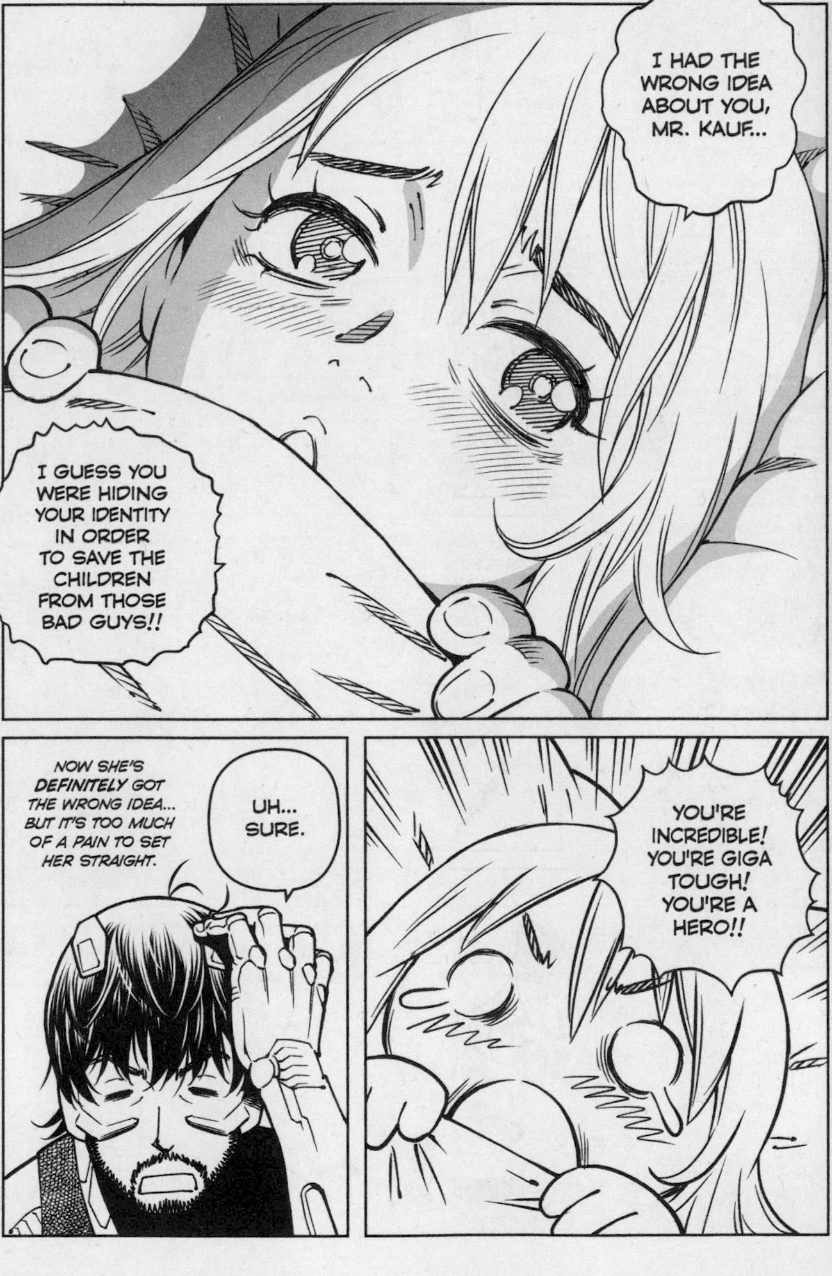
I HAD THE WRONG IDEA ABOUT YOU, MR. KAUF...
I GUESS YOU WERE HIDING YOUR IDENTITY IN ORDER TO SAVE THE CHILDREN FROM THOSE BAD GUYS!!
YOU'RE INCREDIBLE! YOU'RE GIGA TOUGH! YOU'RE A HERO!!
UH... SURE.
NOW SHE'S DEFINITELY GOT THE WRONG IDEA... BUT IT'S TOO MUCH OF A PAIN TO SET HER STRAIGHT.

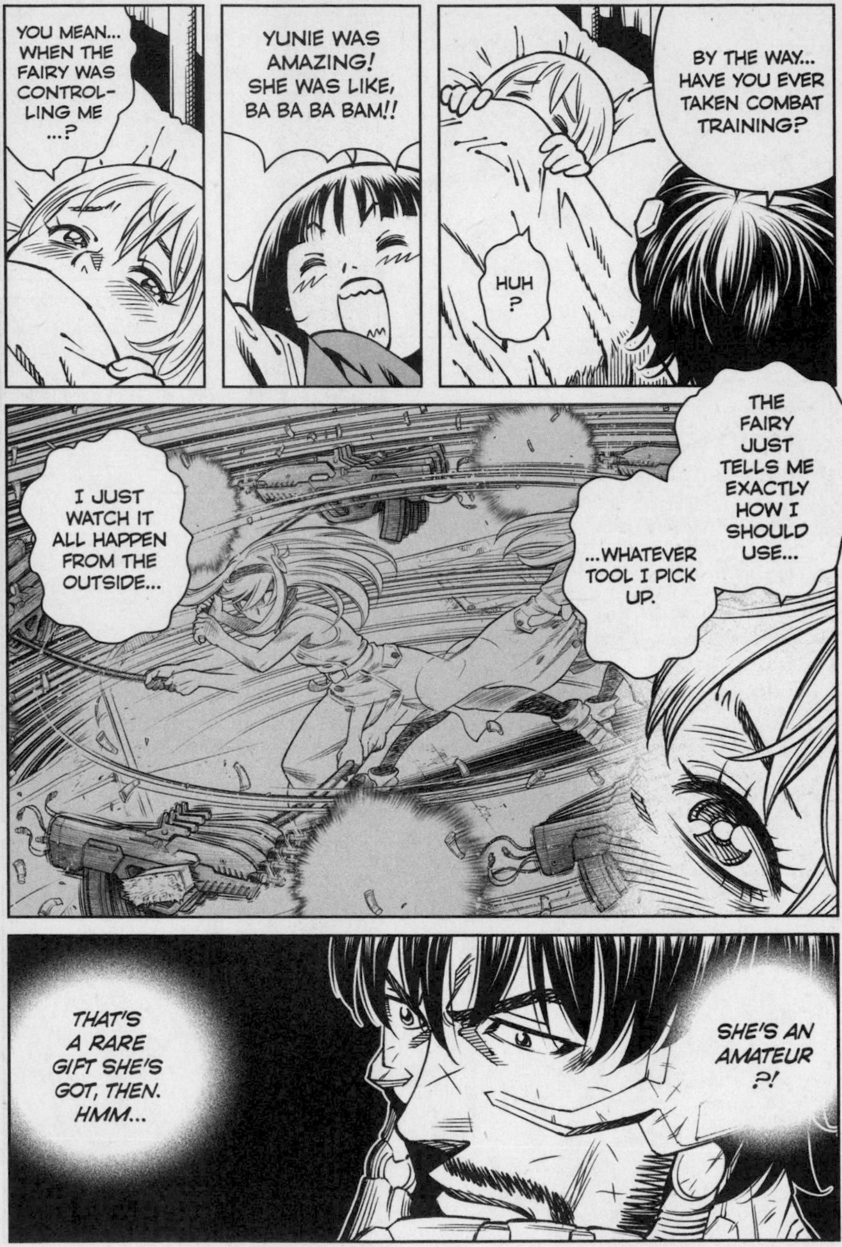
BY THE WAY... HAVE YOU EVER TAKEN COMBAT TRAINING?
HUH?
YUNIE WAS AMAZING! SHE WAS LIKE, BA BA BA BAM!!
YOU MEAN... WHEN THE FAIRY WAS CONTROL-LING ME ...?
THE FAIRY JUST TELLS ME EXACTLY HOW I SHOULD USE...
...WHATEVER TOOL I PICK UP.
I JUST WATCH IT ALL HAPPEN FROM THE OUTSIDE...
SHE'S AN AMATEUR ?!
THAT'S A RARE GIFT SHE'S GOT, THEN. HMM...

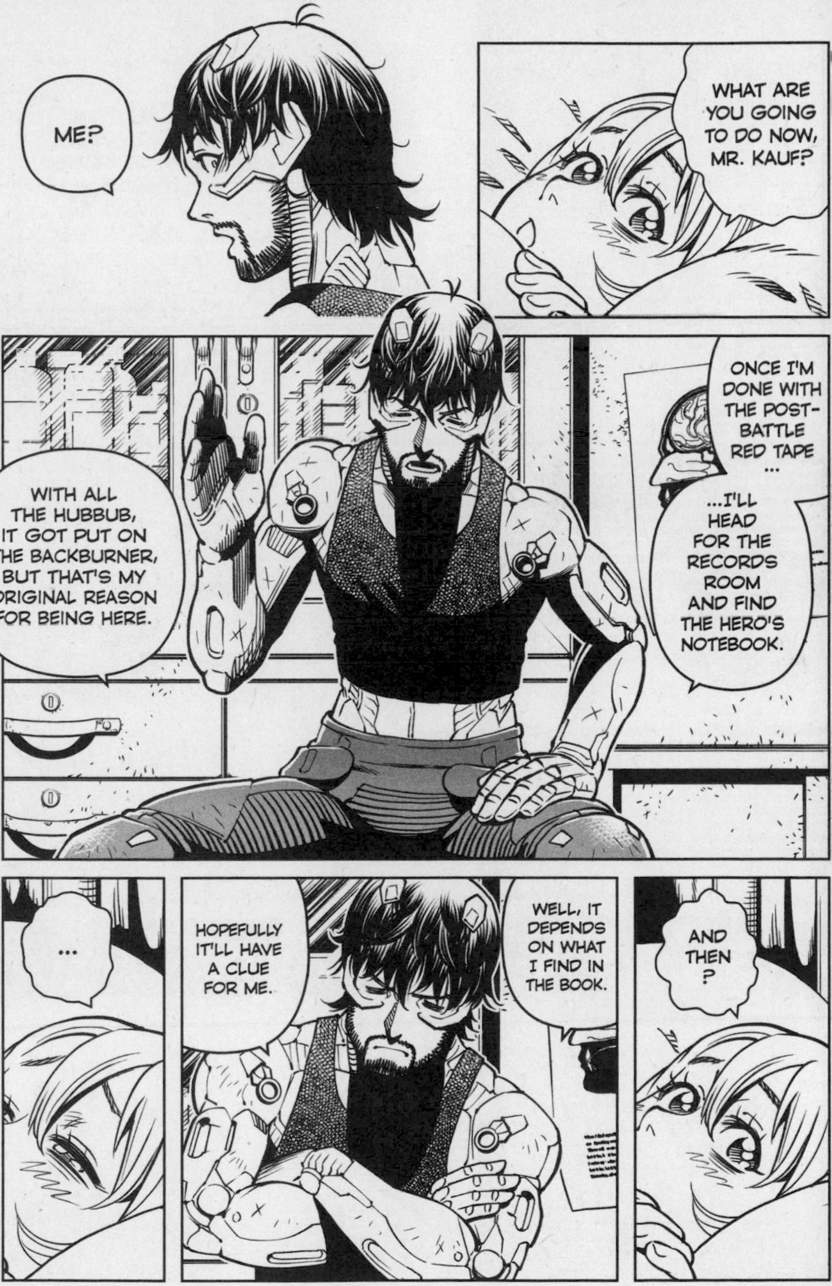
WHAT ARE YOU GOING TO DO NOW, MR. KAUF?
ME?
ONCE I'M DONE WITH THE POST-BATTLE RED TAPE ...
...I'LL HEAD FOR THE RECORDS ROOM AND FIND THE HERO'S NOTEBOOK.
WITH ALL THE HUBBUB, IT GOT PUT ON THE BACKBURNER, BUT THAT'S MY ORIGINAL REASON FOR BEING HERE.
AND THEN ?
WELL, IT DEPENDS ON WHAT I FIND IN THE BOOK.
HOPEFULLY IT'LL HAVE A CLUE FOR ME.
...

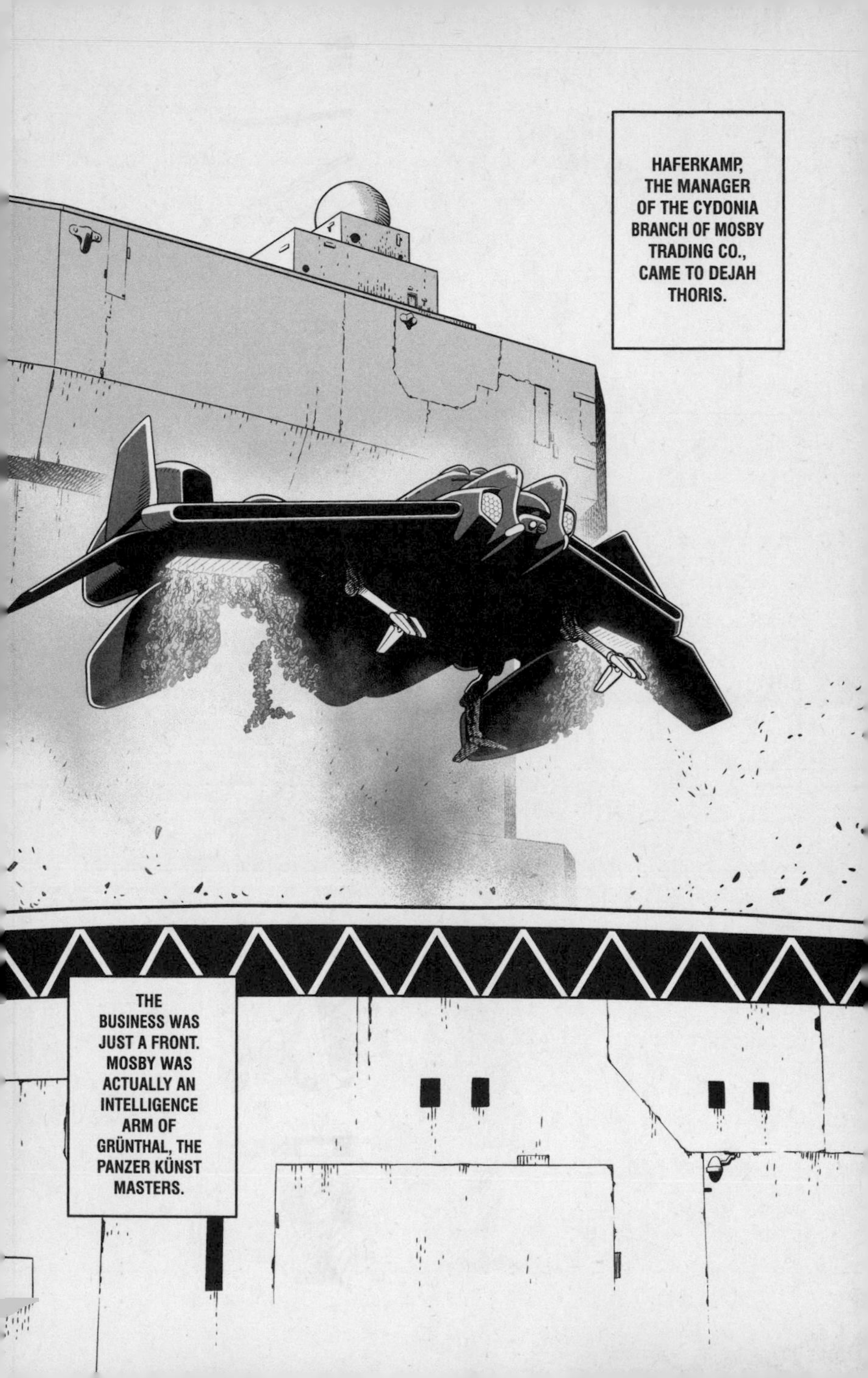
HAFERKAMP, THE MANAGER OF THE CYDONIA BRANCH OF MOSBY TRADING CO., CAME TO DEJAH THORIS.
THE BUSINESS WAS JUST A FRONT. MOSBY WAS ACTUALLY AN INTELLIGENCE ARM OF GRÜNTHAL, THE PANZER KÜNST MASTERS.

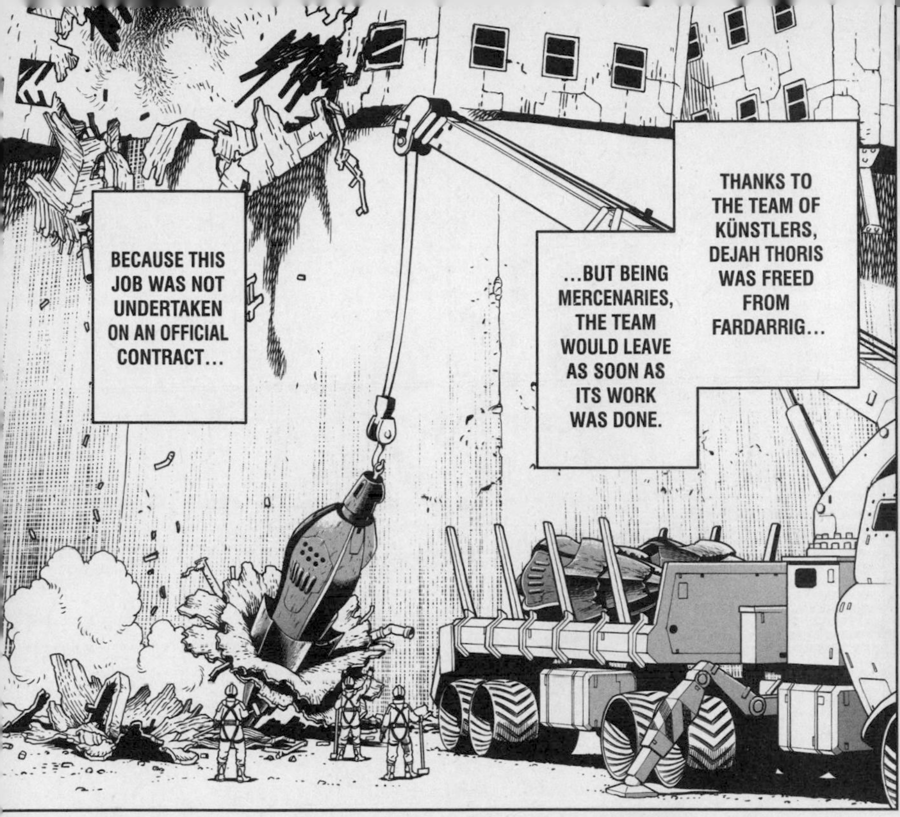
THANKS TO THE TEAM OF KÜNSTLERS, DEJAH THORIS WAS FREED FROM FARDARRIG…
…BUT BEING MERCENARIES, THE TEAM WOULD LEAVE AS SOON AS ITS WORK WAS DONE.
BECAUSE THIS JOB WAS NOT UNDERTAKEN ON AN OFFICIAL CONTRACT…

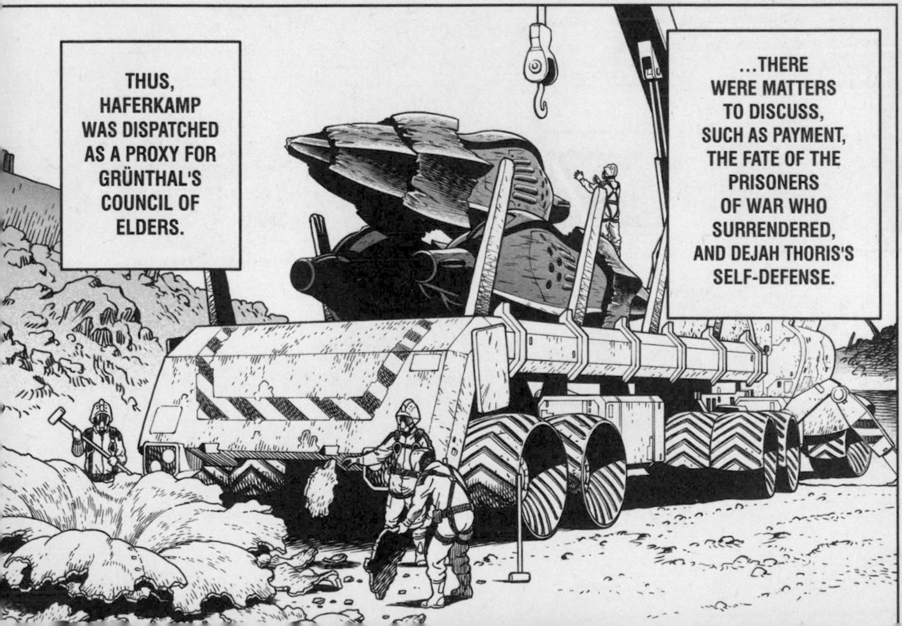
…THERE WERE MATTERS TO DISCUSS, SUCH AS PAYMENT, THE FATE OF THE PRISONERS OF WAR WHO SURRENDERED, AND DEJAH THORIS'S SELF-DEFENSE.
THUS, HAFERKAMP WAS DISPATCHED AS A PROXY FOR GRÜNTHAL'S COUNCIL OF ELDERS.

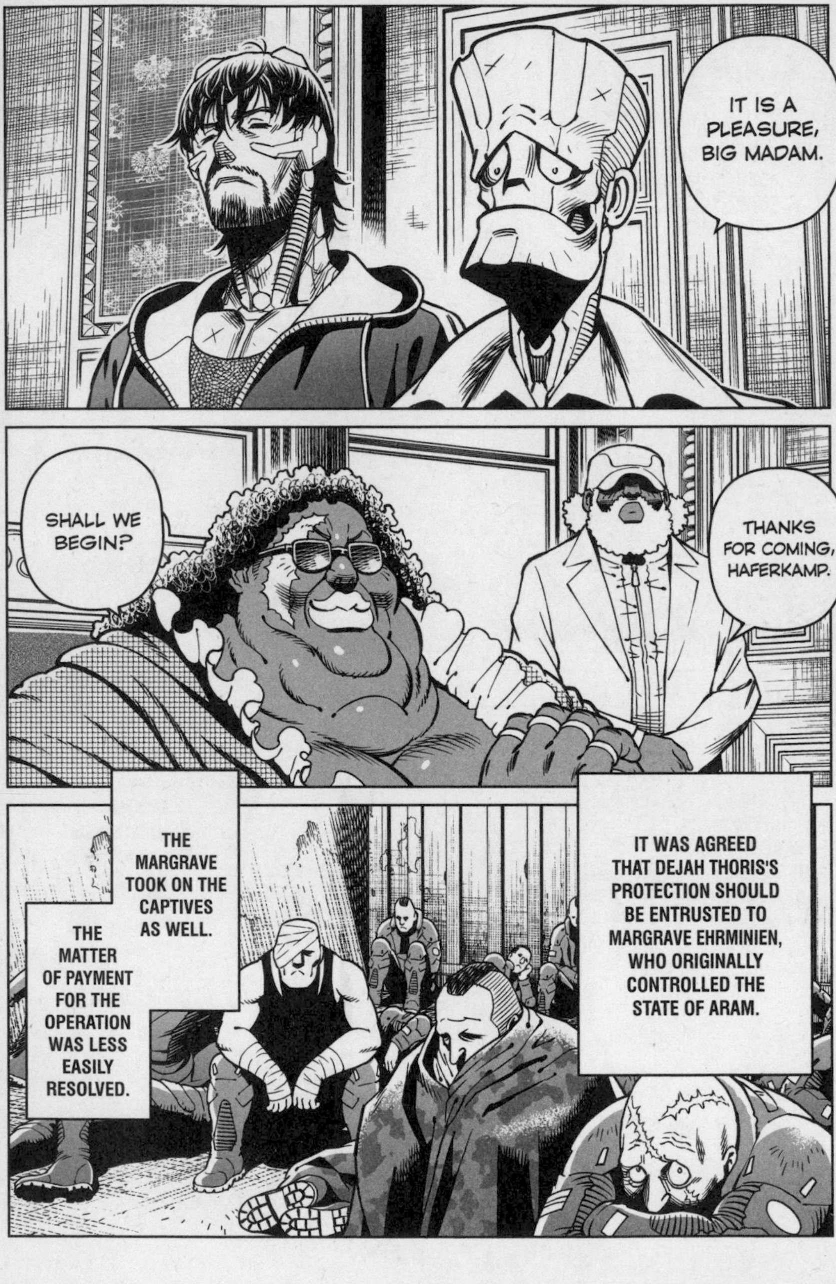
IT IS A PLEASURE, BIG MADAM.
THANKS FOR COMING, HAFERKAMP.
SHALL WE BEGIN?
IT WAS AGREED THAT DEJAH THORIS'S PROTECTION SHOULD BE ENTRUSTED TO MARGRAVE EHRMINIEN, WHO ORIGINALLY CONTROLLED THE STATE OF ARAM.
THE MARGRAVE TOOK ON THE CAPTIVES AS WELL.
THE MATTER OF PAYMENT FOR THE OPERATION WAS LESS EASILY RESOLVED.

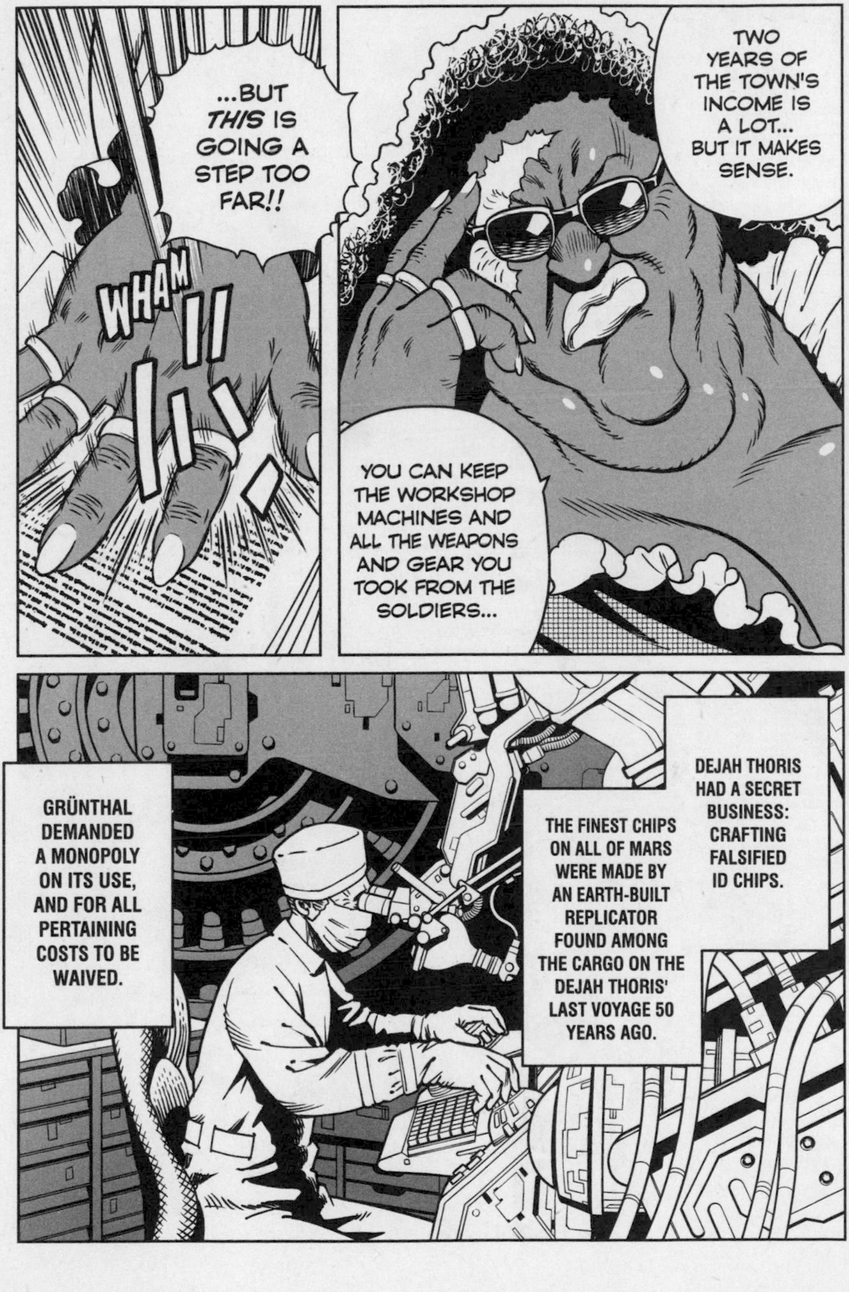
TWO YEARS OF THE TOWN'S INCOME IS A LOT... BUT IT MAKES SENSE.
YOU CAN KEEP THE WORKSHOP MACHINES AND ALL THE WEAPONS AND GEAR YOU TOOK FROM THE SOLDIERS...
...BUT *THIS* IS GOING A STEP TOO FAR!!
WHAM
DEJAH THORIS HAD A SECRET BUSINESS: CRAFTING FALSIFIED ID CHIPS.
THE FINEST CHIPS ON ALL OF MARS WERE MADE BY AN EARTH-BUILT REPLICATOR FOUND AMONG THE CARGO ON THE DEJAH THORIS' LAST VOYAGE 50 YEARS AGO.
GRÜNTHAL DEMANDED A MONOPOLY ON ITS USE, AND FOR ALL PERTAINING COSTS TO BE WAIVED.

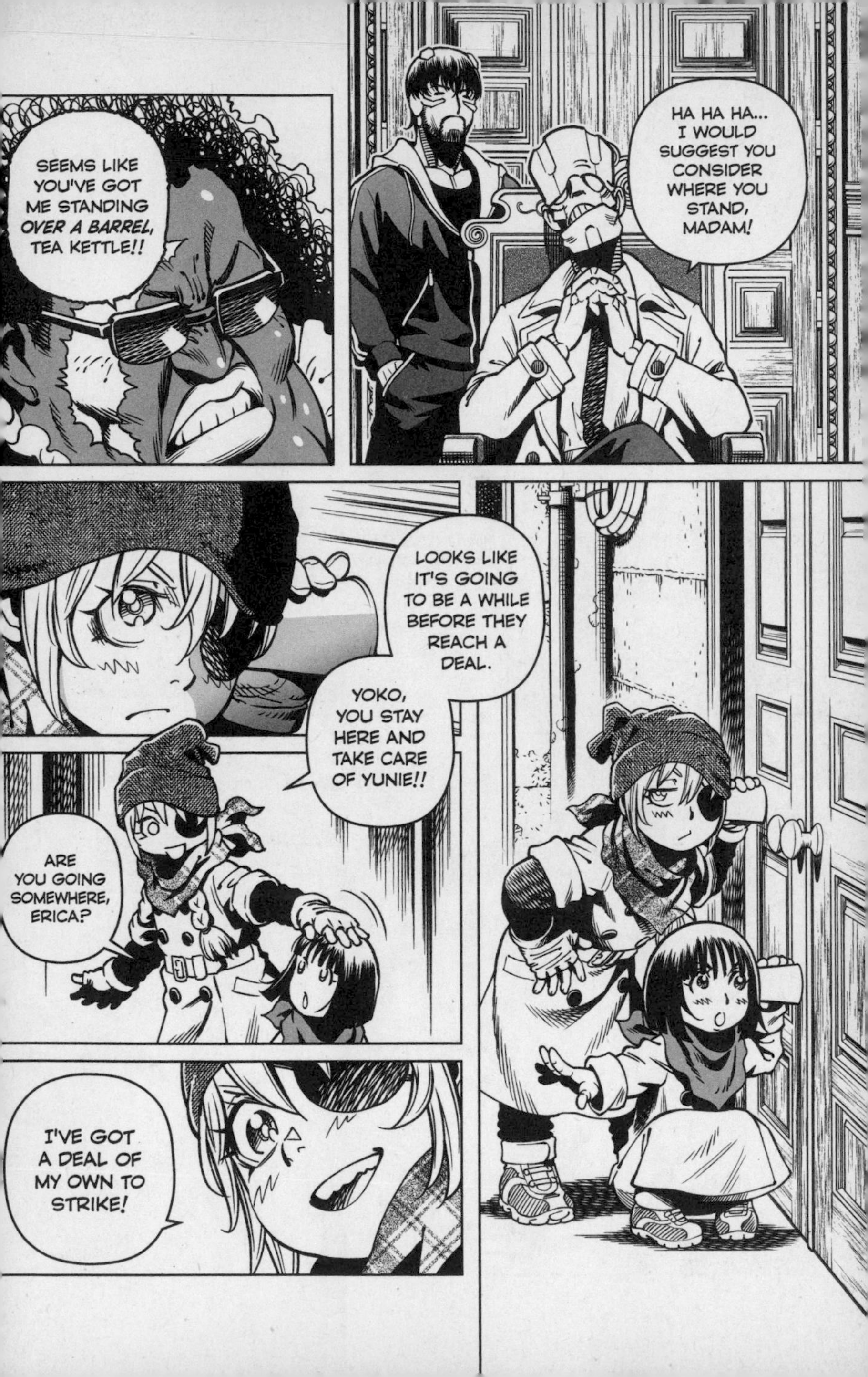
HA HA HA... I WOULD SUGGEST YOU CONSIDER WHERE YOU STAND, MADAM!
SEEMS LIKE YOU'VE GOT ME STANDING *OVER A BARREL*, TEA KETTLE!!
LOOKS LIKE IT'S GOING TO BE A WHILE BEFORE THEY REACH A DEAL.
YOKO, YOU STAY HERE AND TAKE CARE OF YUNIE!!
ARE YOU GOING SOMEWHERE, ERICA?
I'VE GOT A DEAL OF MY OWN TO STRIKE!

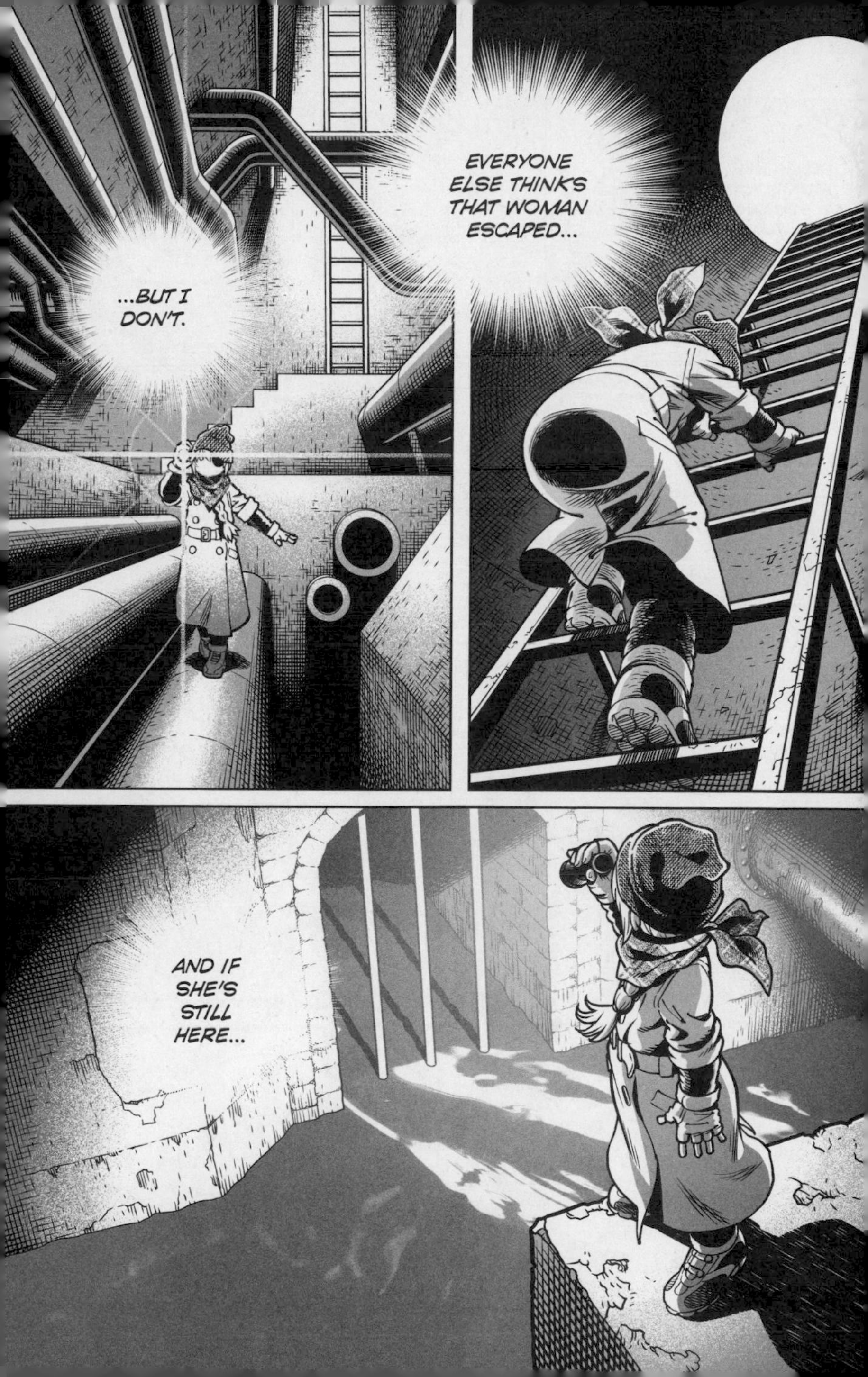
EVERYONE ELSE THINKS THAT WOMAN ESCAPED...
...BUT I DON'T.
AND IF SHE'S STILL HERE...

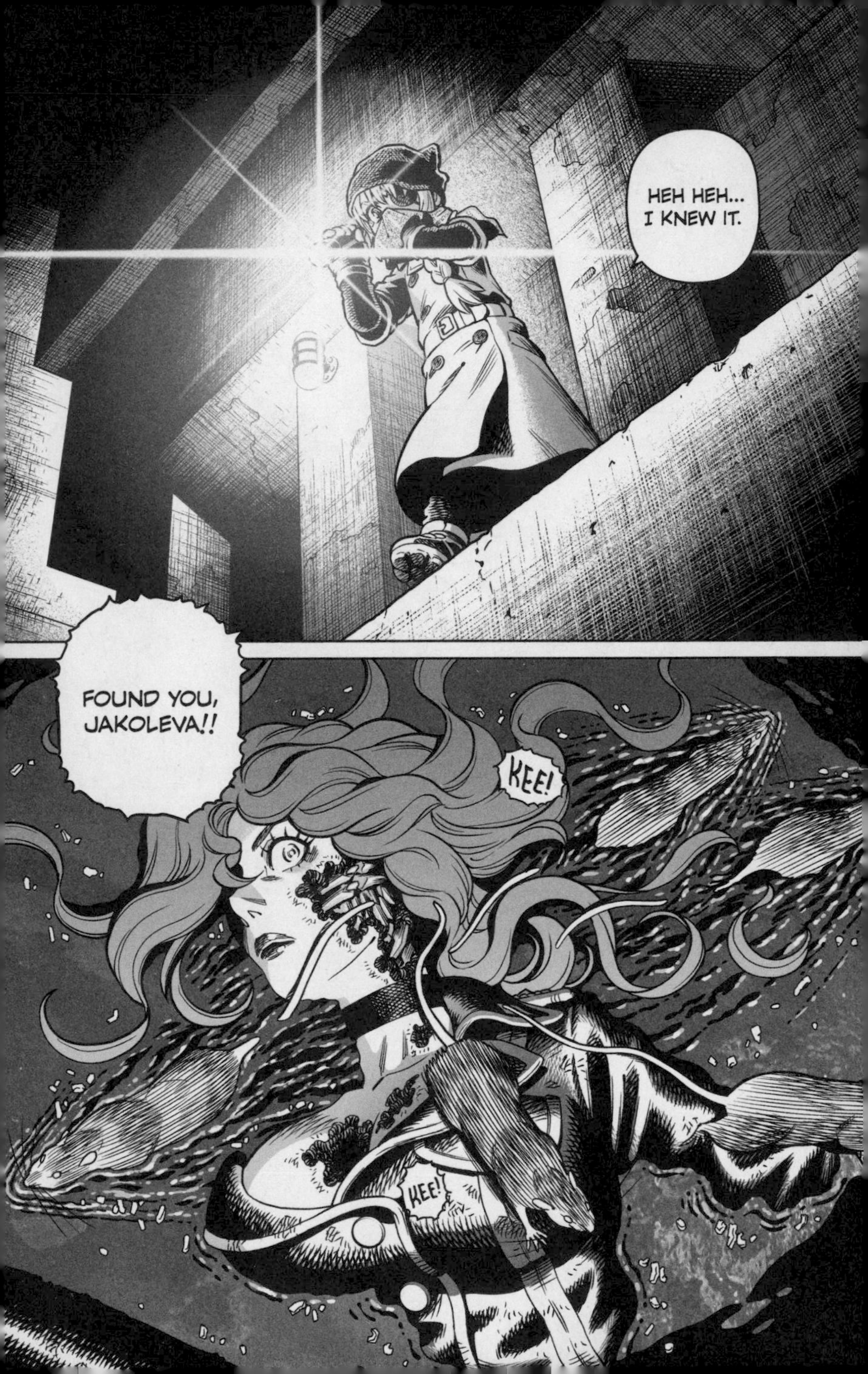
HEH HEH... I KNEW IT.
FOUND YOU, JAKOLEVA!!
KEE!
KEE!

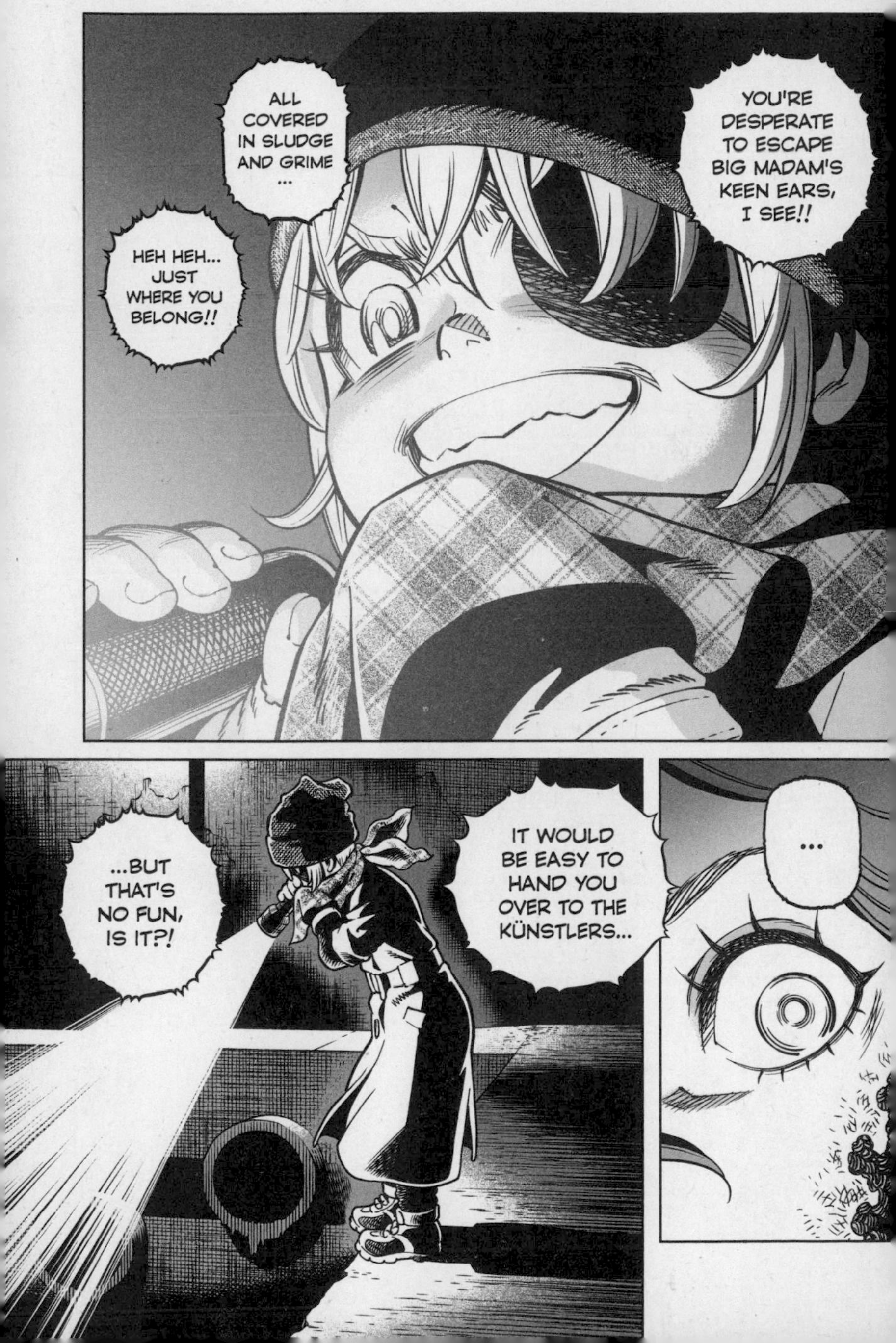
YOU'RE DESPERATE TO ESCAPE BIG MADAM'S KEEN EARS, I SEE!!
ALL COVERED IN SLUDGE AND GRIME ...
HEH HEH... JUST WHERE YOU BELONG!!
...
IT WOULD BE EASY TO HAND YOU OVER TO THE KÜNSTLERS...
...BUT THAT'S NO FUN, IS IT?!

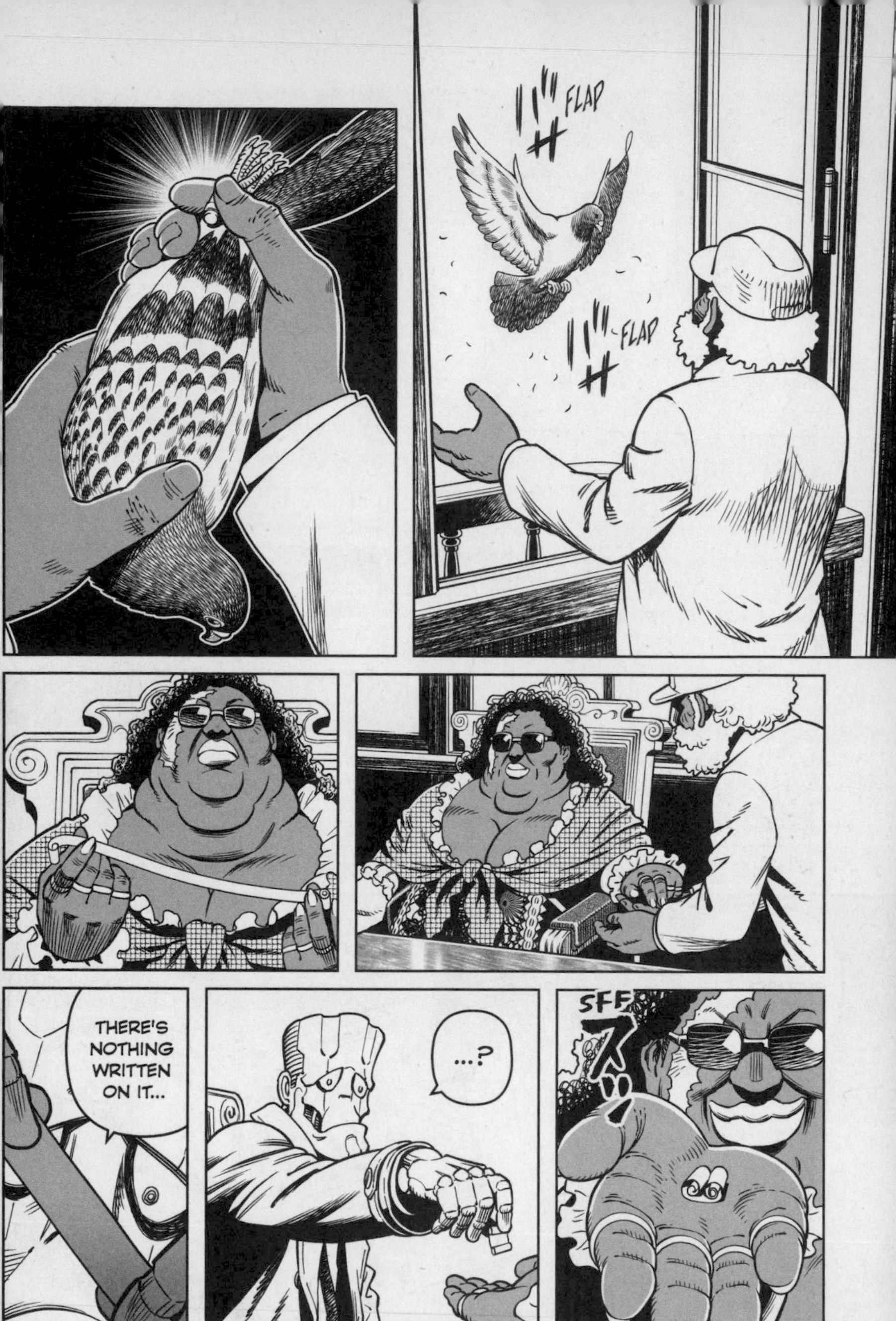
FLAP
FLAP
SFF
...?
THERE'S NOTHING WRITTEN ON IT...

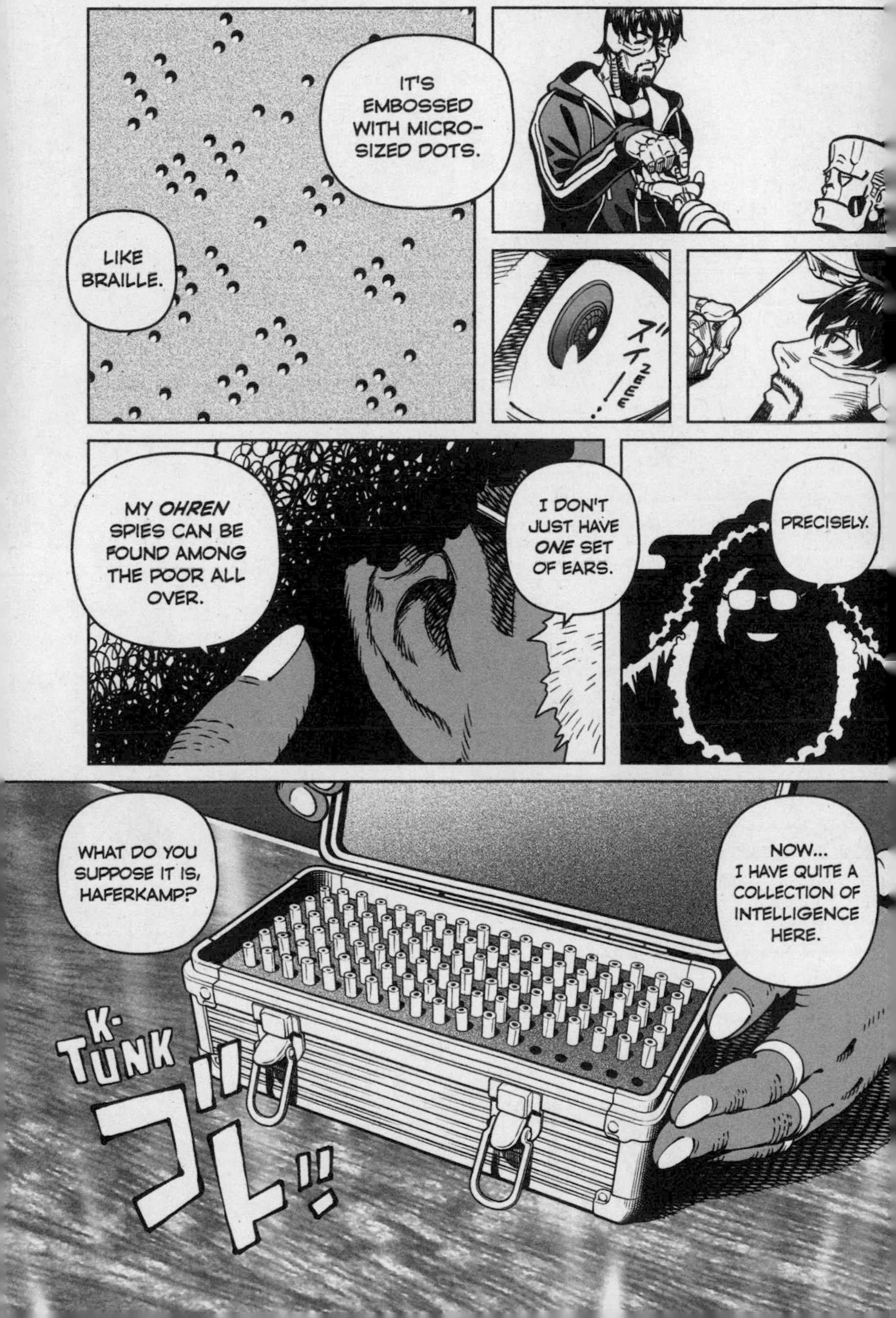
ズイー
ZEEE
IT'S EMBOSSED WITH MICRO-SIZED DOTS.
LIKE BRAILLE.
PRECISELY.
I DON'T JUST HAVE *ONE* SET OF EARS.
MY *OHREN* SPIES CAN BE FOUND AMONG THE POOR ALL OVER.
NOW... I HAVE QUITE A COLLECTION OF INTELLIGENCE HERE.
WHAT DO YOU SUPPOSE IT IS, HAFERKAMP?
コト
K-TUNK

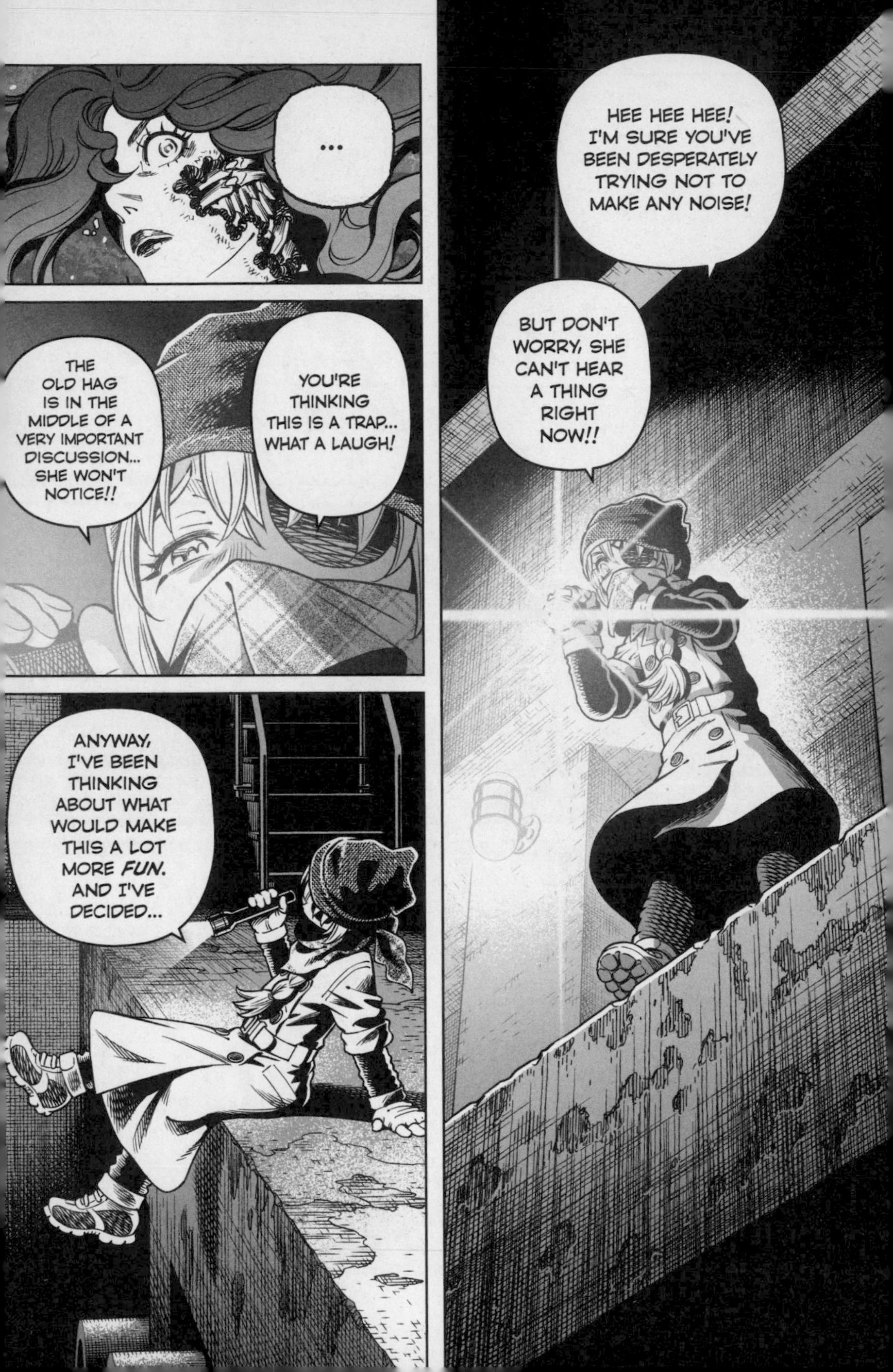
HEE HEE HEE! I'M SURE YOU'VE BEEN DESPERATELY TRYING NOT TO MAKE ANY NOISE!
BUT DON'T WORRY, SHE CAN'T HEAR A THING RIGHT NOW!!
...
YOU'RE THINKING THIS IS A TRAP... WHAT A LAUGH!
THE OLD HAG IS IN THE MIDDLE OF A VERY IMPORTANT DISCUSSION... SHE WON'T NOTICE!!
ANYWAY, I'VE BEEN THINKING ABOUT WHAT WOULD MAKE THIS A LOT MORE *FUN*. AND I'VE DECIDED...

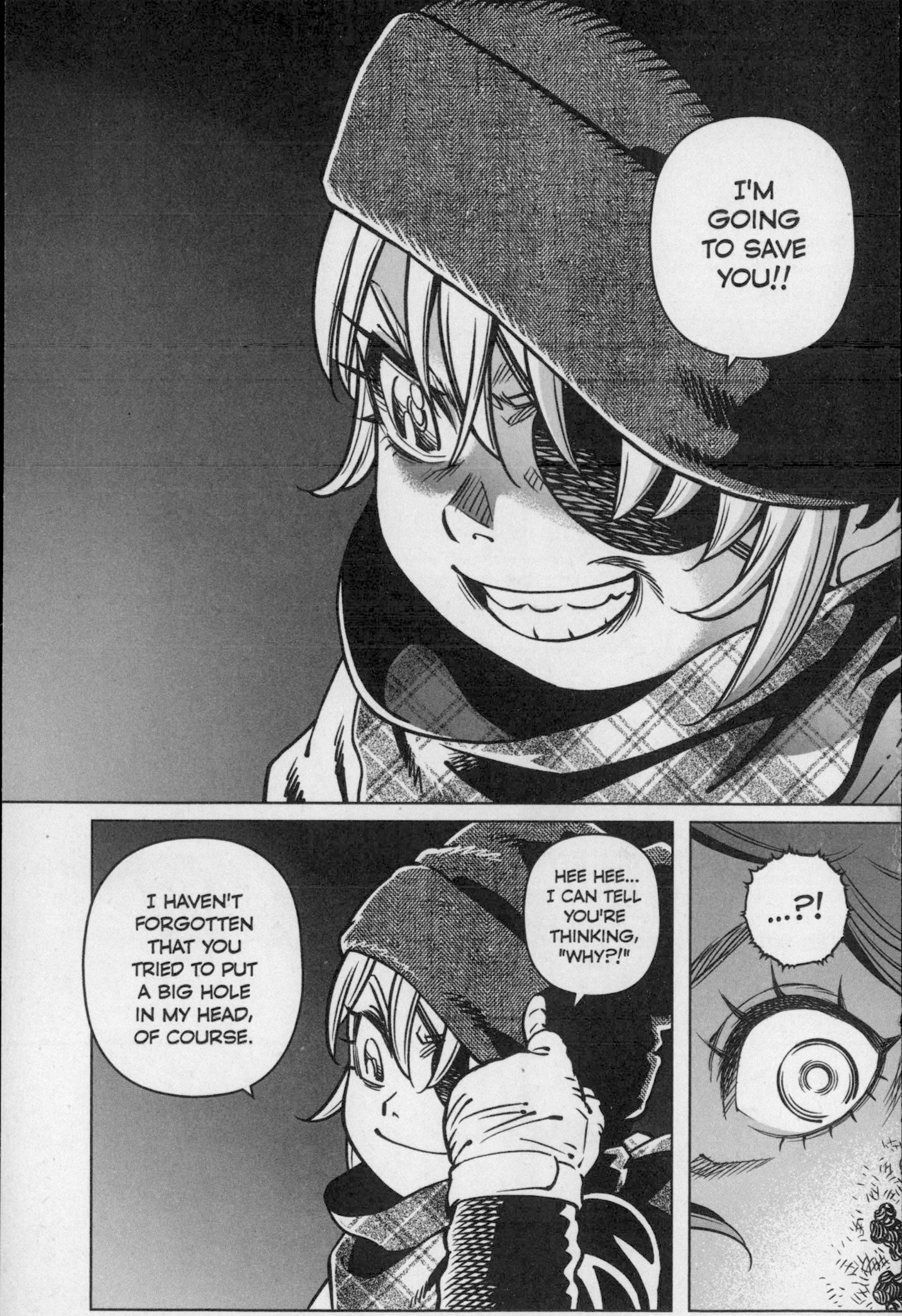
I'M GOING TO SAVE YOU!!
...?!
HEE HEE... I CAN TELL YOU'RE THINKING, "WHY?!"
I HAVEN'T FORGOTTEN THAT YOU TRIED TO PUT A BIG HOLE IN MY HEAD, OF COURSE.

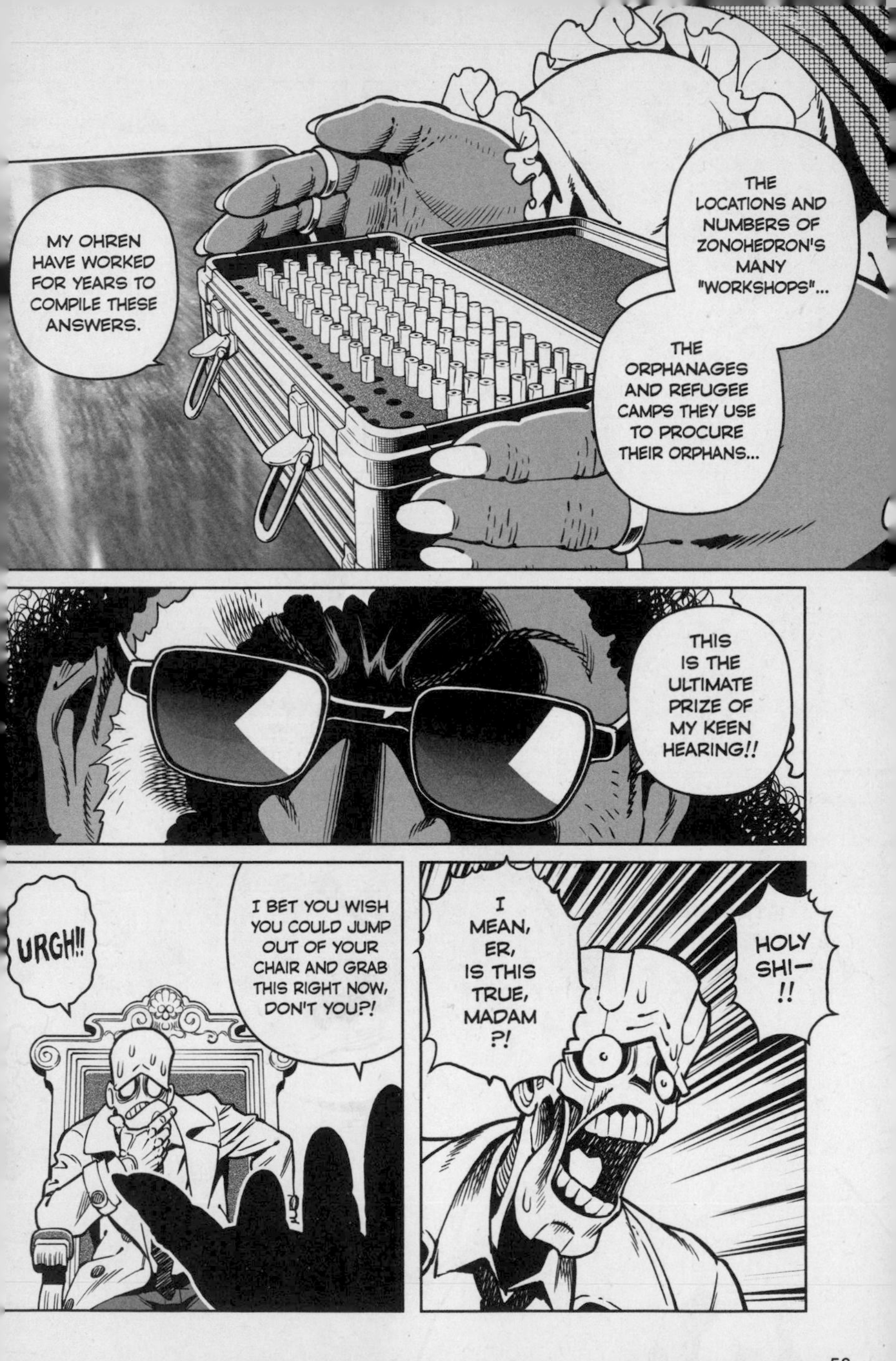
THE LOCATIONS AND NUMBERS OF ZONOHEDRON'S MANY "WORKSHOPS"...
THE ORPHANAGES AND REFUGEE CAMPS THEY USE TO PROCURE THEIR ORPHANS...
MY OHREN HAVE WORKED FOR YEARS TO COMPILE THESE ANSWERS.
THIS IS THE ULTIMATE PRIZE OF MY KEEN HEARING!!
HOLY SHI— !!
I MEAN, ER, IS THIS TRUE, MADAM ?!
I BET YOU WISH YOU COULD JUMP OUT OF YOUR CHAIR AND GRAB THIS RIGHT NOW, DON'T YOU?!
URGH!!

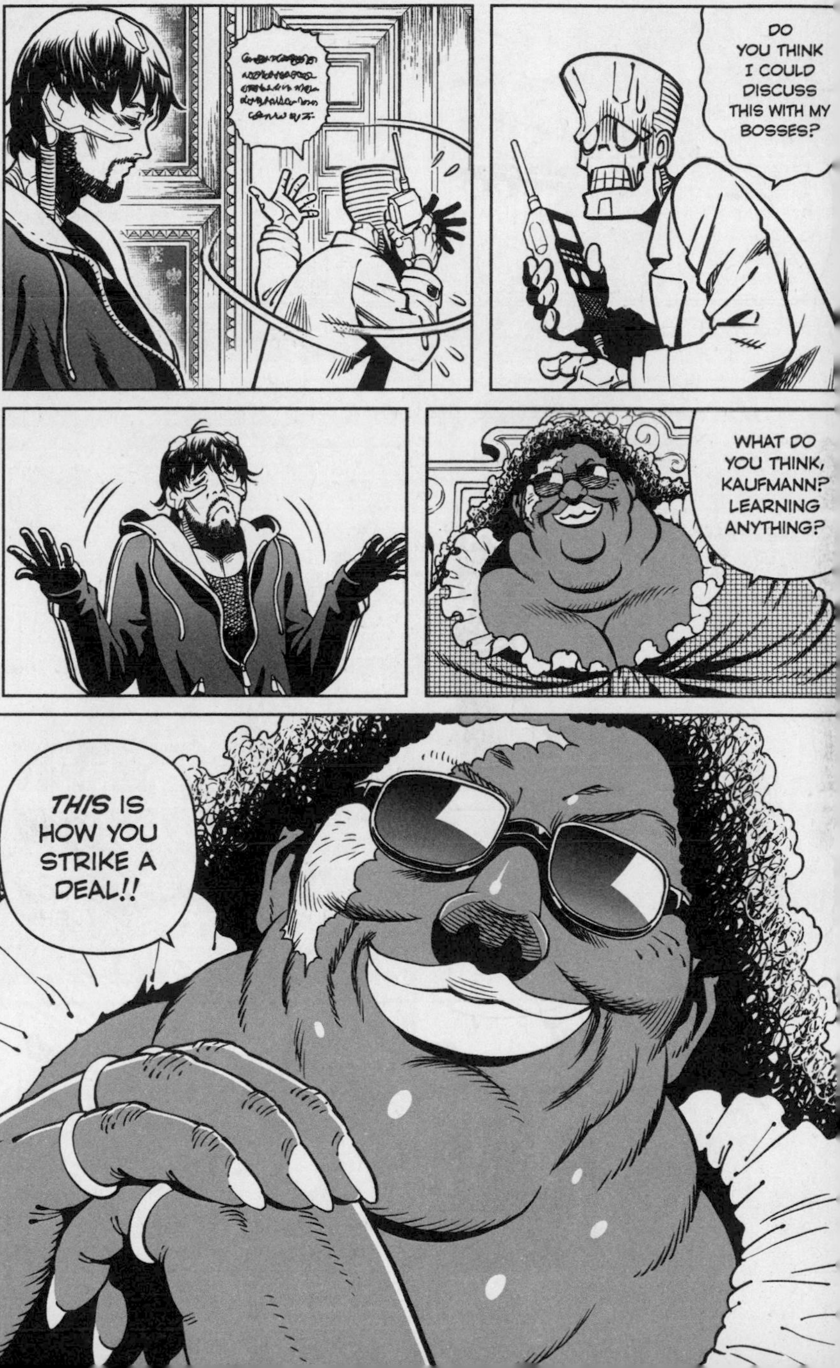
DO YOU THINK I COULD DISCUSS THIS WITH MY BOSSES?
WHAT DO YOU THINK, KAUFMANN? LEARNING ANYTHING?
THIS IS HOW YOU STRIKE A DEAL!!

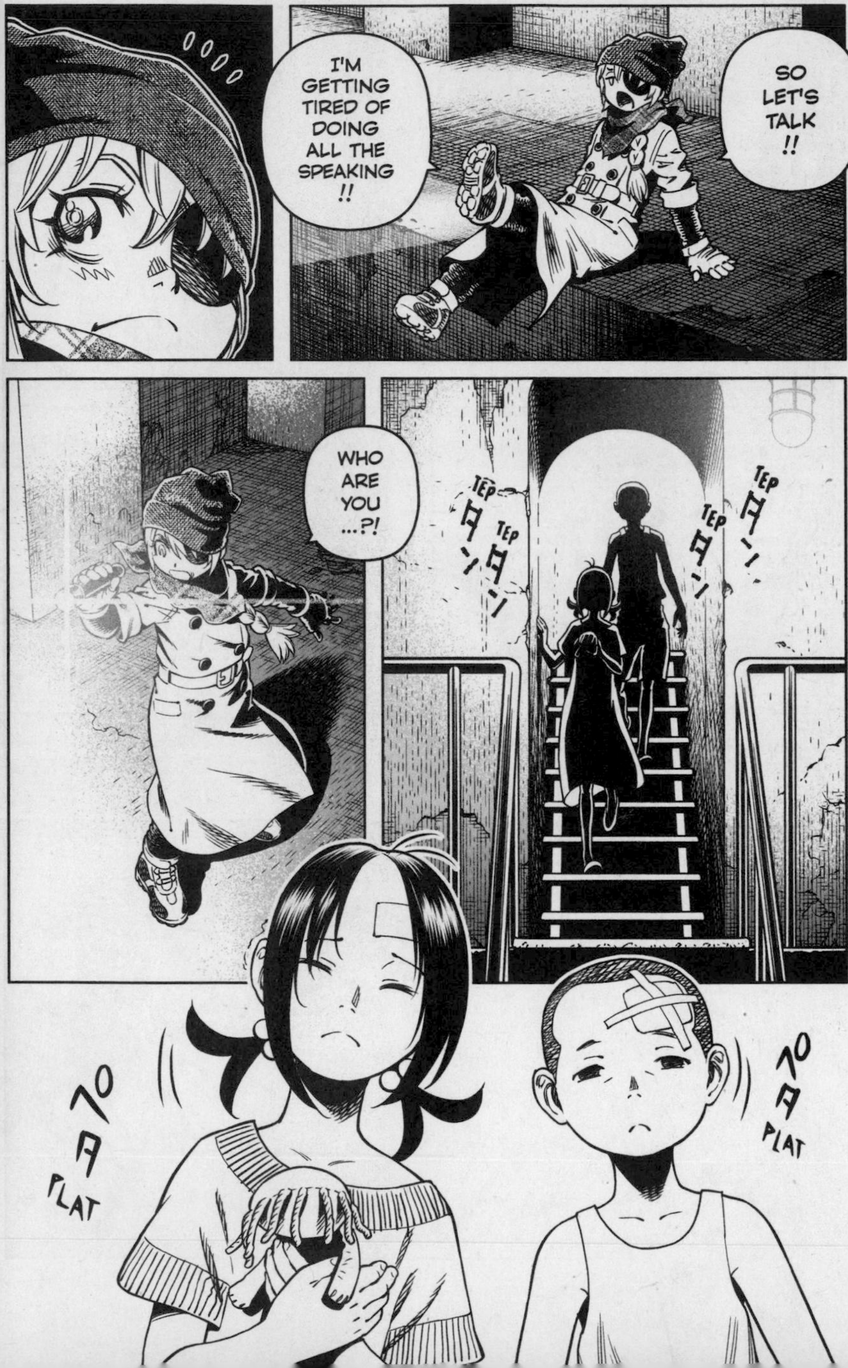
SO LET'S TALK!!
I'M GETTING TIRED OF DOING ALL THE SPEAKING!!
TEP
TEP
TEP
TEP
WHO ARE YOU...?!
PLAT
PLAT

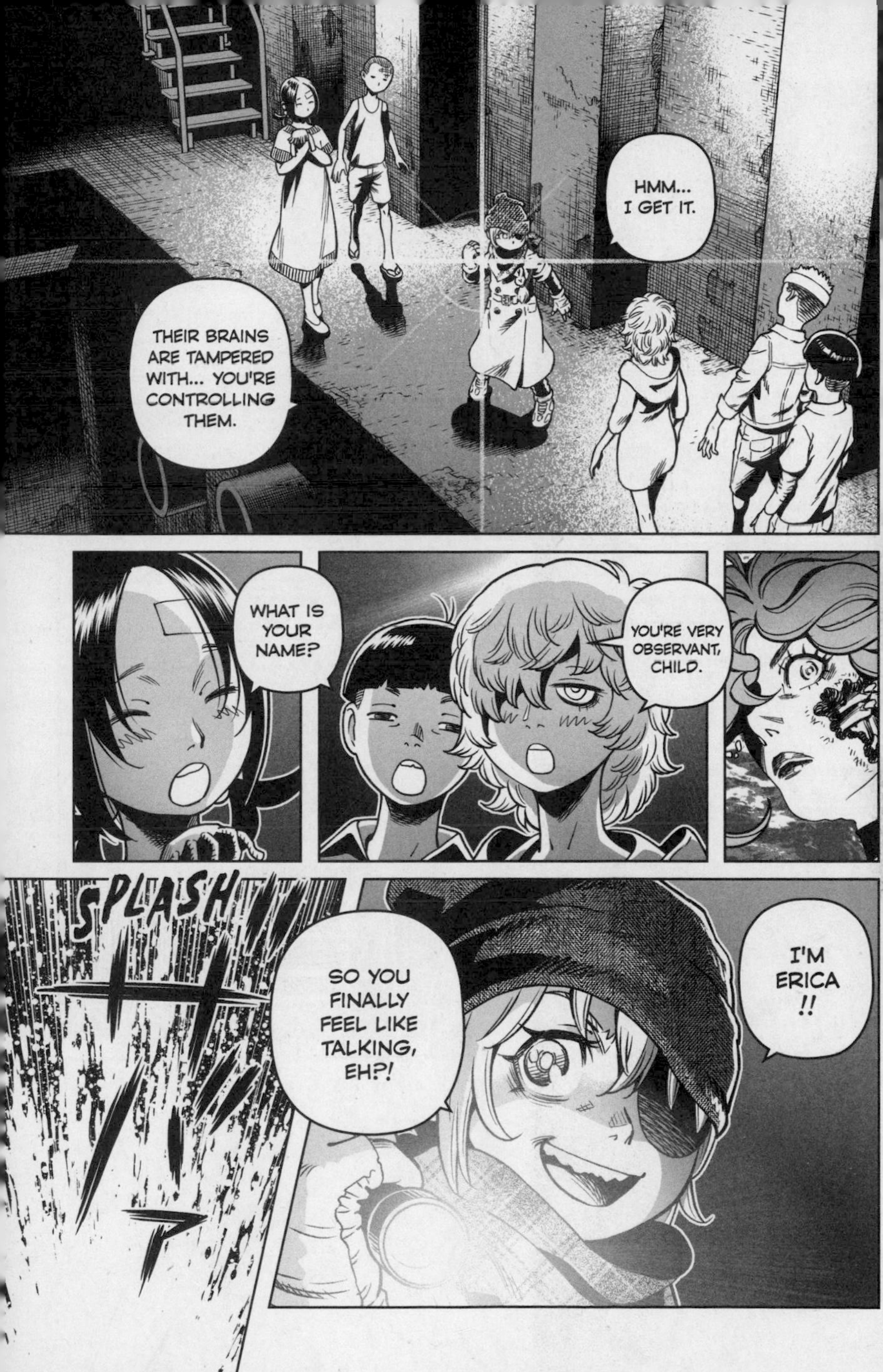
HMM... I GET IT.
THEIR BRAINS ARE TAMPERED WITH... YOU'RE CONTROLLING THEM.
YOU'RE VERY OBSERVANT, CHILD.
WHAT IS YOUR NAME?
I'M ERICA!!
SO YOU FINALLY FEEL LIKE TALKING, EH?!
SPLASH

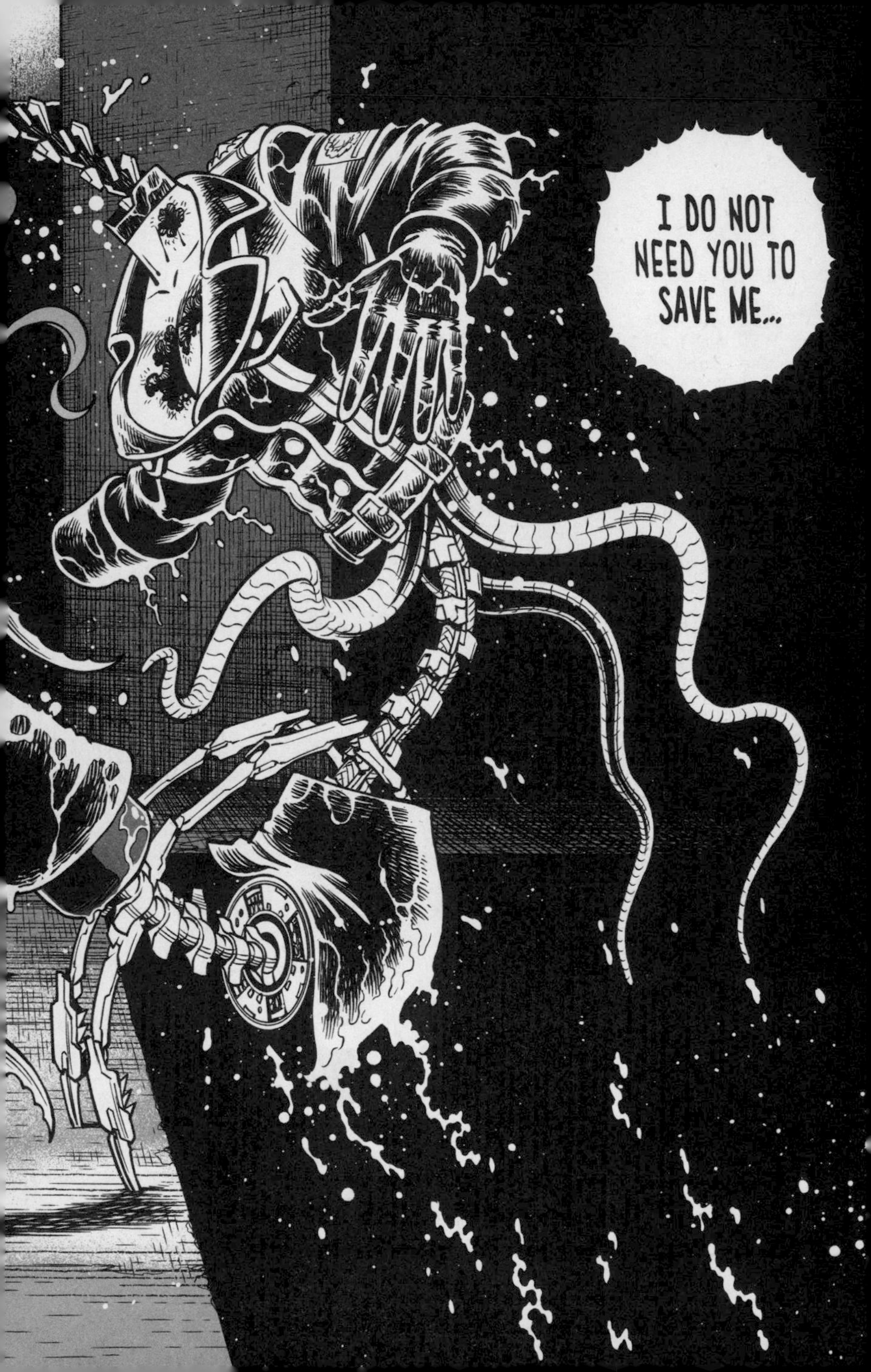
I DO NOT NEED YOU TO SAVE ME...

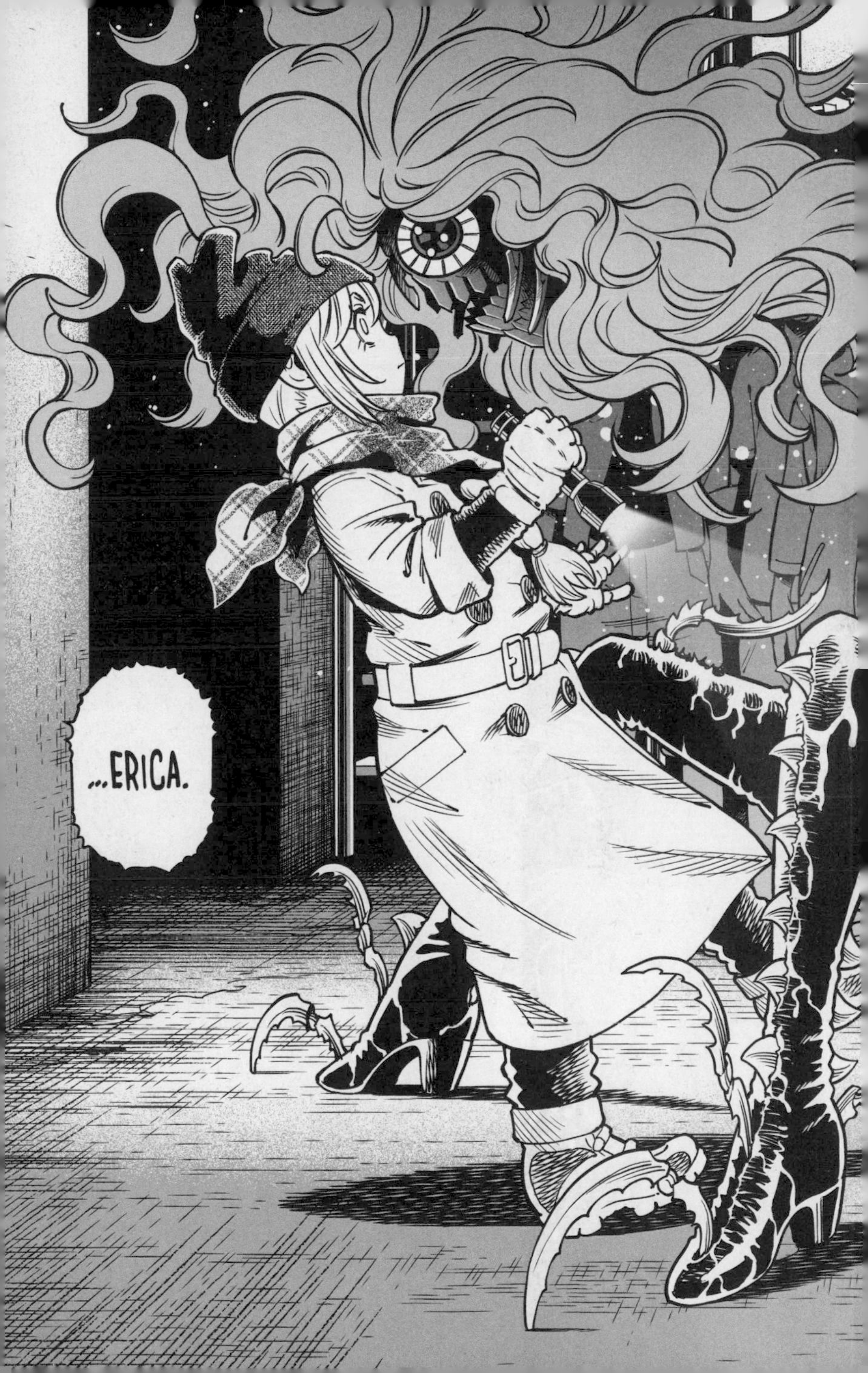
...ERICA.

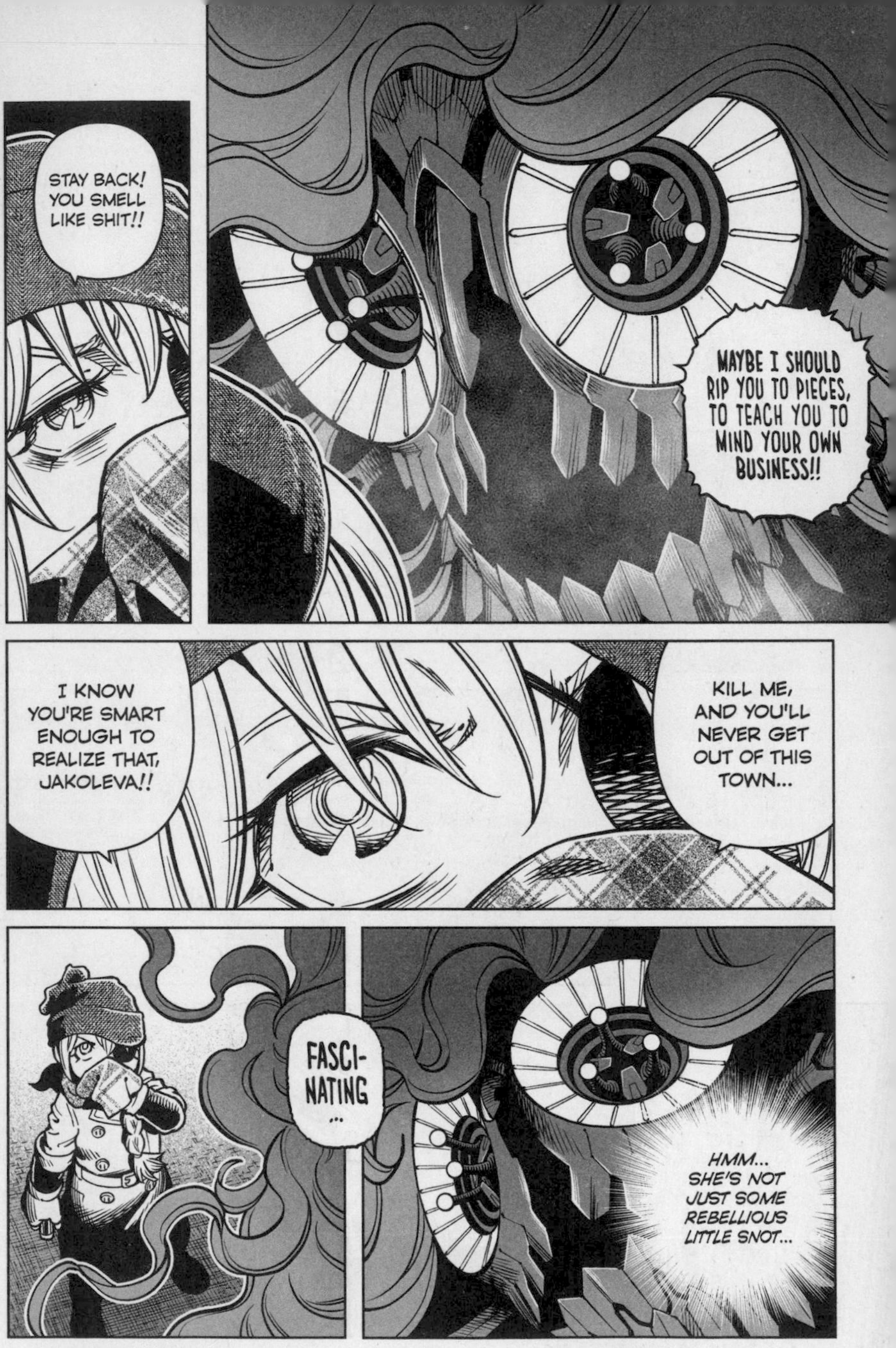
MAYBE I SHOULD RIP YOU TO PIECES, TO TEACH YOU TO MIND YOUR OWN BUSINESS!!
STAY BACK! YOU SMELL LIKE SHIT!!
KILL ME, AND YOU'LL NEVER GET OUT OF THIS TOWN...
I KNOW YOU'RE SMART ENOUGH TO REALIZE THAT, JAKOLEVA!!
HMM... SHE'S NOT JUST SOME REBELLIOUS LITTLE SNOT...
FASCI- NATING ...

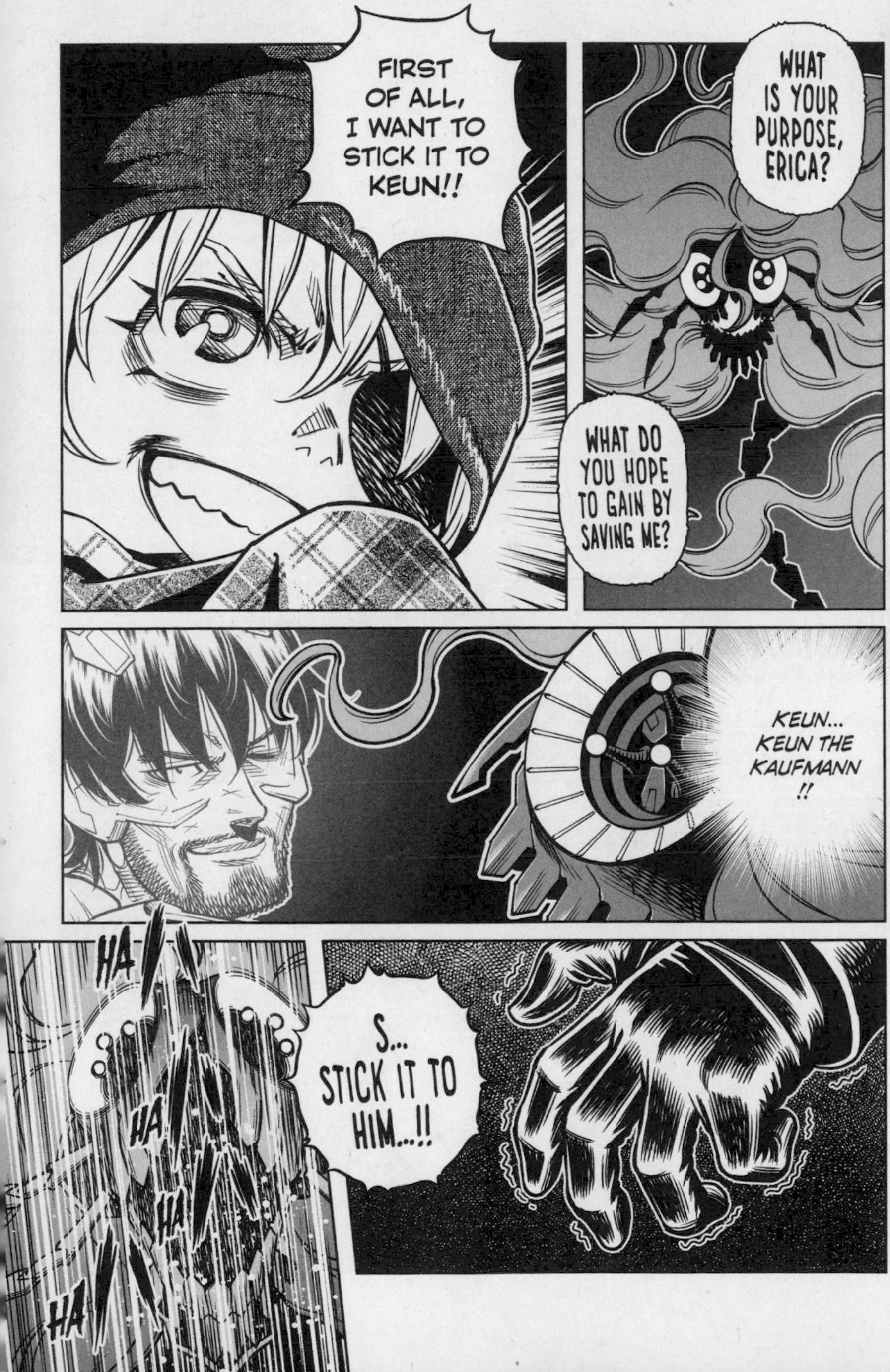
WHAT IS YOUR PURPOSE, ERICA?
WHAT DO YOU HOPE TO GAIN BY SAVING ME?
FIRST OF ALL, I WANT TO STICK IT TO KEUN!!
KEUN... KEUN THE KAUFMANN !!
S... STICK IT TO HIM...!!
HA
HA
HA
HA

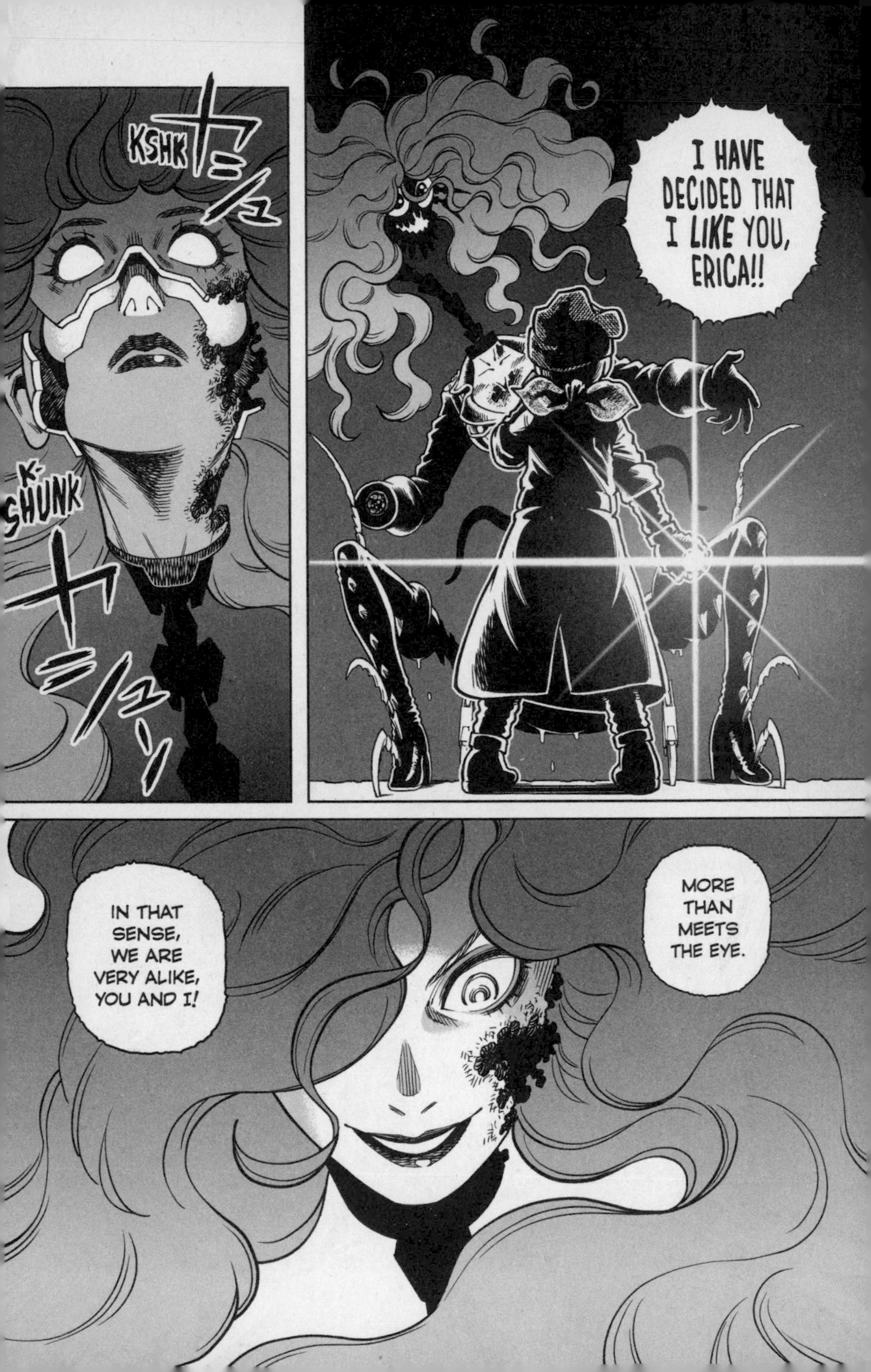
I HAVE DECIDED THAT I LIKE YOU, ERICA!!
KSHK
K-SHUNK
MORE THAN MEETS THE EYE.
IN THAT SENSE, WE ARE VERY ALIKE, YOU AND I!

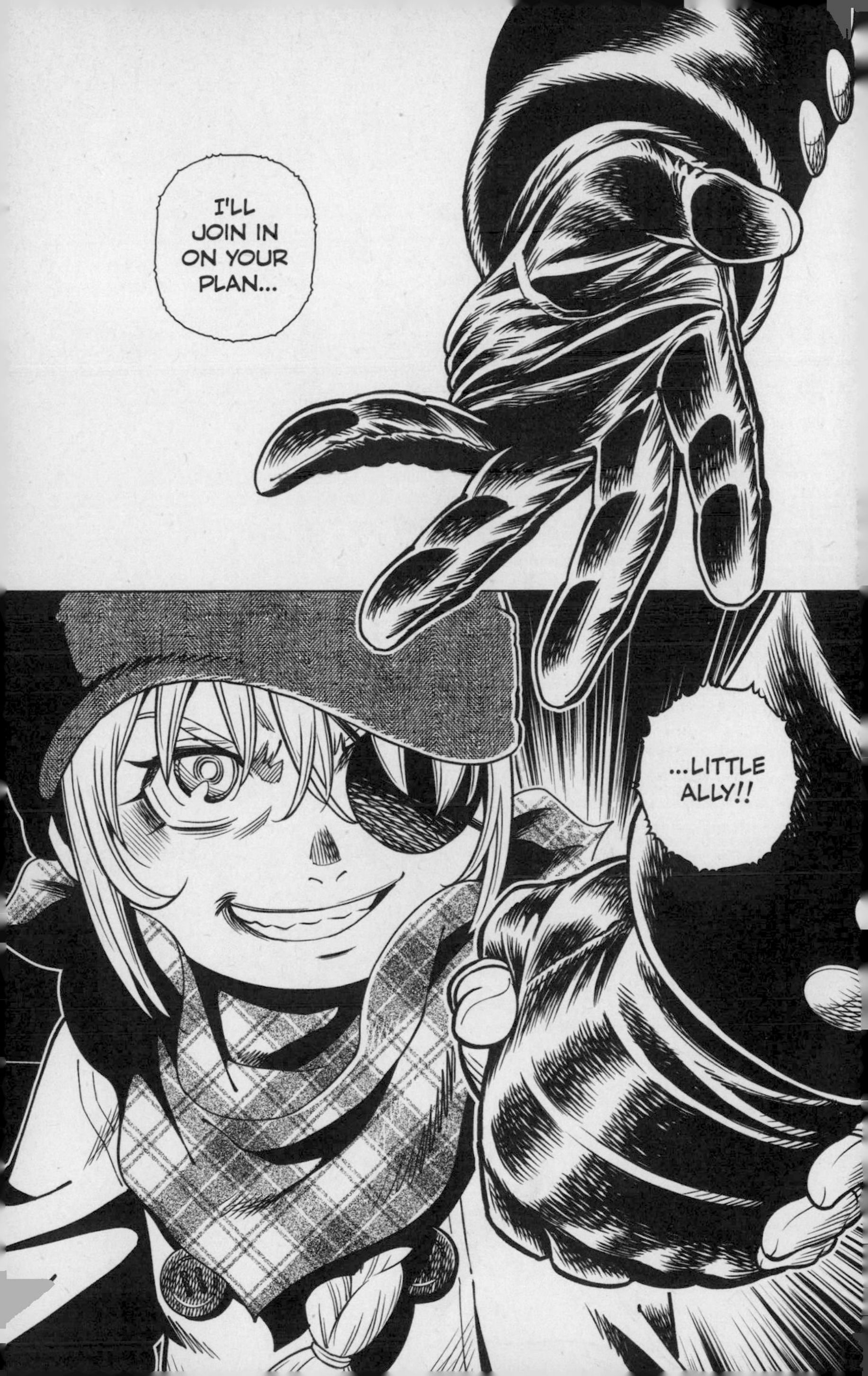
I'LL JOIN IN ON YOUR PLAN...
...LITTLE ALLY!!

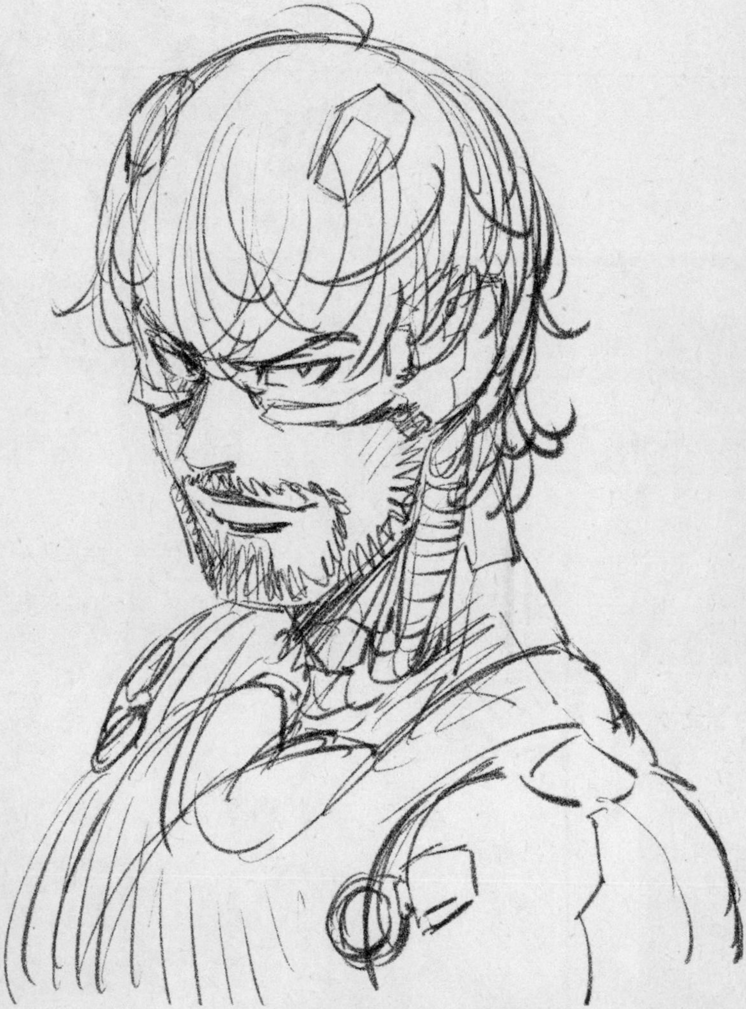

LOG:039

THE WISEHEART REPORT

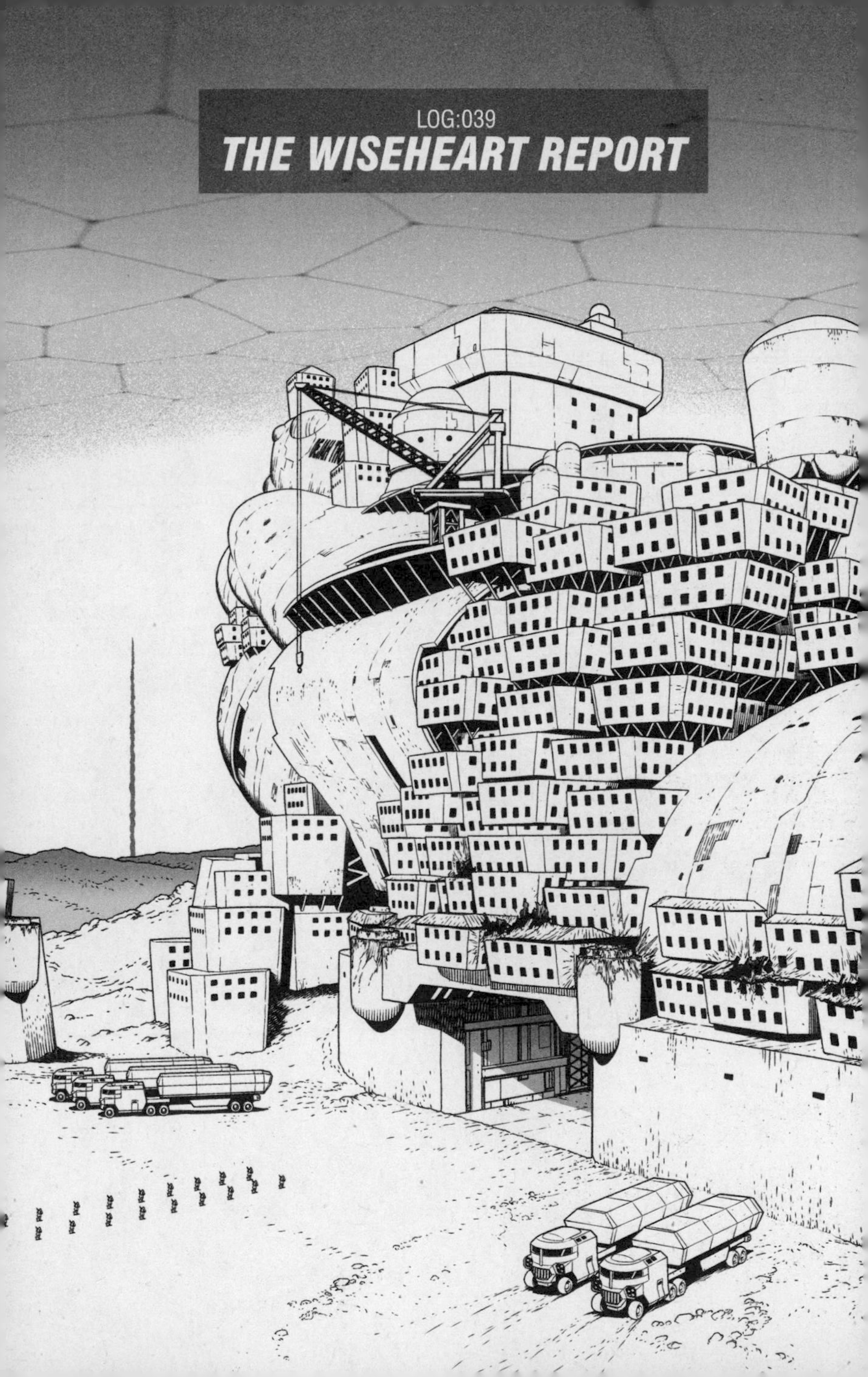

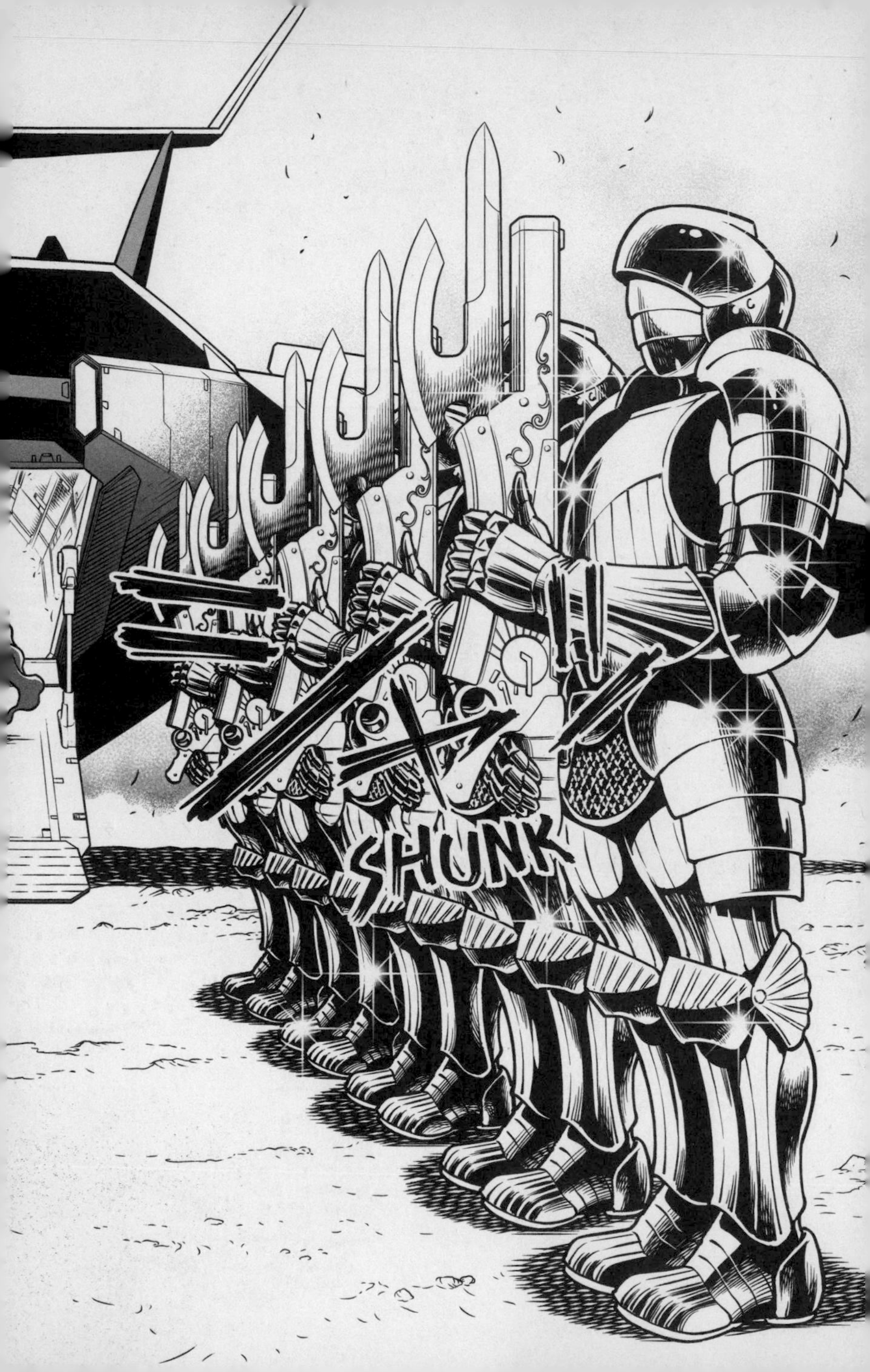
SHUNK

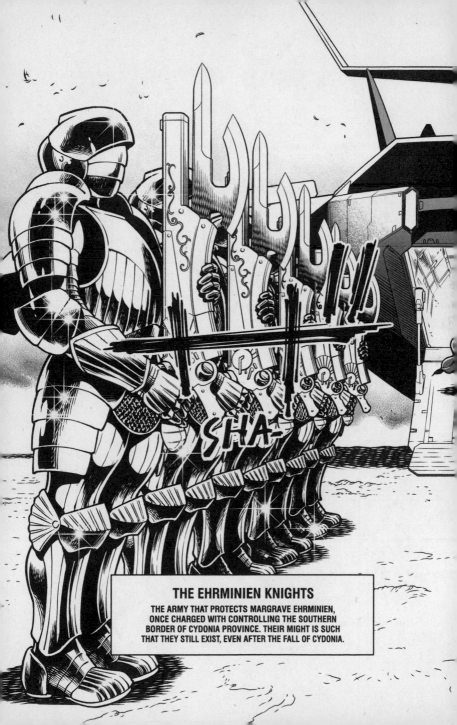

THE EHRMINIEN KNIGHTS

THE ARMY THAT PROTECTS MARGRAVE EHRMINIEN,
ONCE CHARGED WITH CONTROLLING THE SOUTHERN
BORDER OF CYDONIA PROVINCE. THEIR MIGHT IS SUCH
THAT THEY STILL EXIST, EVEN AFTER THE FALL OF CYDONIA.

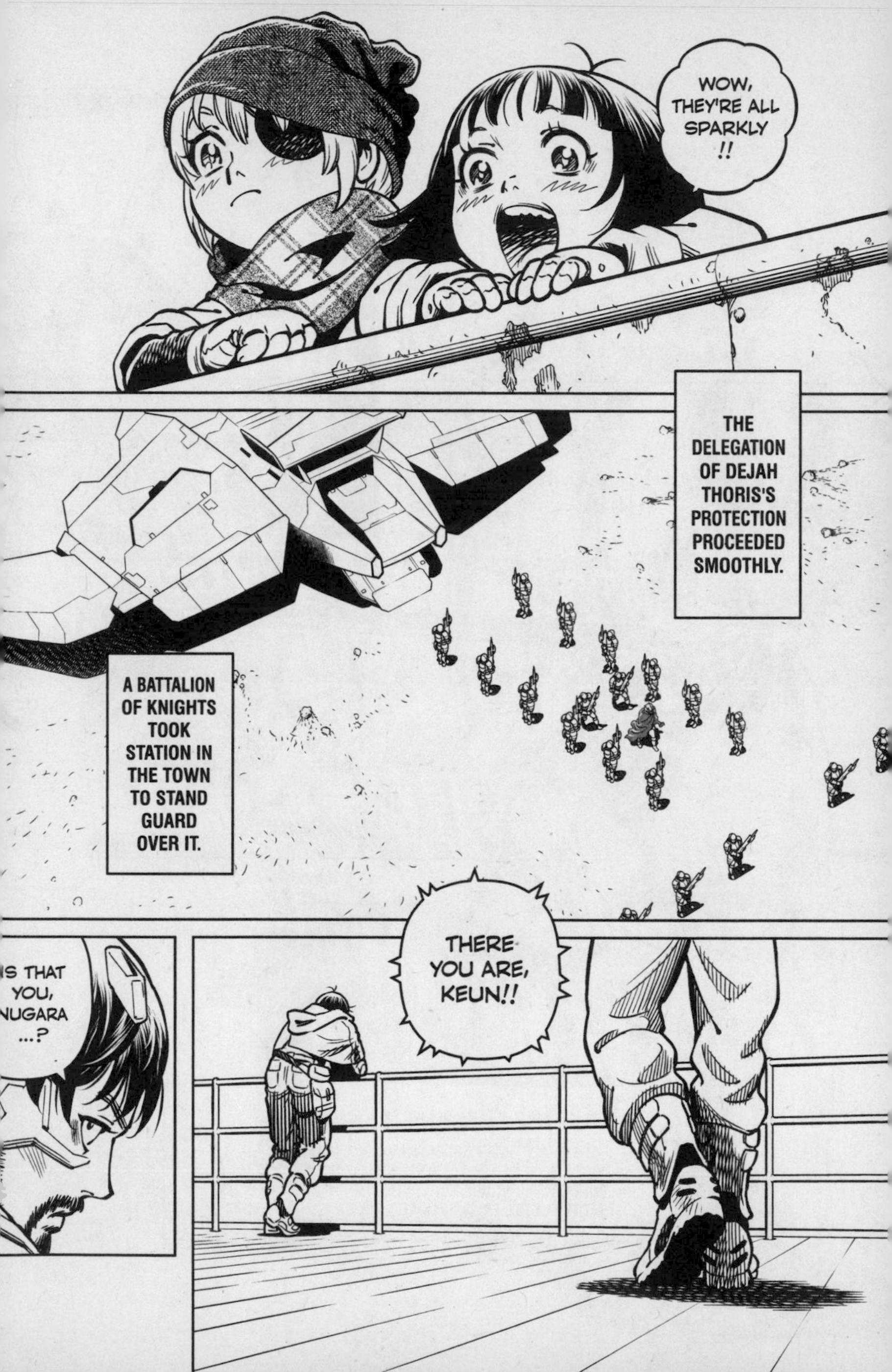

WOW, THEY'RE ALL SPARKLY !!
THE DELEGATION OF DEJAH THORIS'S PROTECTION PROCEEDED SMOOTHLY.
A BATTALION OF KNIGHTS TOOK STATION IN THE TOWN TO STAND GUARD OVER IT.
THERE YOU ARE, KEUN!!
IS THAT YOU, NUGARA ...?

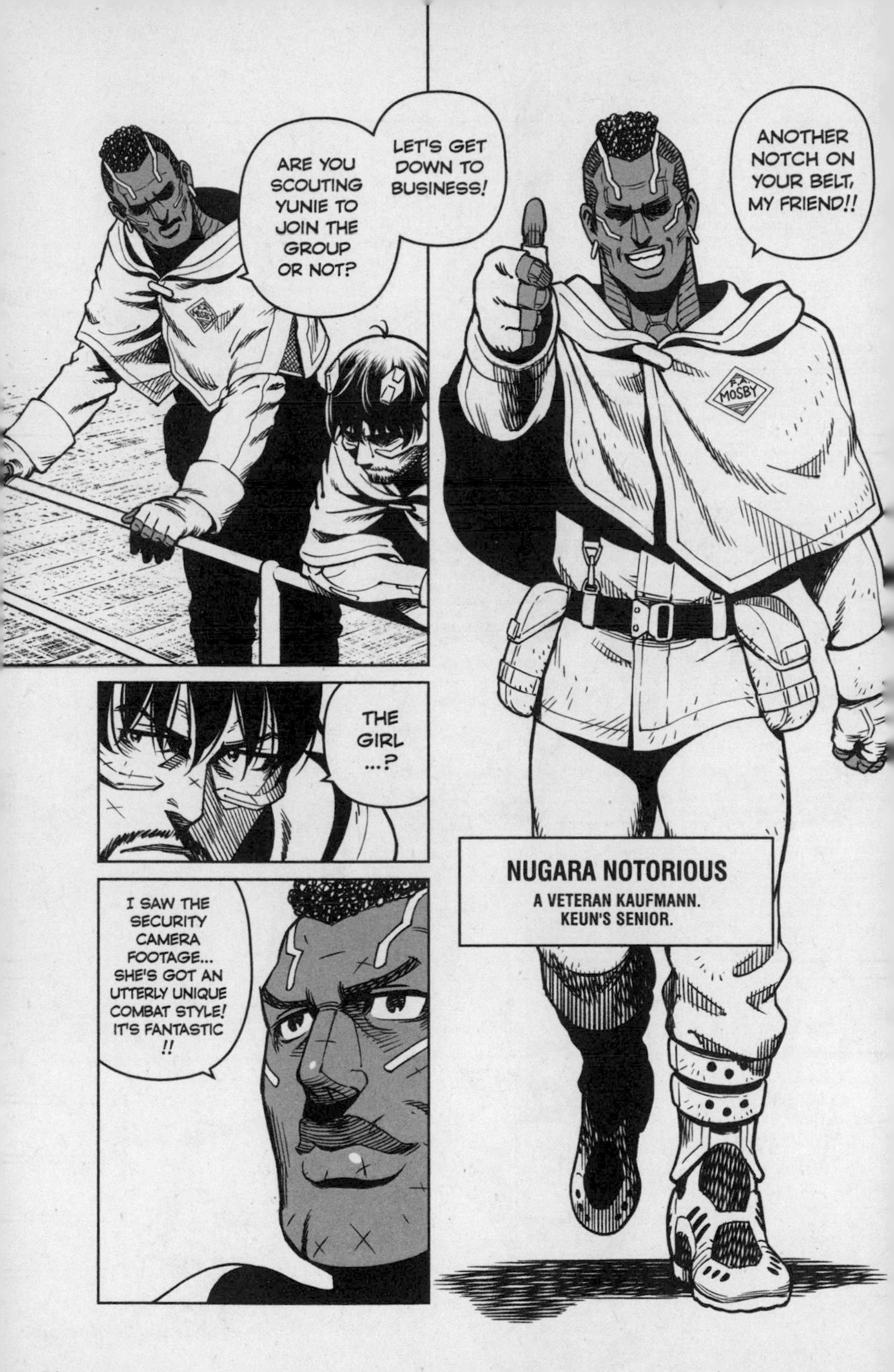
ANOTHER NOTCH ON YOUR BELT, MY FRIEND!!
NUGARA NOTORIOUS
A VETERAN KAUFMANN. KEUN'S SENIOR.
LET'S GET DOWN TO BUSINESS!
ARE YOU SCOUTING YUNIE TO JOIN THE GROUP OR NOT?
THE GIRL ...?
I SAW THE SECURITY CAMERA FOOTAGE... SHE'S GOT AN UTTERLY UNIQUE COMBAT STYLE! IT'S FANTASTIC !!

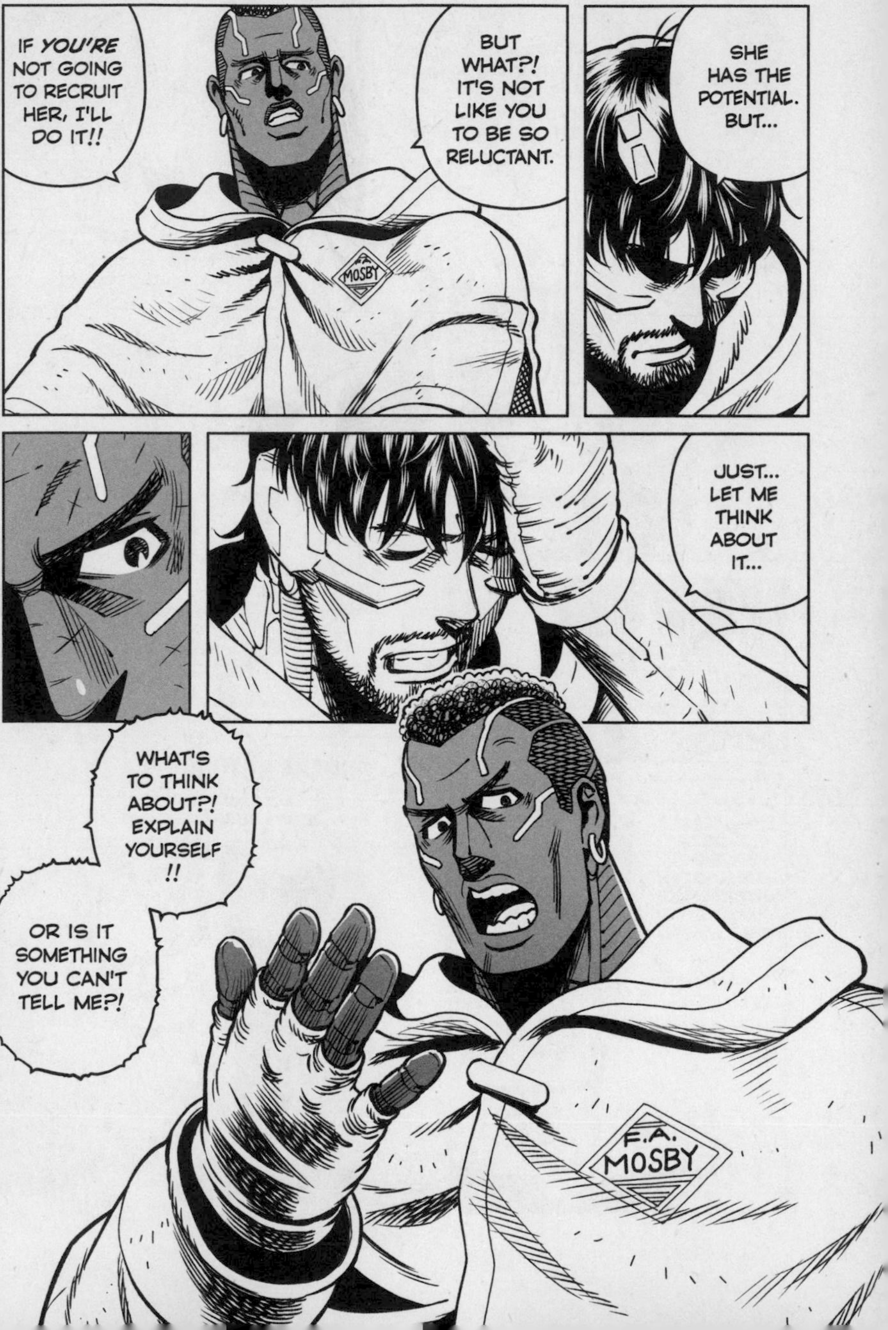
SHE HAS THE POTENTIAL. BUT...
BUT WHAT?! IT'S NOT LIKE YOU TO BE SO RELUCTANT.
MOSBY
IF *YOU'RE* NOT GOING TO RECRUIT HER, I'LL DO IT!!
JUST... LET ME THINK ABOUT IT...
WHAT'S TO THINK ABOUT?! EXPLAIN YOURSELF!!
OR IS IT SOMETHING YOU CAN'T TELL ME?!
F.A. MOSBY

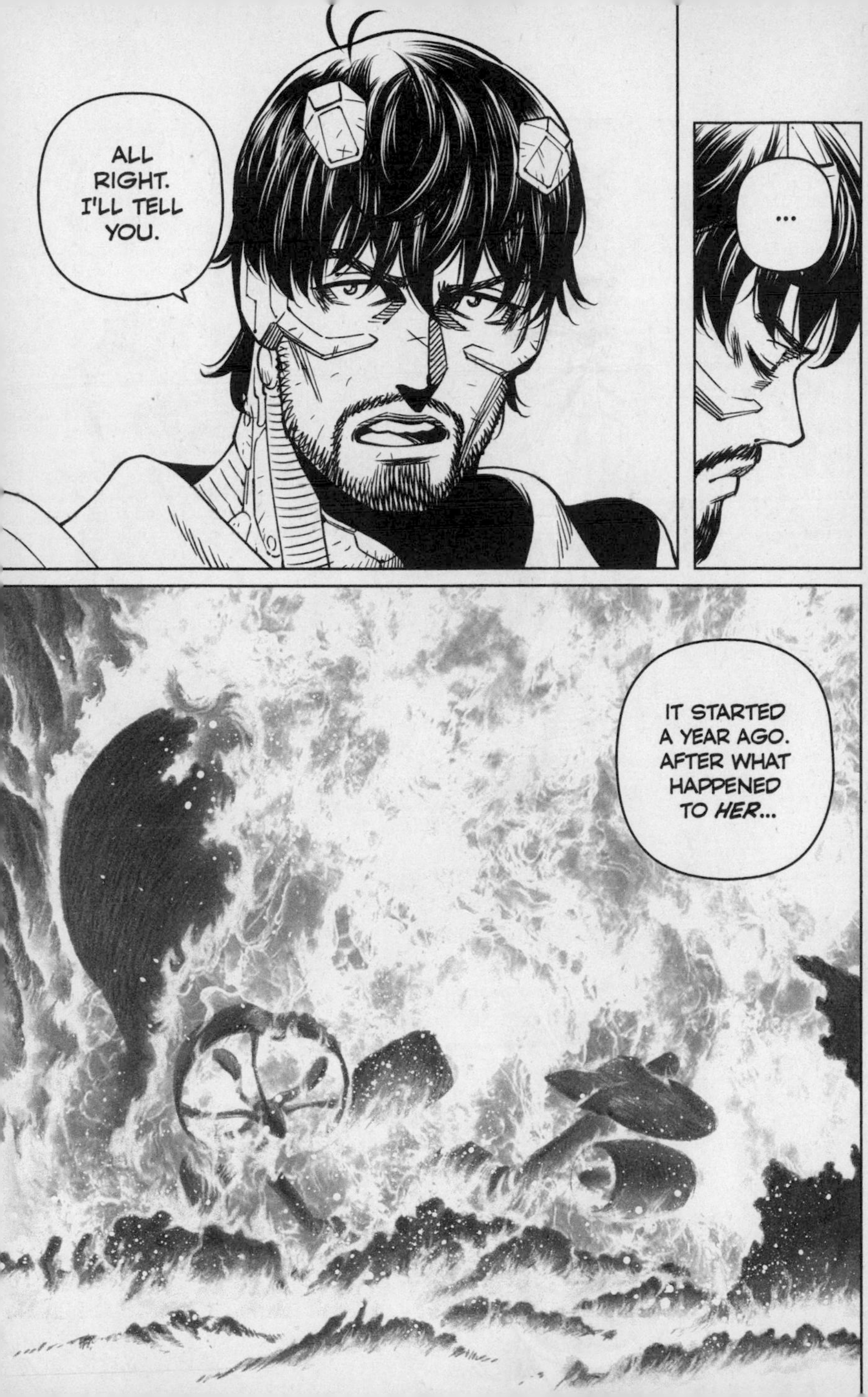
...
ALL RIGHT. I'LL TELL YOU.
IT STARTED A YEAR AGO. AFTER WHAT HAPPENED TO *HER*...

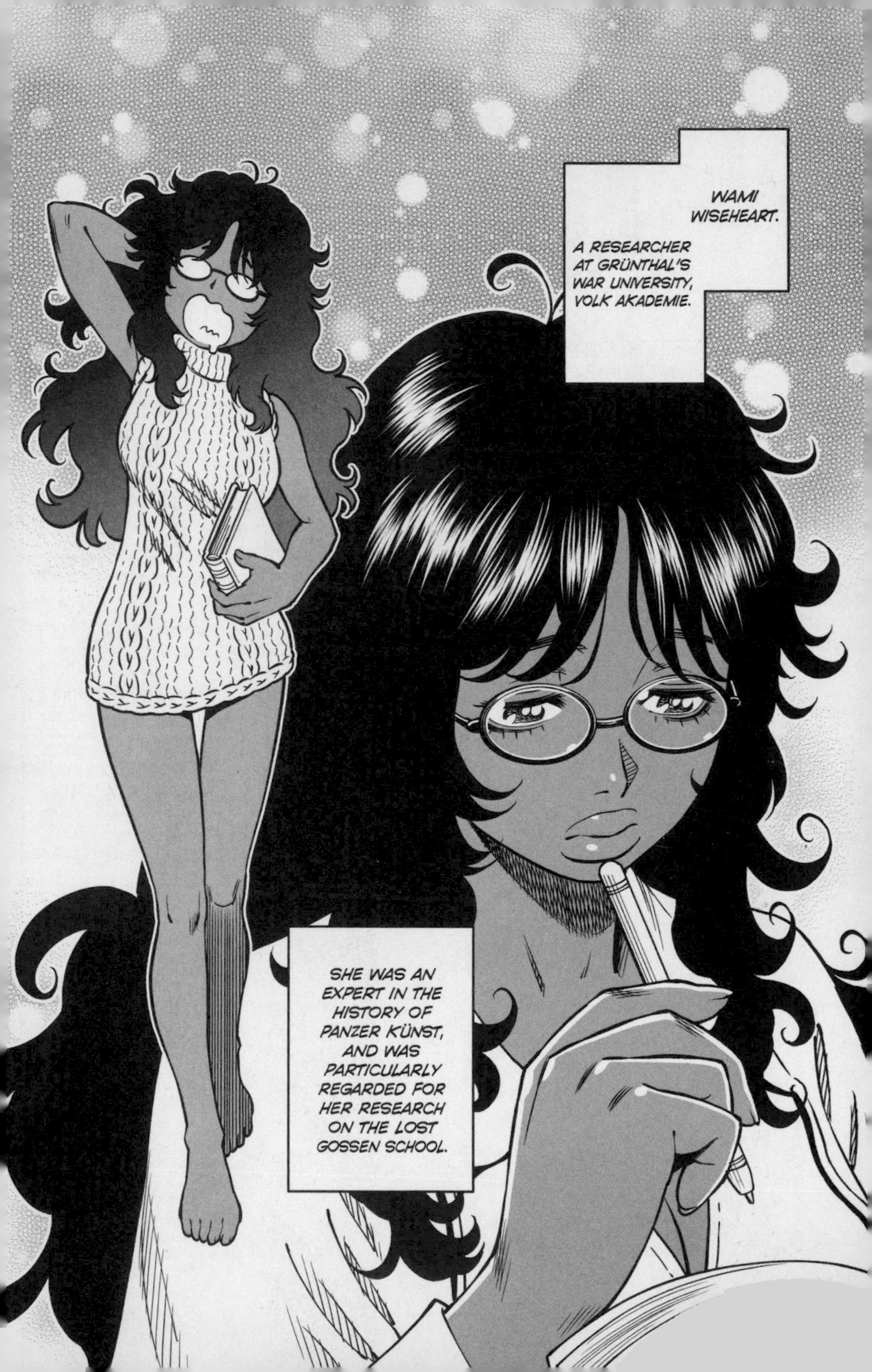
WAMI WISEHEART.
A RESEARCHER AT GRÜNTHAL'S WAR UNIVERSITY, VOLK AKADEMIE.
SHE WAS AN EXPERT IN THE HISTORY OF PANZER KÜNST, AND WAS PARTICULARLY REGARDED FOR HER RESEARCH ON THE LOST GOSSEN SCHOOL.

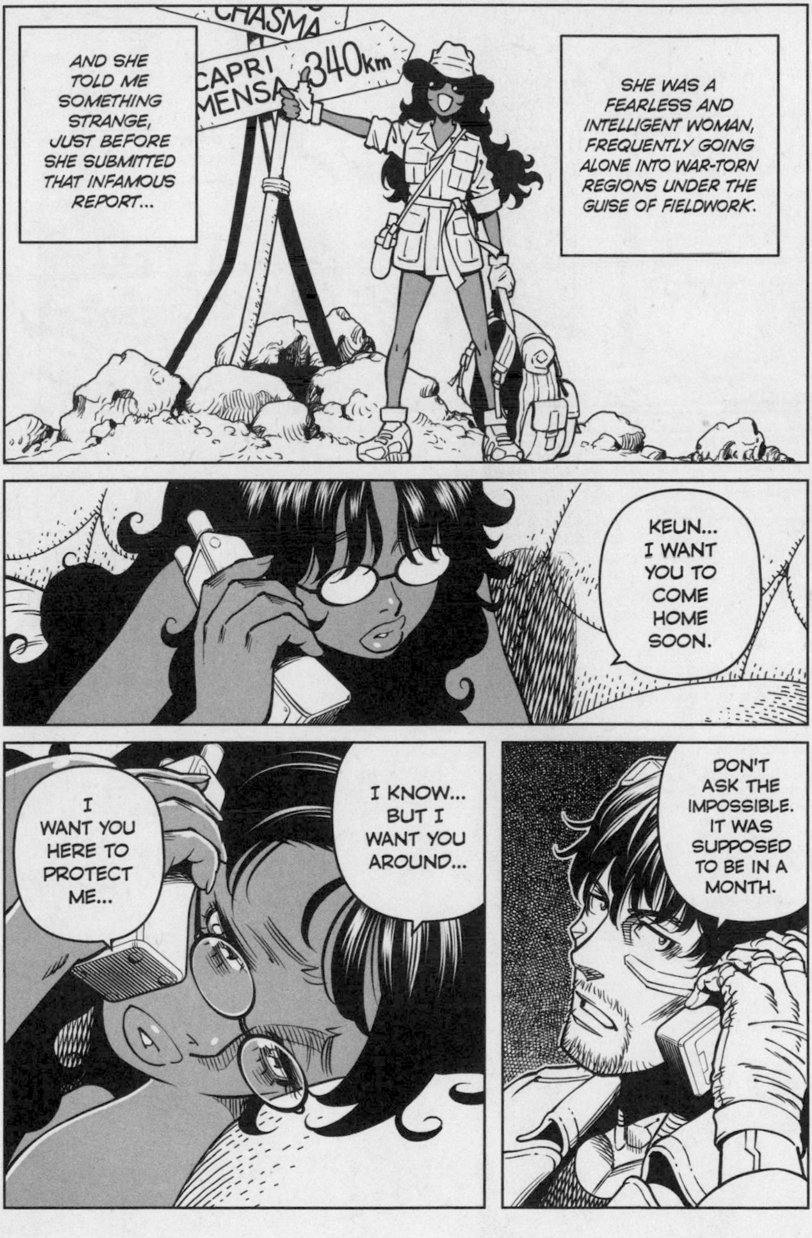
SHE WAS A FEARLESS AND INTELLIGENT WOMAN, FREQUENTLY GOING ALONE INTO WAR-TORN REGIONS UNDER THE GUISE OF FIELDWORK.
CHASMA
CAPRI MENSA 340km
AND SHE TOLD ME SOMETHING STRANGE, JUST BEFORE SHE SUBMITTED THAT INFAMOUS REPORT...
KEUN... I WANT YOU TO COME HOME SOON.
DON'T ASK THE IMPOSSIBLE. IT WAS SUPPOSED TO BE IN A MONTH.
I KNOW... BUT I WANT YOU AROUND...
I WANT YOU HERE TO PROTECT ME...

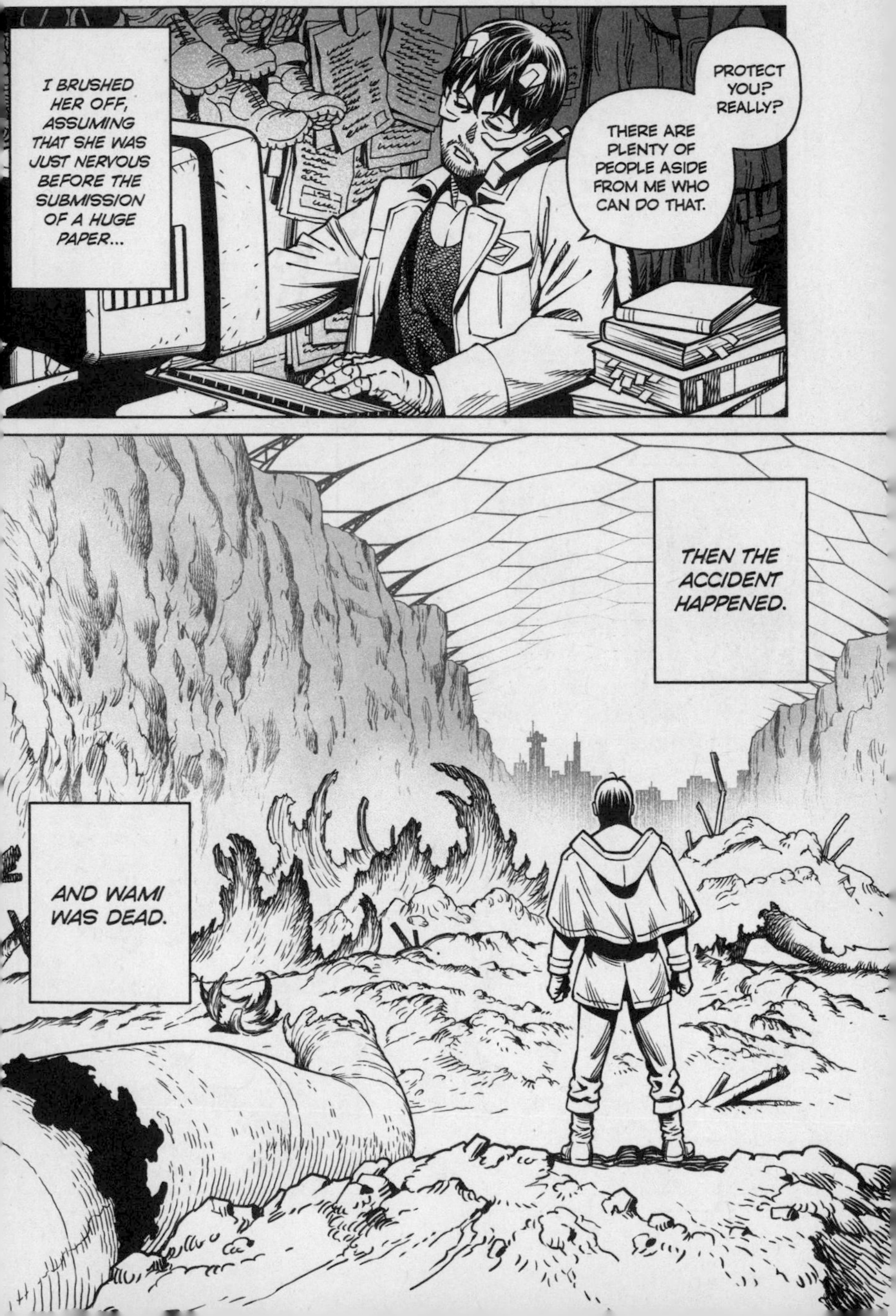
PROTECT YOU? REALLY?
THERE ARE PLENTY OF PEOPLE ASIDE FROM ME WHO CAN DO THAT.
I BRUSHED HER OFF, ASSUMING THAT SHE WAS JUST NERVOUS BEFORE THE SUBMISSION OF A HUGE PAPER...
THEN THE ACCIDENT HAPPENED.
AND WAMI WAS DEAD.

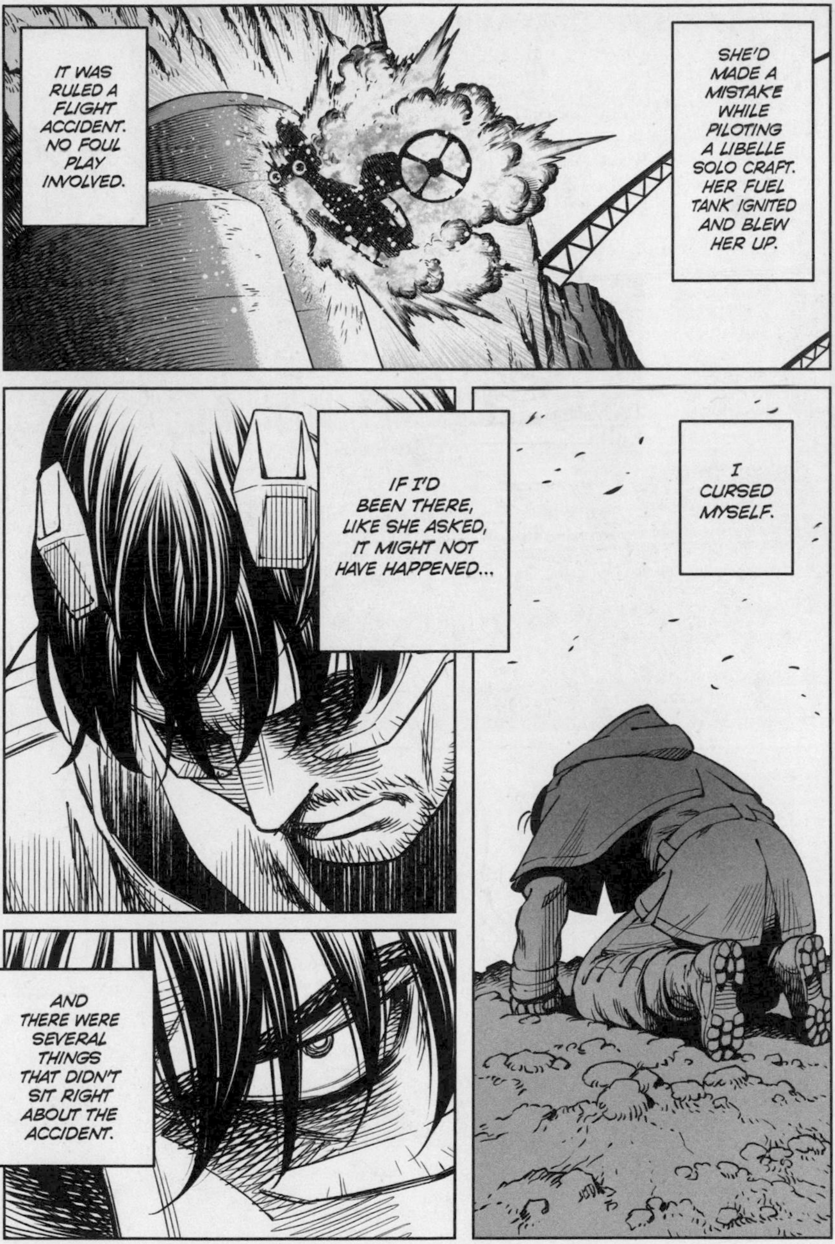
SHE'D MADE A MISTAKE WHILE PILOTING A LIBELLE SOLO CRAFT. HER FUEL TANK IGNITED AND BLEW HER UP.
IT WAS RULED A FLIGHT ACCIDENT. NO FOUL PLAY INVOLVED.
I CURSED MYSELF.
IF I'D BEEN THERE, LIKE SHE ASKED, IT MIGHT NOT HAVE HAPPENED...
AND THERE WERE SEVERAL THINGS THAT DIDN'T SIT RIGHT ABOUT THE ACCIDENT.

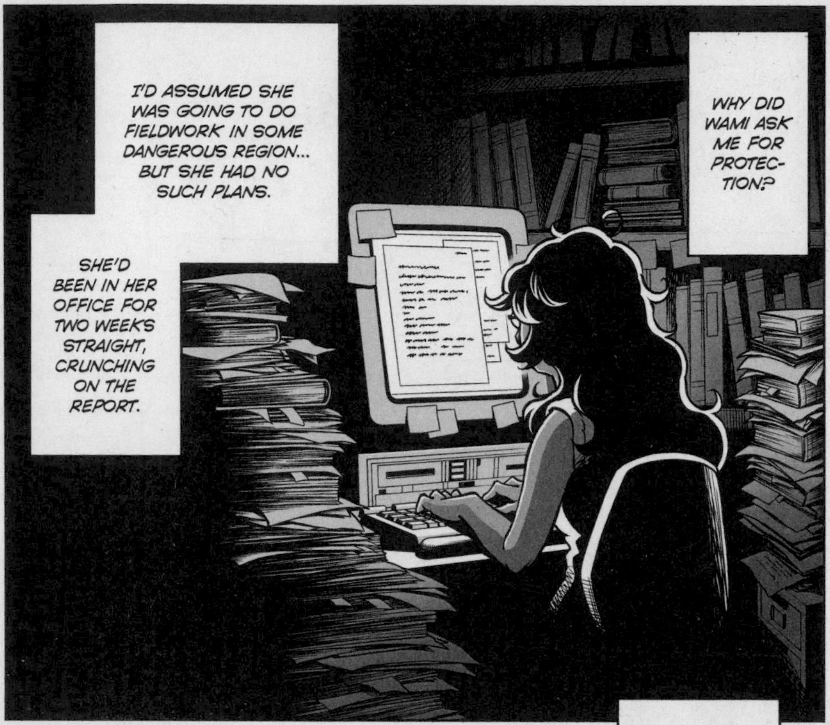
WHY DID WAMI ASK ME FOR PROTEC- TION?
I'D ASSUMED SHE WAS GOING TO DO FIELDWORK IN SOME DANGEROUS REGION... BUT SHE HAD NO SUCH PLANS.
SHE'D BEEN IN HER OFFICE FOR TWO WEEKS STRAIGHT, CRUNCHING ON THE REPORT.

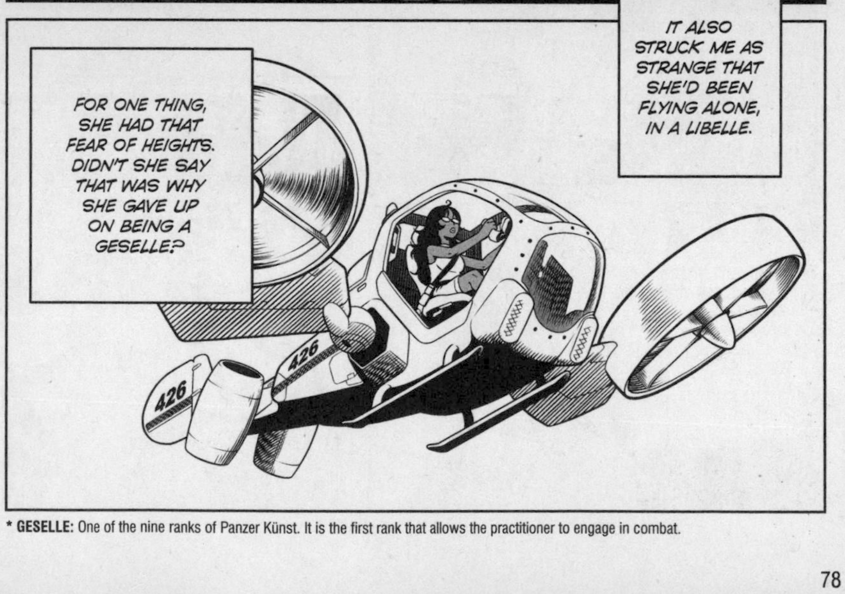
IT ALSO STRUCK ME AS STRANGE THAT SHE'D BEEN FLYING ALONE, IN A LIBELLE.
FOR ONE THING, SHE HAD THAT FEAR OF HEIGHTS. DIDN'T SHE SAY THAT WAS WHY SHE GAVE UP ON BEING A GESELLE?
426
426

* **GESELLE:** One of the nine ranks of Panzer Künst. It is the first rank that allows the practitioner to engage in combat.

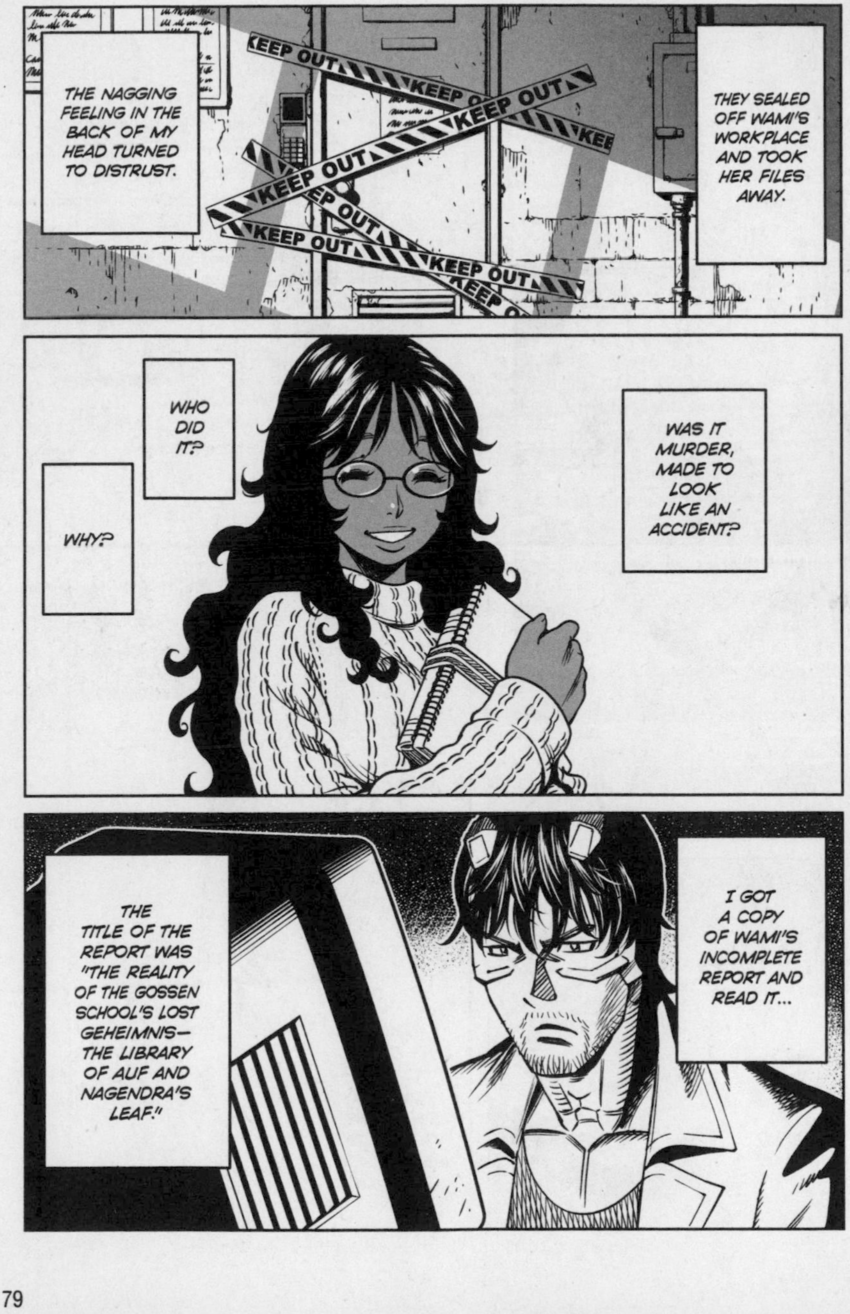
THEY SEALED OFF WAMI'S WORKPLACE AND TOOK HER FILES AWAY.
THE NAGGING FEELING IN THE BACK OF MY HEAD TURNED TO DISTRUST.
WAS IT MURDER, MADE TO LOOK LIKE AN ACCIDENT?
WHO DID IT?
WHY?
I GOT A COPY OF WAMI'S INCOMPLETE REPORT AND READ IT...
THE TITLE OF THE REPORT WAS "THE REALITY OF THE GOSSEN SCHOOL'S LOST GEHEIMNIS—THE LIBRARY OF AUF AND NAGENDRA'S LEAF."

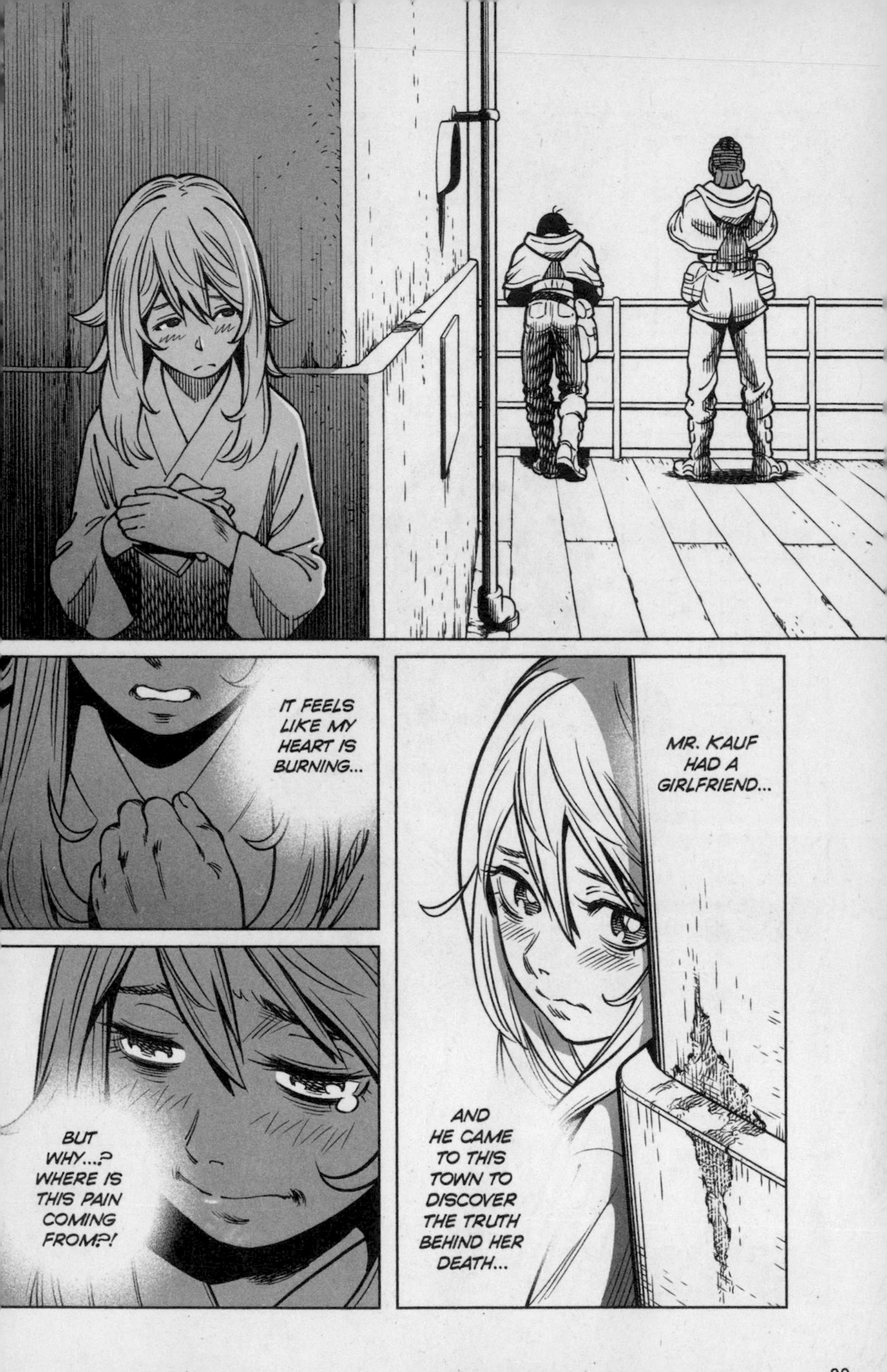
MR. KAUF HAD A GIRLFRIEND...
AND HE CAME TO THIS TOWN TO DISCOVER THE TRUTH BEHIND HER DEATH...
IT FEELS LIKE MY HEART IS BURNING...
BUT WHY...?! WHERE IS THIS PAIN COMING FROM?!

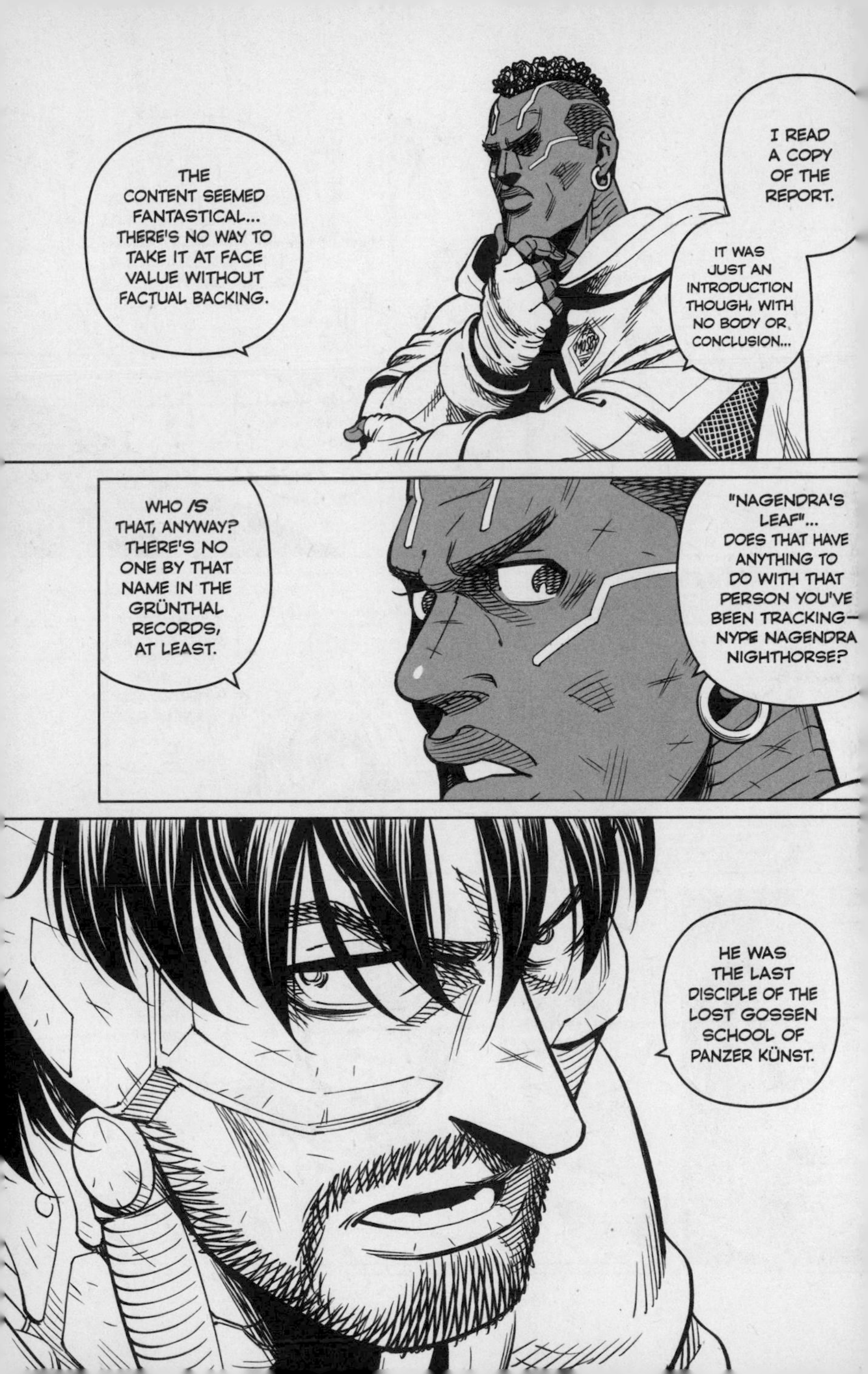
I READ A COPY OF THE REPORT.
IT WAS JUST AN INTRODUCTION THOUGH, WITH NO BODY OR CONCLUSION...
THE CONTENT SEEMED FANTASTICAL... THERE'S NO WAY TO TAKE IT AT FACE VALUE WITHOUT FACTUAL BACKING.
"NAGENDRA'S LEAF"... DOES THAT HAVE ANYTHING TO DO WITH THAT PERSON YOU'VE BEEN TRACKING—NYPE NAGENDRA NIGHTHORSE?
WHO *IS* THAT, ANYWAY? THERE'S NO ONE BY THAT NAME IN THE GRÜNTHAL RECORDS, AT LEAST.
HE WAS THE LAST DISCIPLE OF THE LOST GOSSEN SCHOOL OF PANZER KÜNST.

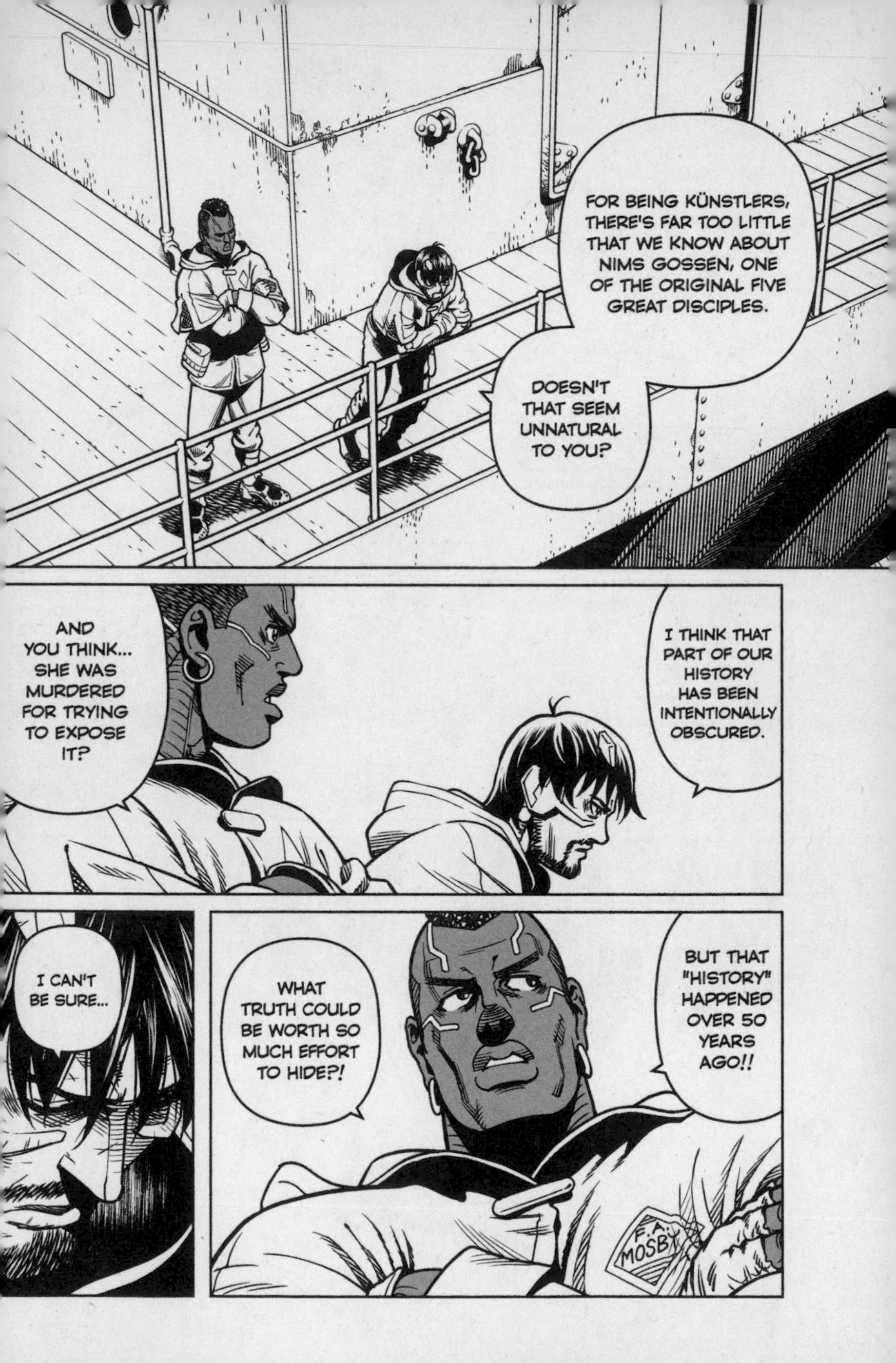
FOR BEING KÜNSTLERS, THERE'S FAR TOO LITTLE THAT WE KNOW ABOUT NIMS GOSSEN, ONE OF THE ORIGINAL FIVE GREAT DISCIPLES.
DOESN'T THAT SEEM UNNATURAL TO YOU?
I THINK THAT PART OF OUR HISTORY HAS BEEN INTENTIONALLY OBSCURED.
AND YOU THINK... SHE WAS MURDERED FOR TRYING TO EXPOSE IT?
BUT THAT "HISTORY" HAPPENED OVER 50 YEARS AGO!!
WHAT TRUTH COULD BE WORTH SO MUCH EFFORT TO HIDE?!
F.A. MOSBY
I CAN'T BE SURE...

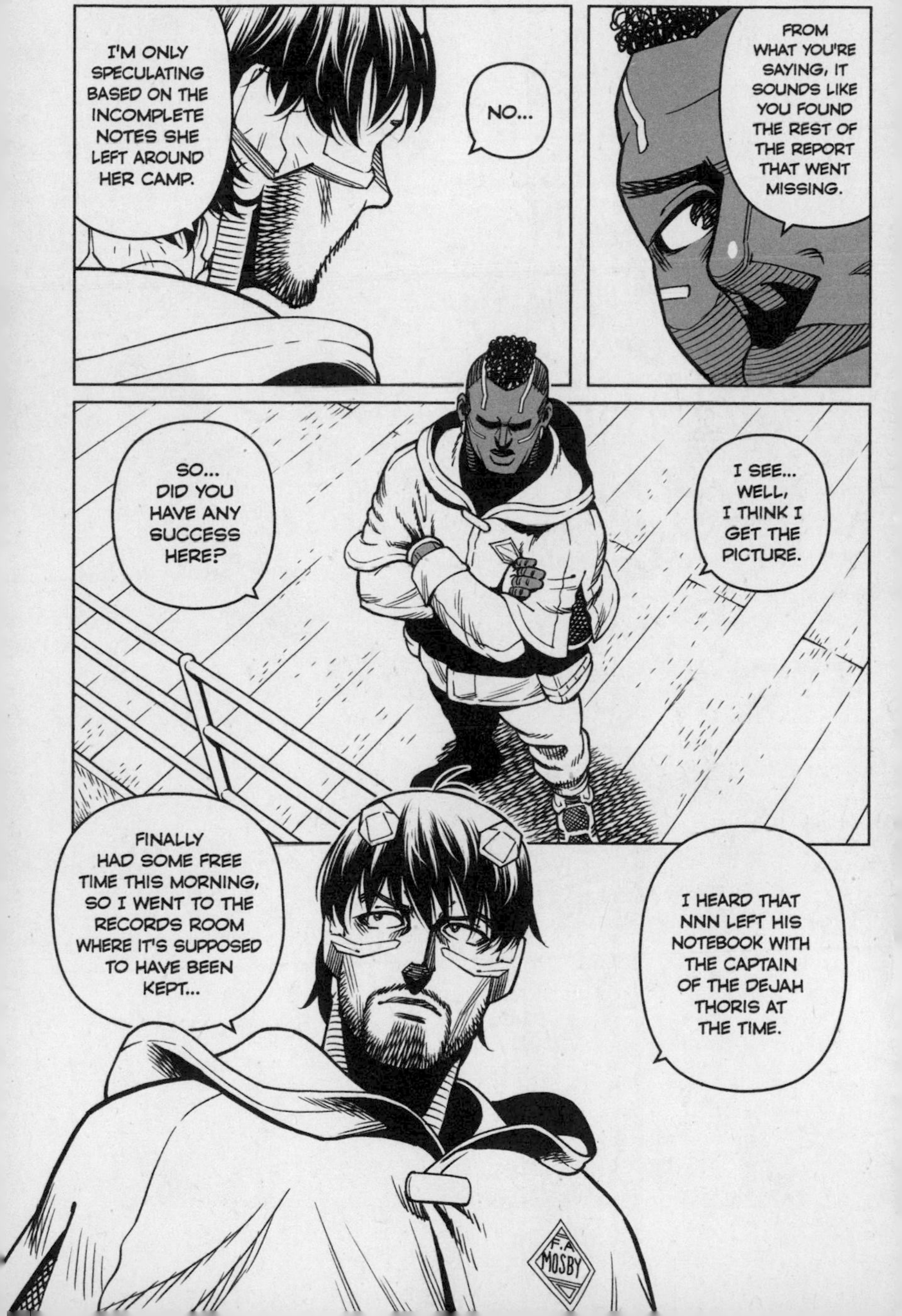
FROM WHAT YOU'RE SAYING, IT SOUNDS LIKE YOU FOUND THE REST OF THE REPORT THAT WENT MISSING.
NO...
I'M ONLY SPECULATING BASED ON THE INCOMPLETE NOTES SHE LEFT AROUND HER CAMP.
I SEE... WELL, I THINK I GET THE PICTURE.
SO... DID YOU HAVE ANY SUCCESS HERE?
I HEARD THAT NNN LEFT HIS NOTEBOOK WITH THE CAPTAIN OF THE DEJAH THORIS AT THE TIME.
FINALLY HAD SOME FREE TIME THIS MORNING, SO I WENT TO THE RECORDS ROOM WHERE IT'S SUPPOSED TO HAVE BEEN KEPT...
F.A MOSBY

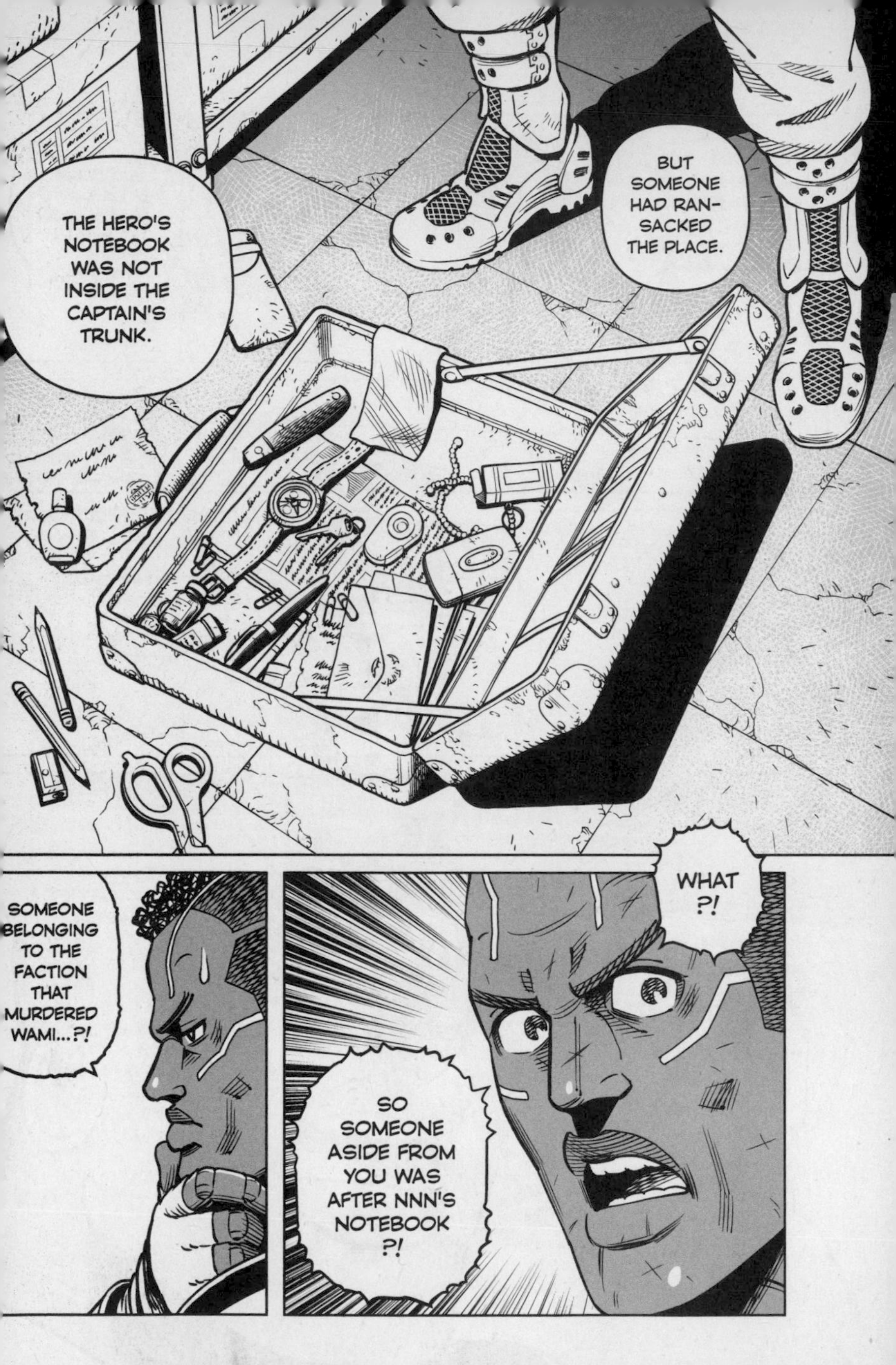
BUT SOMEONE HAD RAN-SACKED THE PLACE.
THE HERO'S NOTEBOOK WAS NOT INSIDE THE CAPTAIN'S TRUNK.
WHAT ?!
SO SOMEONE ASIDE FROM YOU WAS AFTER NNN'S NOTEBOOK ?!
SOMEONE BELONGING TO THE FACTION THAT MURDERED WAMI...?!

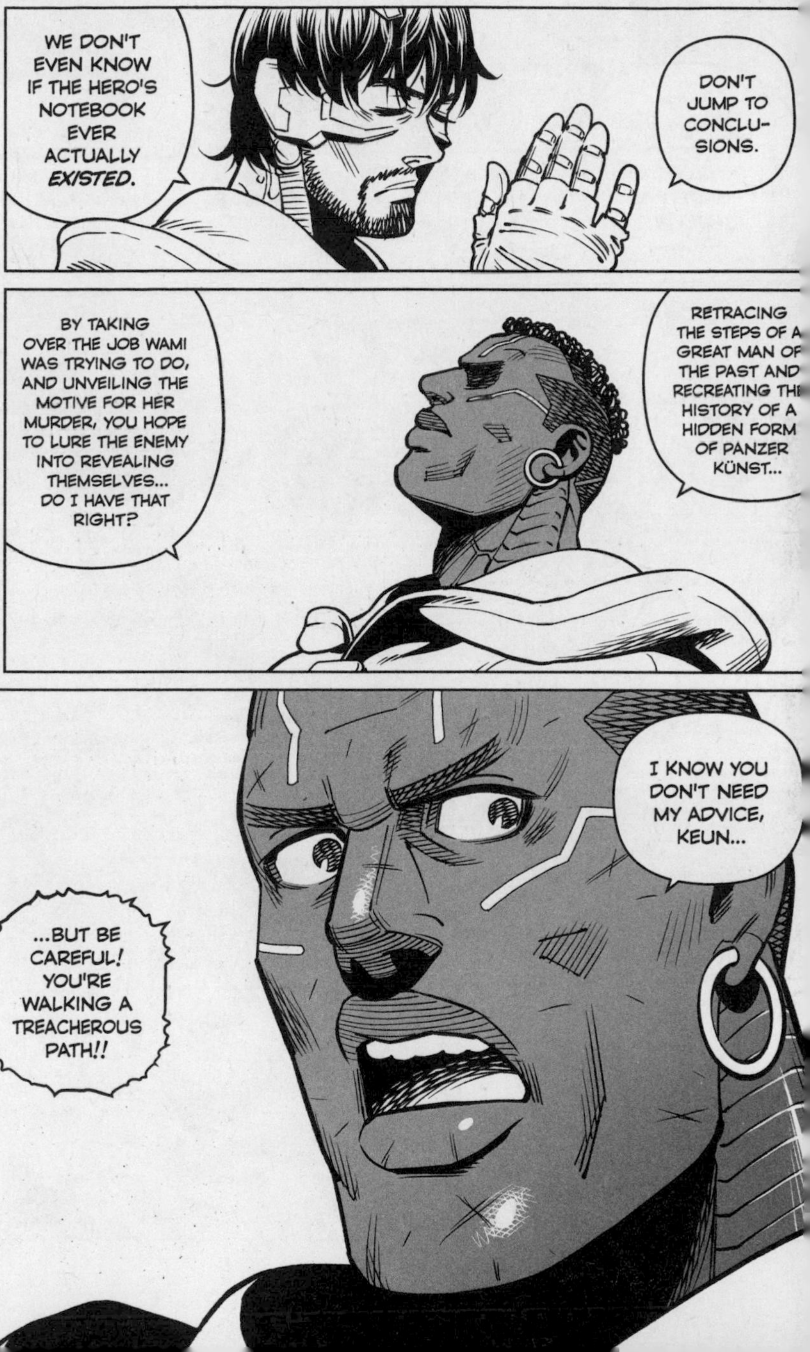
DON'T JUMP TO CONCLUSIONS.
WE DON'T EVEN KNOW IF THE HERO'S NOTEBOOK EVER ACTUALLY *EXISTED*.
RETRACING THE STEPS OF A GREAT MAN OF THE PAST AND RECREATING THE HISTORY OF A HIDDEN FORM OF PANZER KÜNST...
BY TAKING OVER THE JOB WAMI WAS TRYING TO DO, AND UNVEILING THE MOTIVE FOR HER MURDER, YOU HOPE TO LURE THE ENEMY INTO REVEALING THEMSELVES... DO I HAVE THAT RIGHT?
I KNOW YOU DON'T NEED MY ADVICE, KEUN...
...BUT BE CAREFUL! YOU'RE WALKING A TREACHEROUS PATH!!

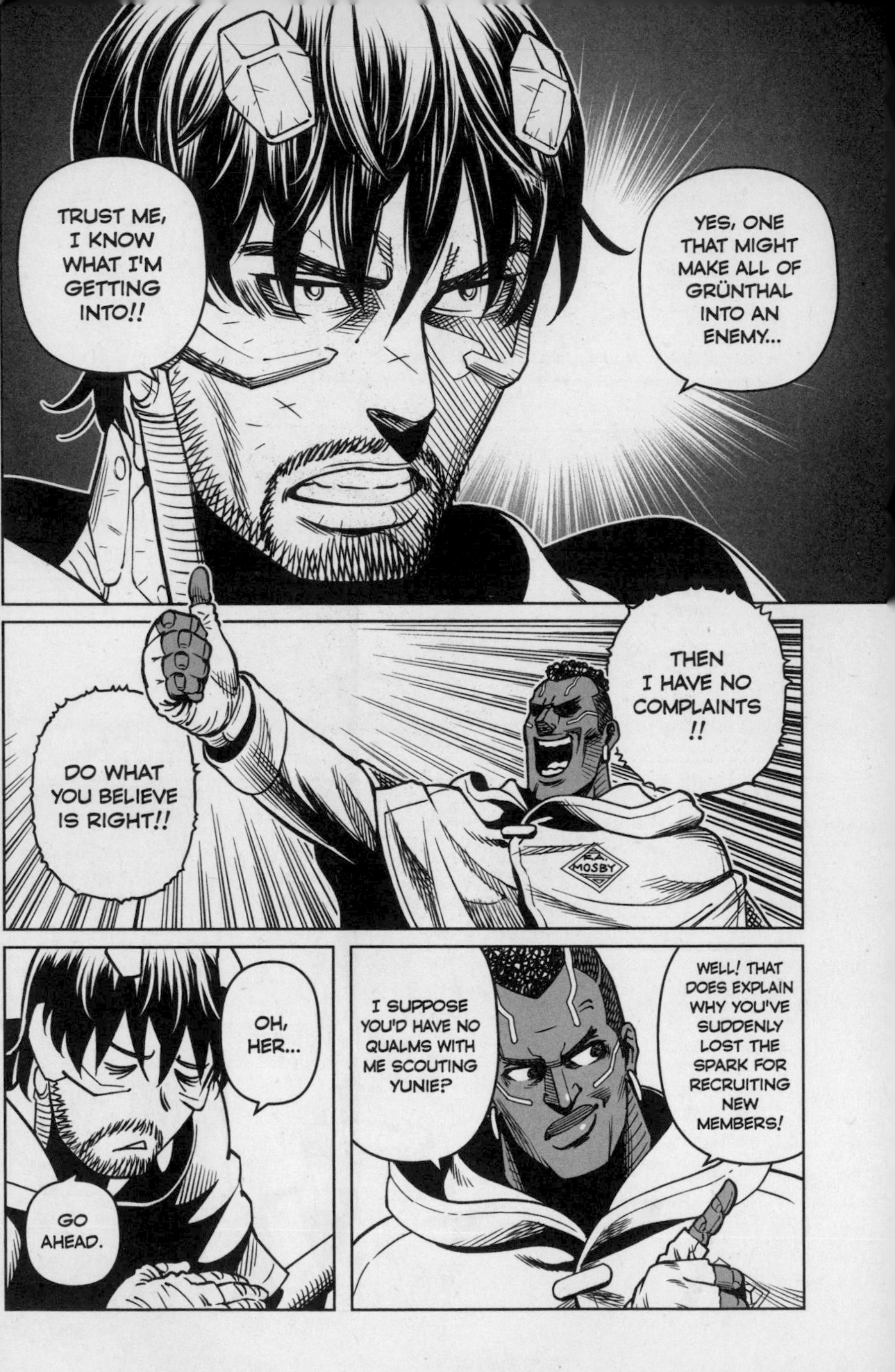
YES, ONE THAT MIGHT MAKE ALL OF GRÜNTHAL INTO AN ENEMY...
TRUST ME, I KNOW WHAT I'M GETTING INTO!!
THEN I HAVE NO COMPLAINTS!!
DO WHAT YOU BELIEVE IS RIGHT!!
WELL! THAT DOES EXPLAIN WHY YOU'VE SUDDENLY LOST THE SPARK FOR RECRUITING NEW MEMBERS!
I SUPPOSE YOU'D HAVE NO QUALMS WITH ME SCOUTING YUNIE?
OH, HER...
GO AHEAD.

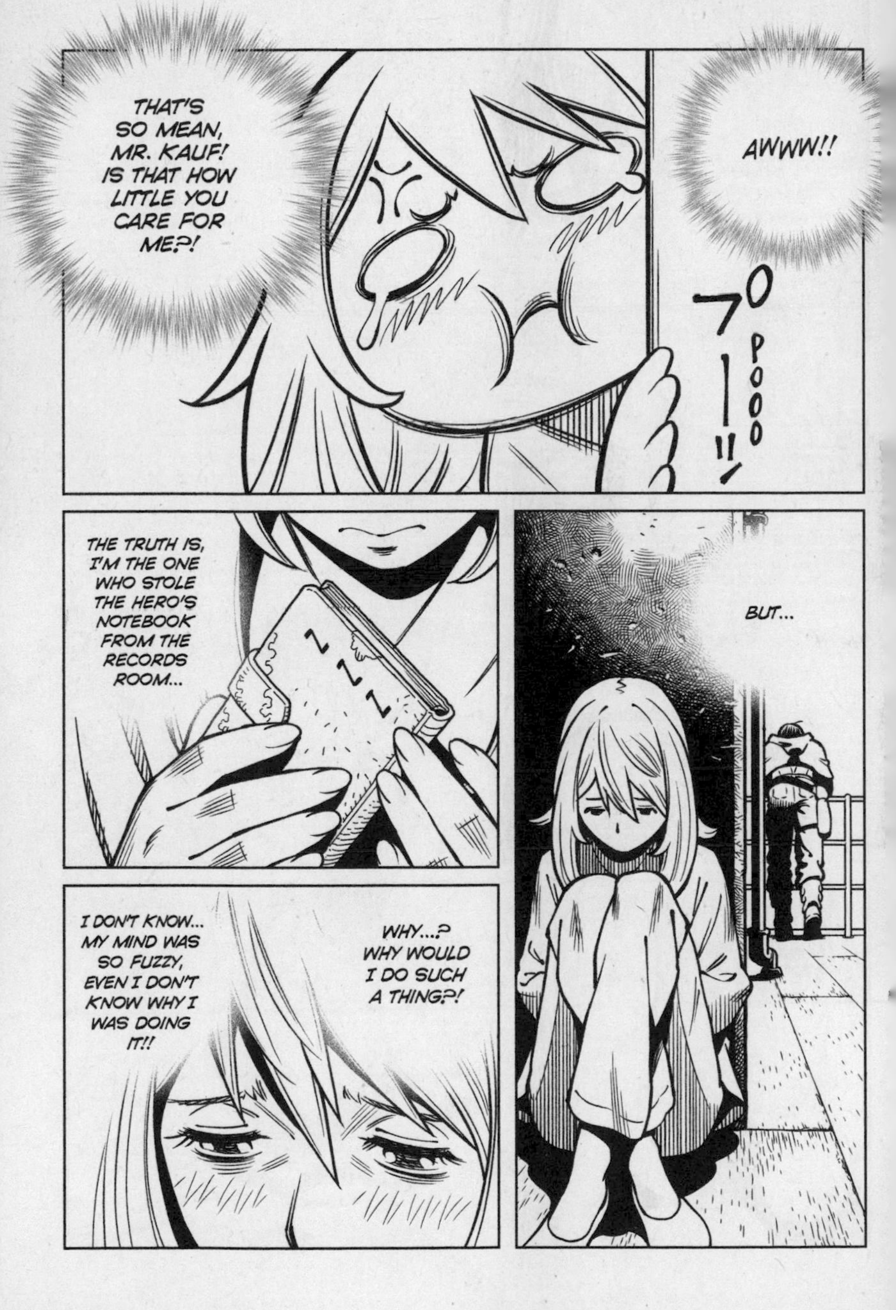
AWWW!!
POOO
THAT'S SO MEAN, MR. KAUF! IS THAT HOW LITTLE YOU CARE FOR ME?!
BUT...
THE TRUTH IS, I'M THE ONE WHO STOLE THE HERO'S NOTEBOOK FROM THE RECORDS ROOM...
WHY...? WHY WOULD I DO SUCH A THING?!
I DON'T KNOW... MY MIND WAS SO FUZZY, EVEN I DON'T KNOW WHY I WAS DOING IT!!

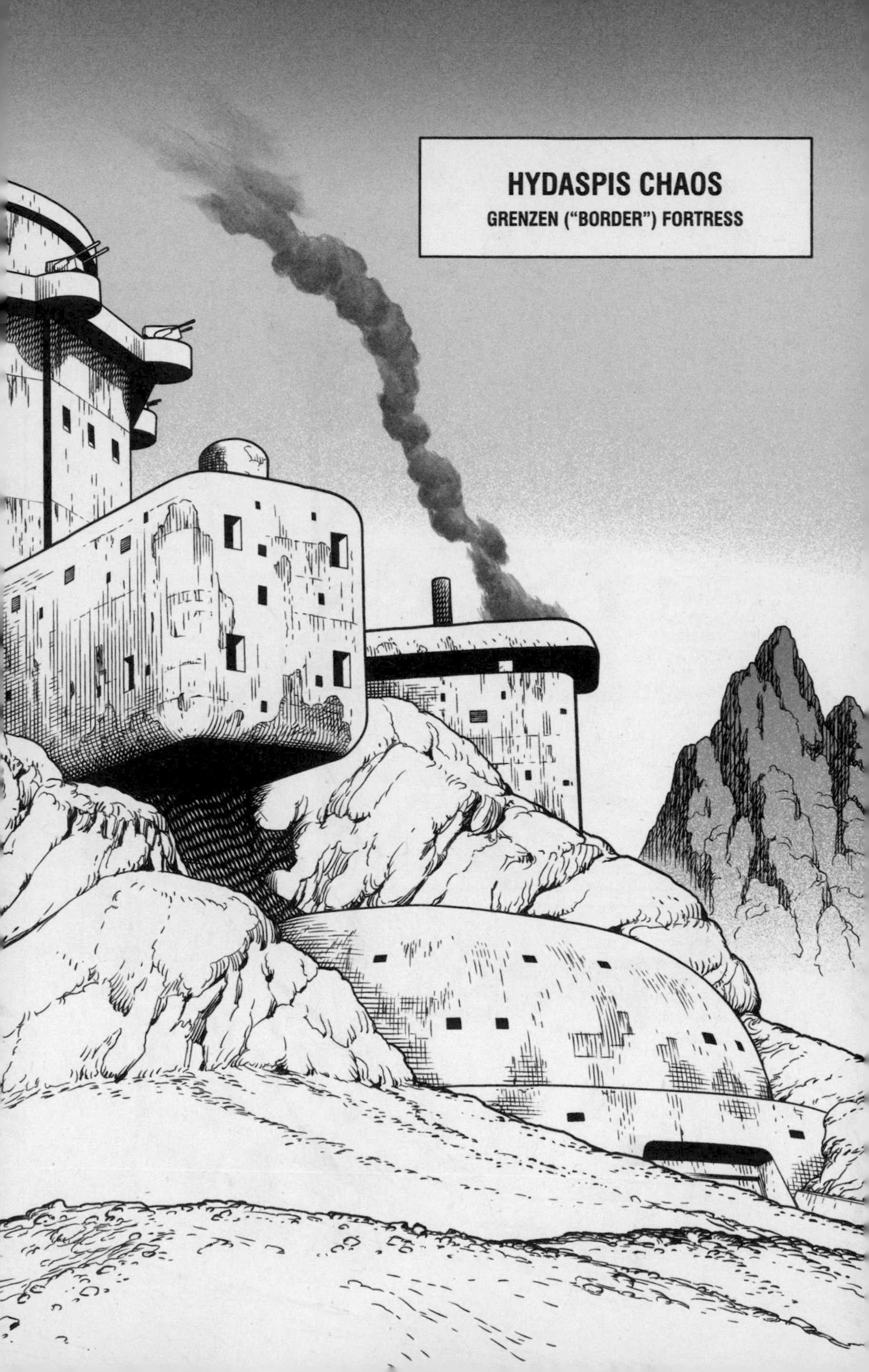
HYDASPIS CHAOS
GRENZEN ("BORDER") FORTRESS

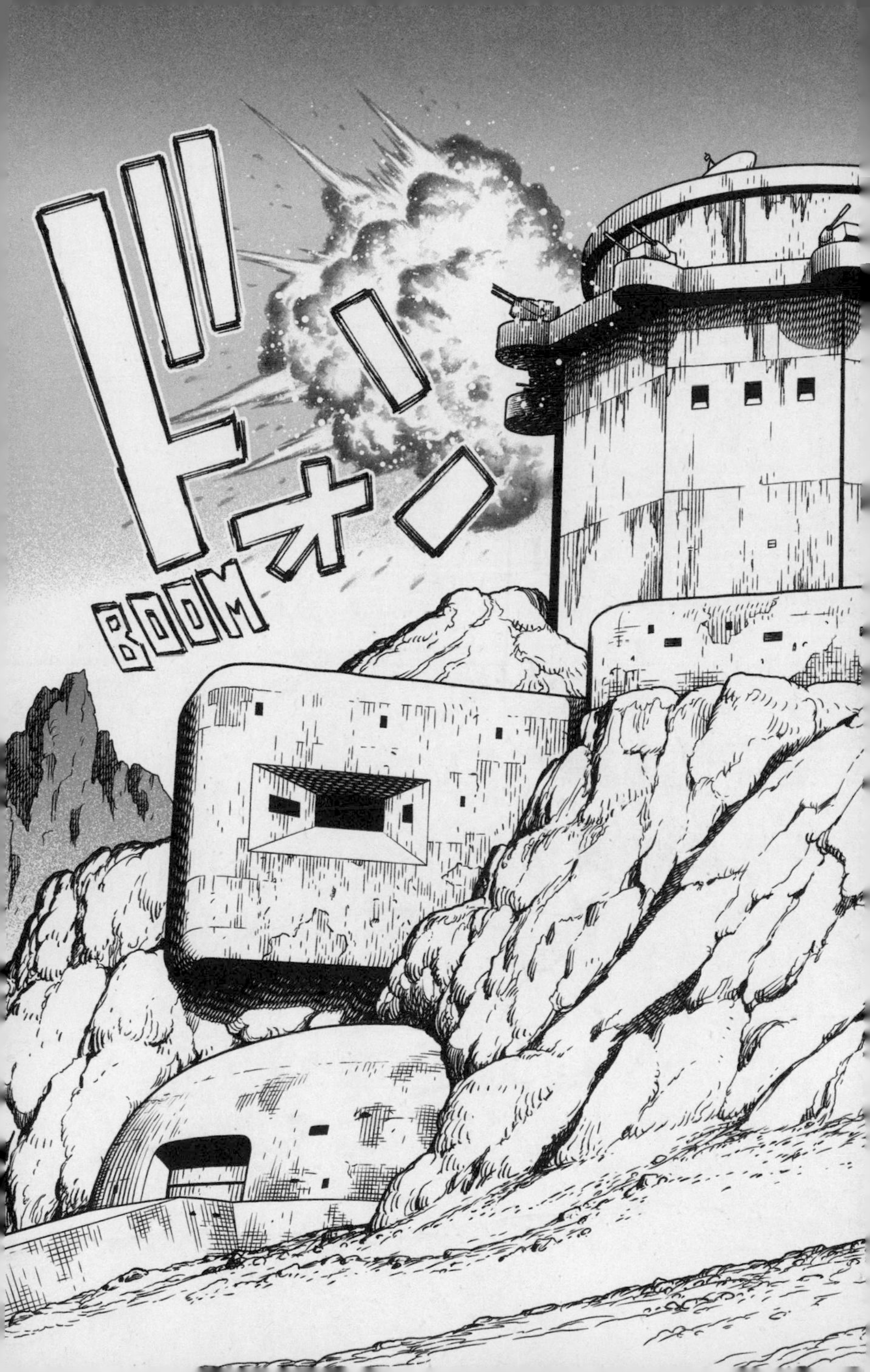
ドオーン
BOOM

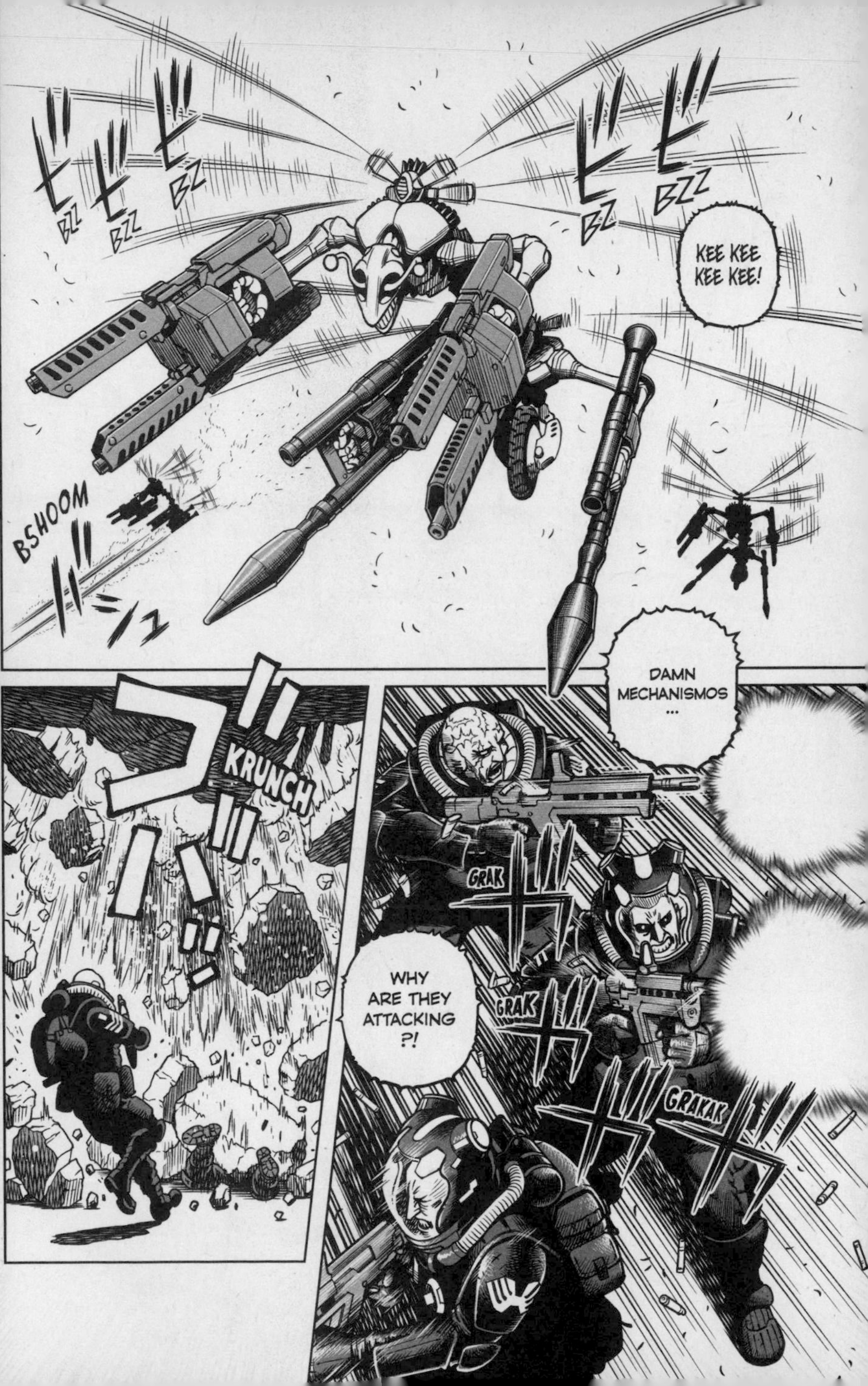
BZZ
BZZ
KEE KEE
KEE KEE!
BZZ
BZZ
BZZ
BSHOOM
DAMN MECHANISMOS
...
GRAK
GRAK
WHY ARE THEY ATTACKING ?!
GRAKAK
KRUNCH

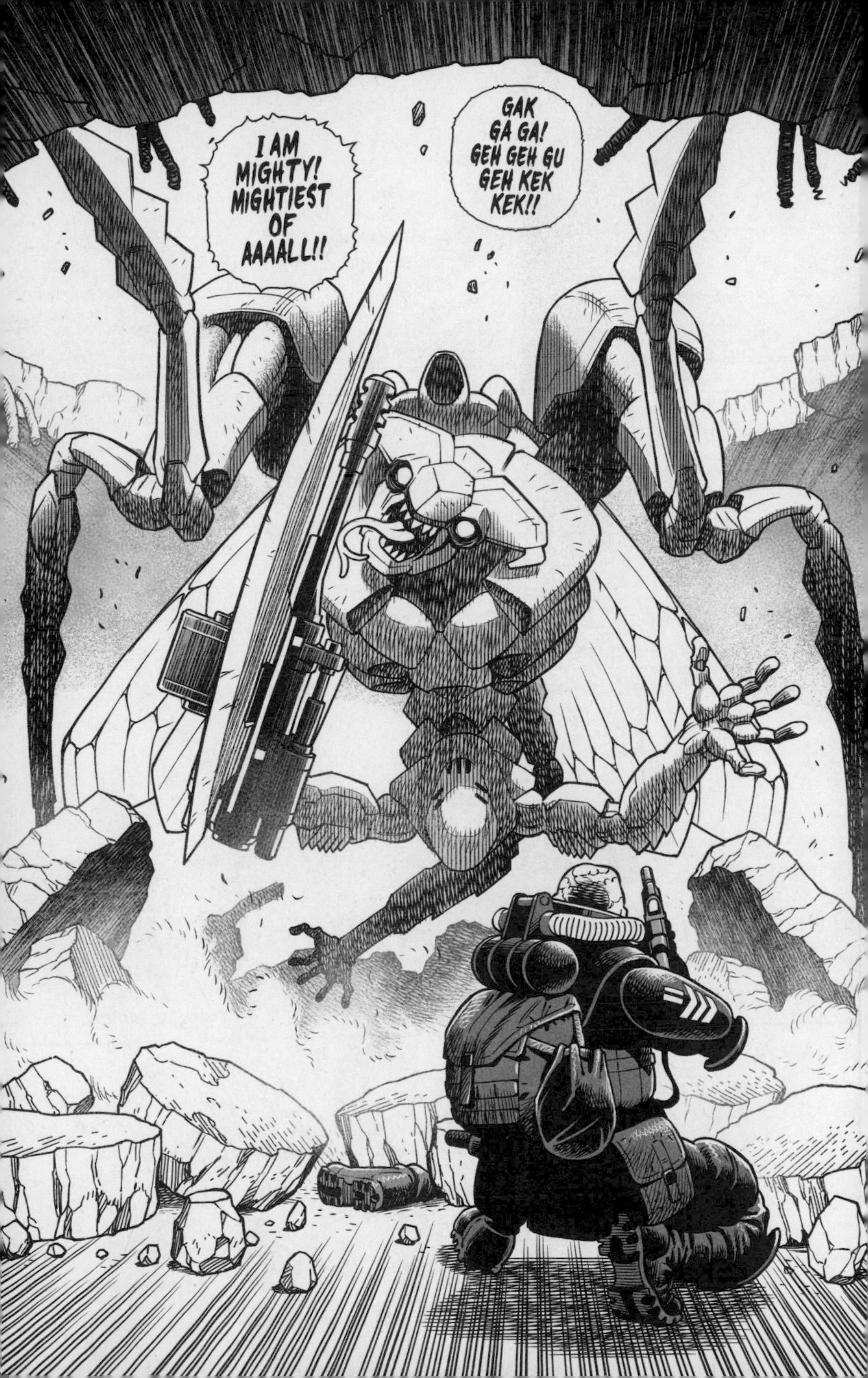
GAK GA GA! GEH GEH GU GEH KEK KEK!!
I AM MIGHTY! MIGHTIEST OF AAAALL!!

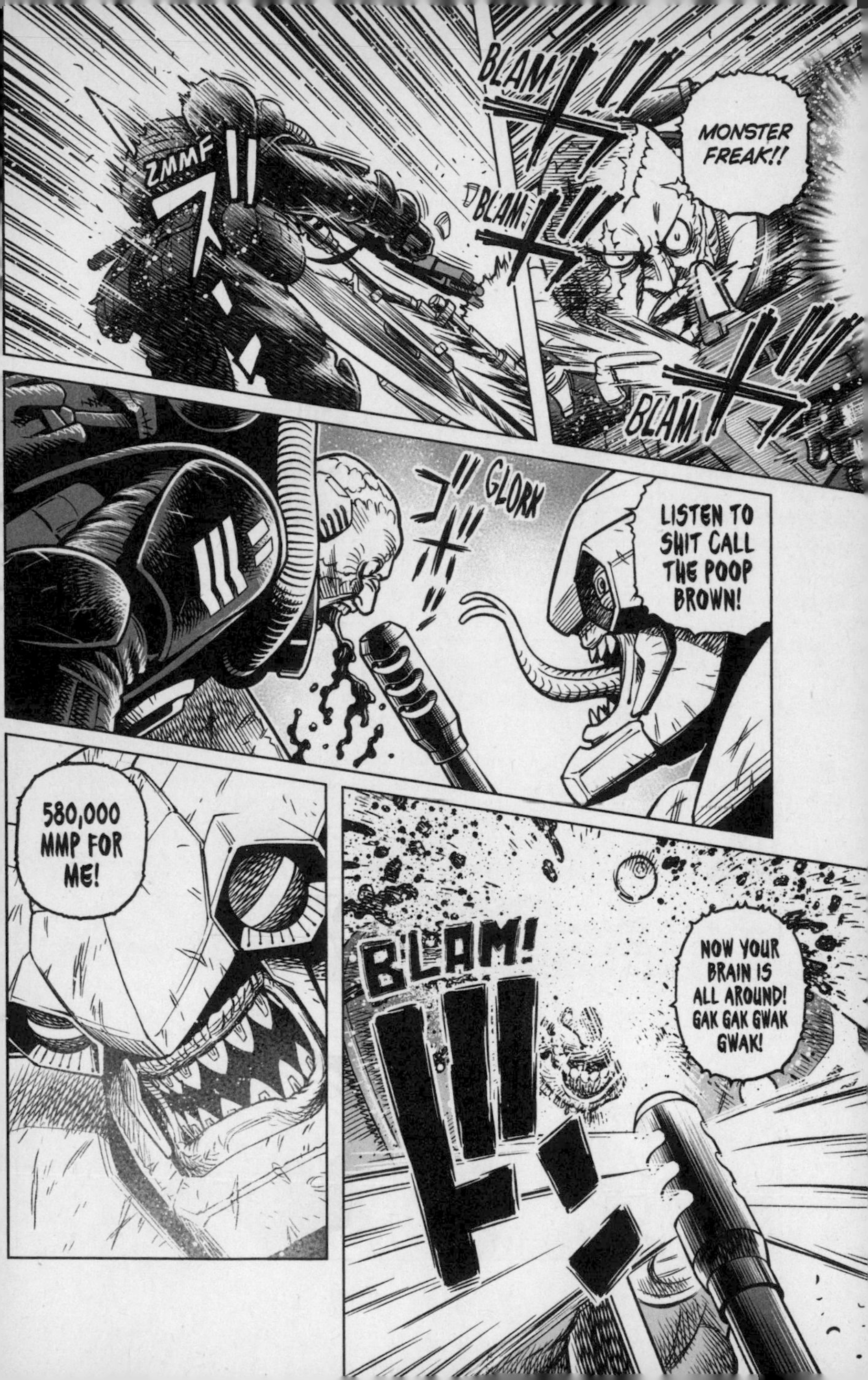
BLAM
MONSTER FREAK!!
BLAM
BLAM
ZMMF
GLORK
LISTEN TO SHIT CALL THE POOP BROWN!
BLAM!
NOW YOUR BRAIN IS ALL AROUND! GAK GAK GWAK GWAK!
580,000 MMP FOR ME!

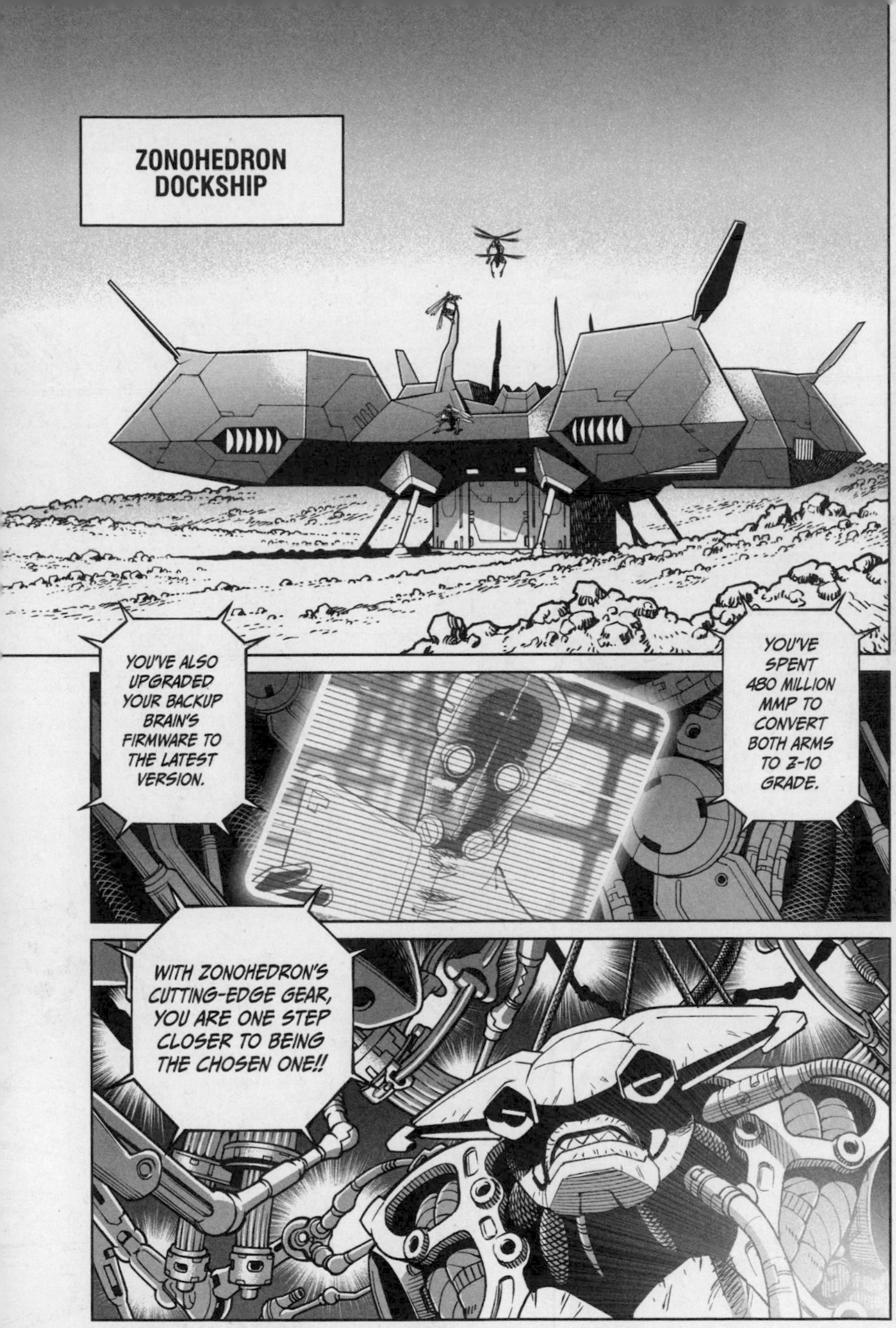
ZONOHEDRON DOCKSHIP
YOU'VE SPENT 480 MILLION MMP TO CONVERT BOTH ARMS TO Z-10 GRADE.
YOU'VE ALSO UPGRADED YOUR BACKUP BRAIN'S FIRMWARE TO THE LATEST VERSION.
WITH ZONOHEDRON'S CUTTING-EDGE GEAR, YOU ARE ONE STEP CLOSER TO BEING THE CHOSEN ONE!!

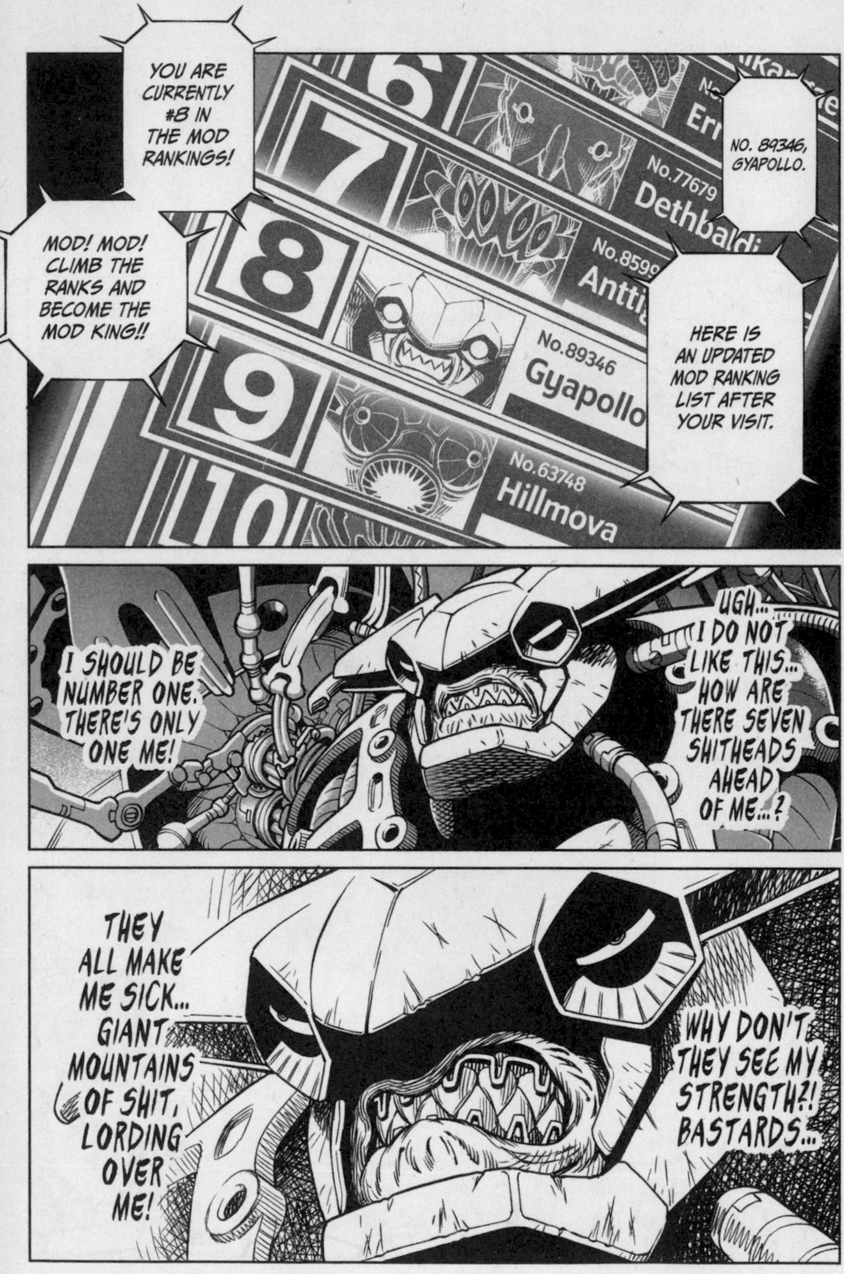
NO. 89346, GYAPOLLO.
HERE IS AN UPDATED MOD RANKING LIST AFTER YOUR VISIT.
YOU ARE CURRENTLY #8 IN THE MOD RANKINGS!
MOD! MOD! CLIMB THE RANKS AND BECOME THE MOD KING!!
No.77679 Dethbaldi
No.89346 Gyapollo
No.63748 Hillmova
UGH... I DO NOT LIKE THIS... HOW ARE THERE SEVEN SHITHEADS AHEAD OF ME...?
I SHOULD BE NUMBER ONE. THERE'S ONLY ONE ME!
WHY DON'T THEY SEE MY STRENGTH?! BASTARDS...
THEY ALL MAKE ME SICK... GIANT MOUNTAINS OF SHIT, LORDING OVER ME!

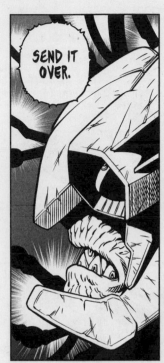

BZZZZ!!
PWIT!!
GYAPOLLO! YOU HAVE A ZONOFLY FROM MAJOR JAKOLEVA! SECURE LINE!!
SEND IT OVER.
IT'S BEEN A LO TIME, GYAPOLLO.
VOICE ONLY
I APOLOGIZE FOR THE POOR SI UALITY.
BZZK
Major Jakoleva Jantzen
monaural
BZK

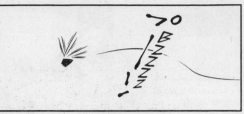

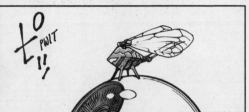

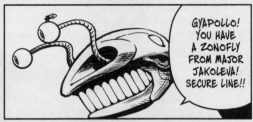

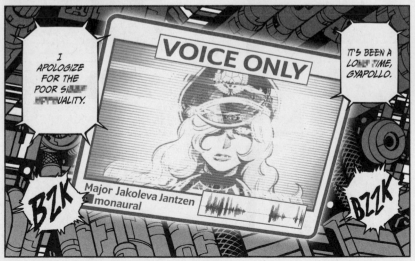

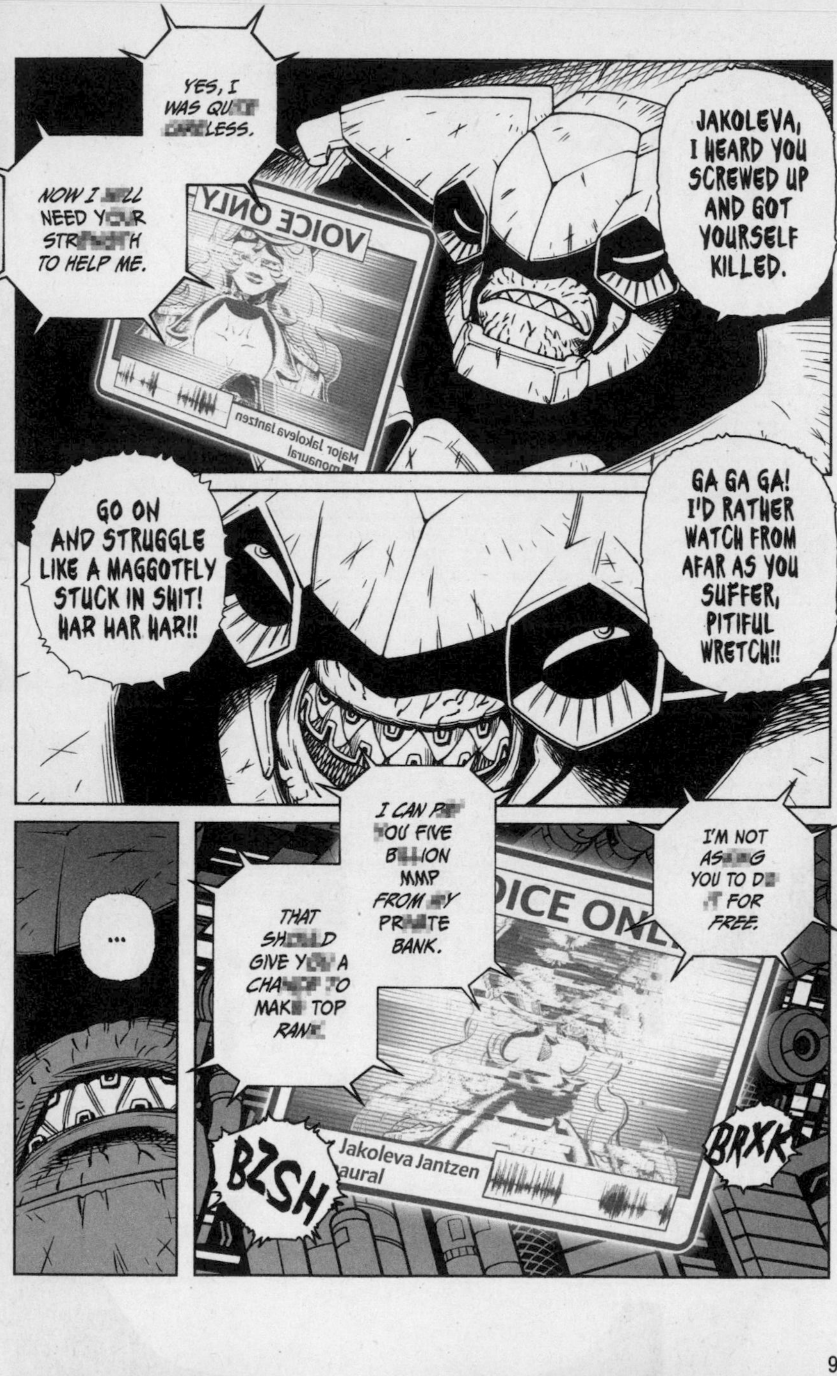
JAKOLEVA, I HEARD YOU SCREWED UP AND GOT YOURSELF KILLED.
YES, I WAS QU LESS.
NOW I LL NEED Y R STR H TO HELP ME.
GA GA GA! I'D RATHER WATCH FROM AFAR AS YOU SUFFER, PITIFUL WRETCH!!
GO ON AND STRUGGLE LIKE A MAGGOTFLY STUCK IN SHIT! HAR HAR HAR!!
I'M NOT AS G YOU TO D T FOR FREE.
I CAN P OU FIVE B ION MMP FROM Y PR TE BANK.
THAT SH D GIVE Y A CHA TO MAK TOP RAN
BRXK
OICE ONL
Jakoleva Jantzen
aural
BZSH
...

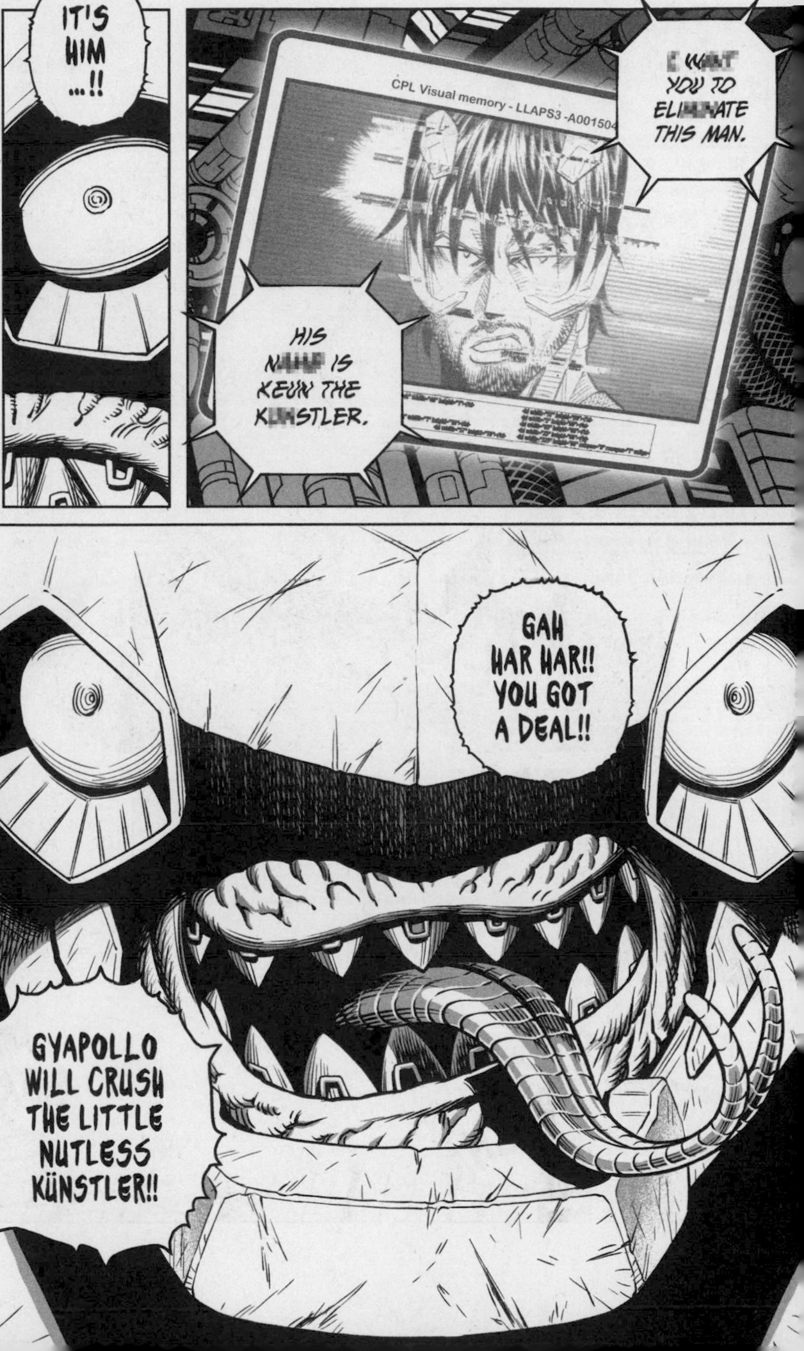
CPL Visual memory - LLAPS3 -A001504
I WANT YOU TO ELIMINATE THIS MAN.
HIS NAME IS KEVIN THE KÜNSTLER.
IT'S HIM ...!!
GAH HAR HAR!! YOU GOT A DEAL!!
GYAPOLLO WILL CRUSH THE LITTLE NUTLESS KÜNSTLER!!

LOG:040

GYAPOLLO ATTACKS

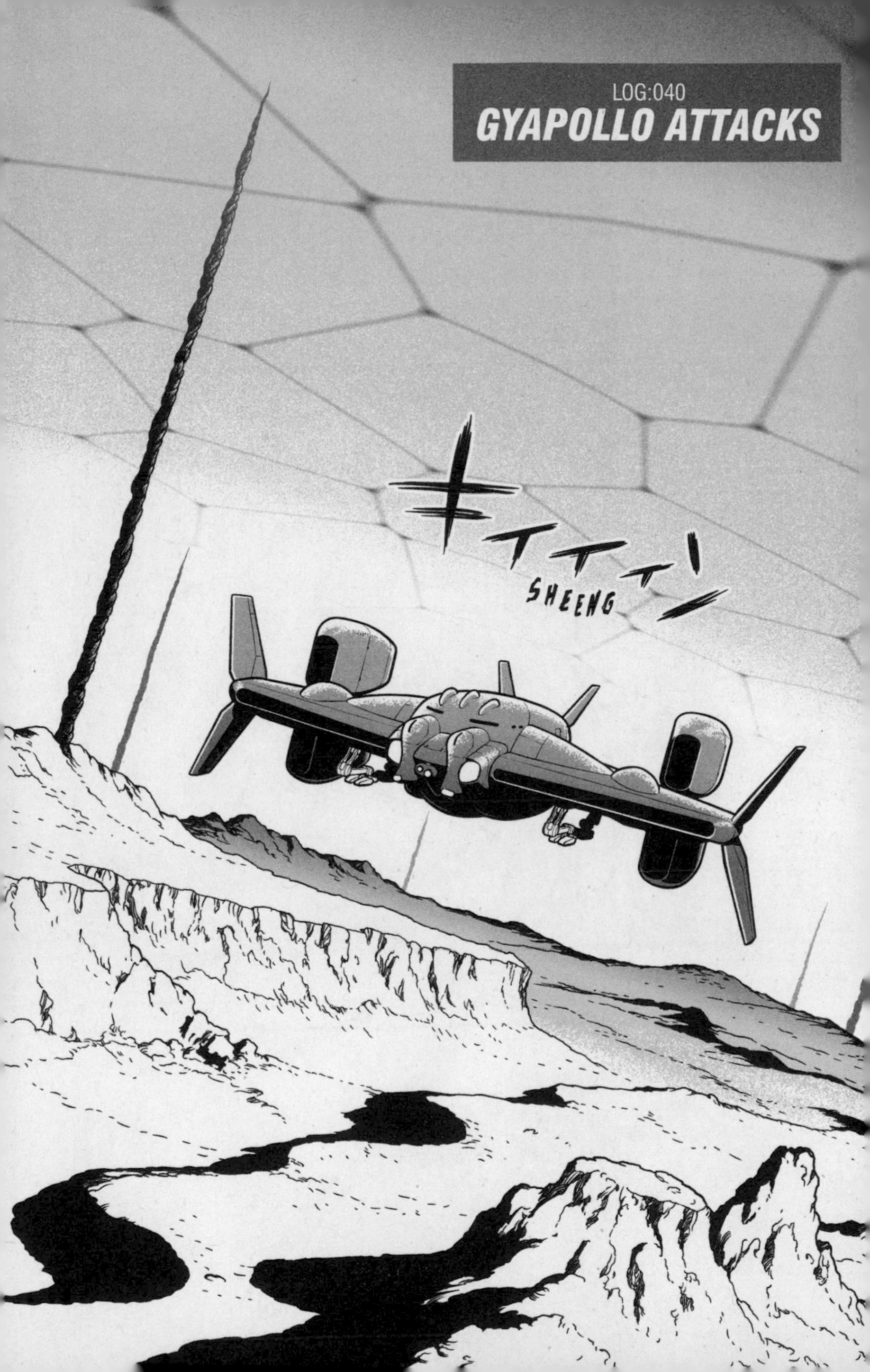
SHEENG

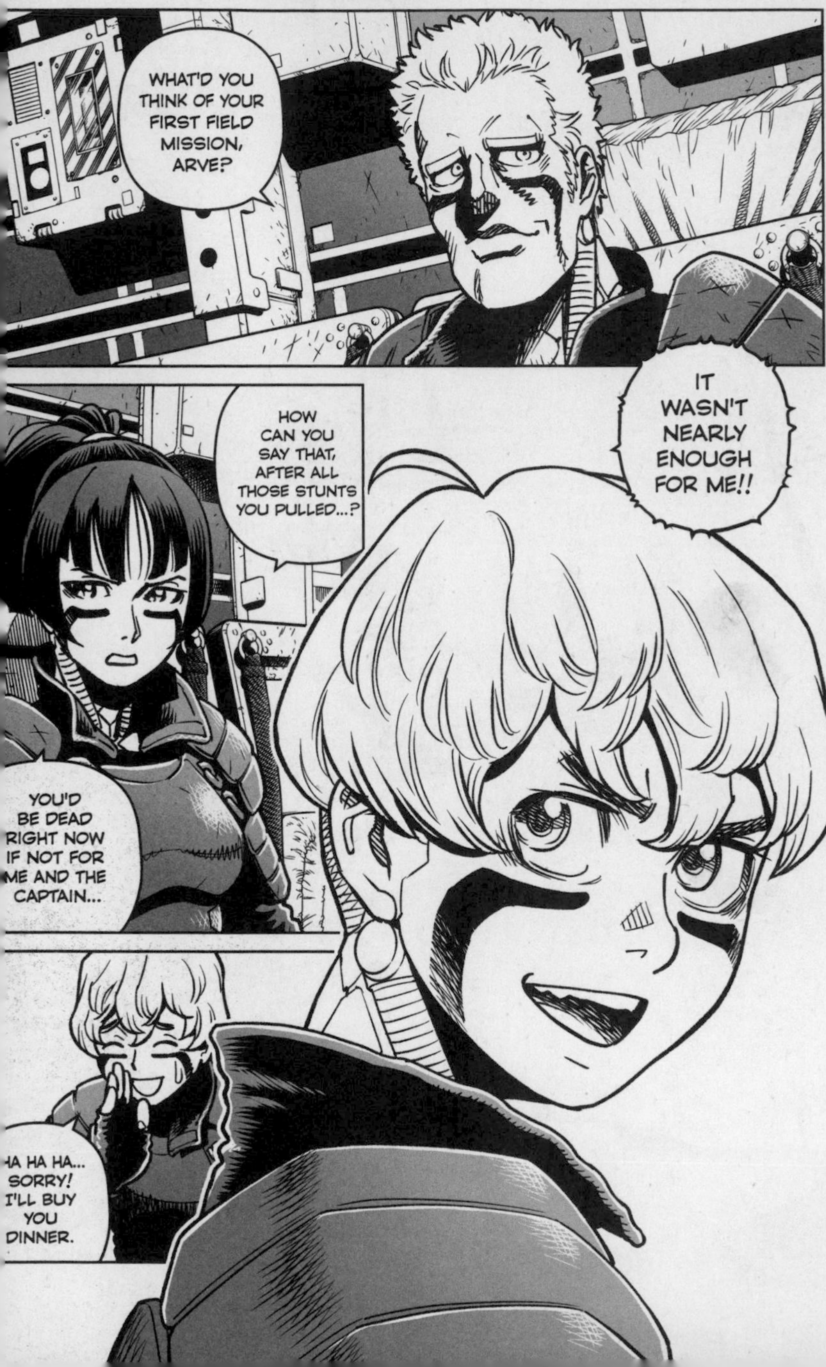
WHAT'D YOU THINK OF YOUR FIRST FIELD MISSION, ARVE?
IT WASN'T NEARLY ENOUGH FOR ME!!
HOW CAN YOU SAY THAT, AFTER ALL THOSE STUNTS YOU PULLED...?
YOU'D BE DEAD RIGHT NOW IF NOT FOR ME AND THE CAPTAIN...
HA HA HA... SORRY! I'LL BUY YOU DINNER.

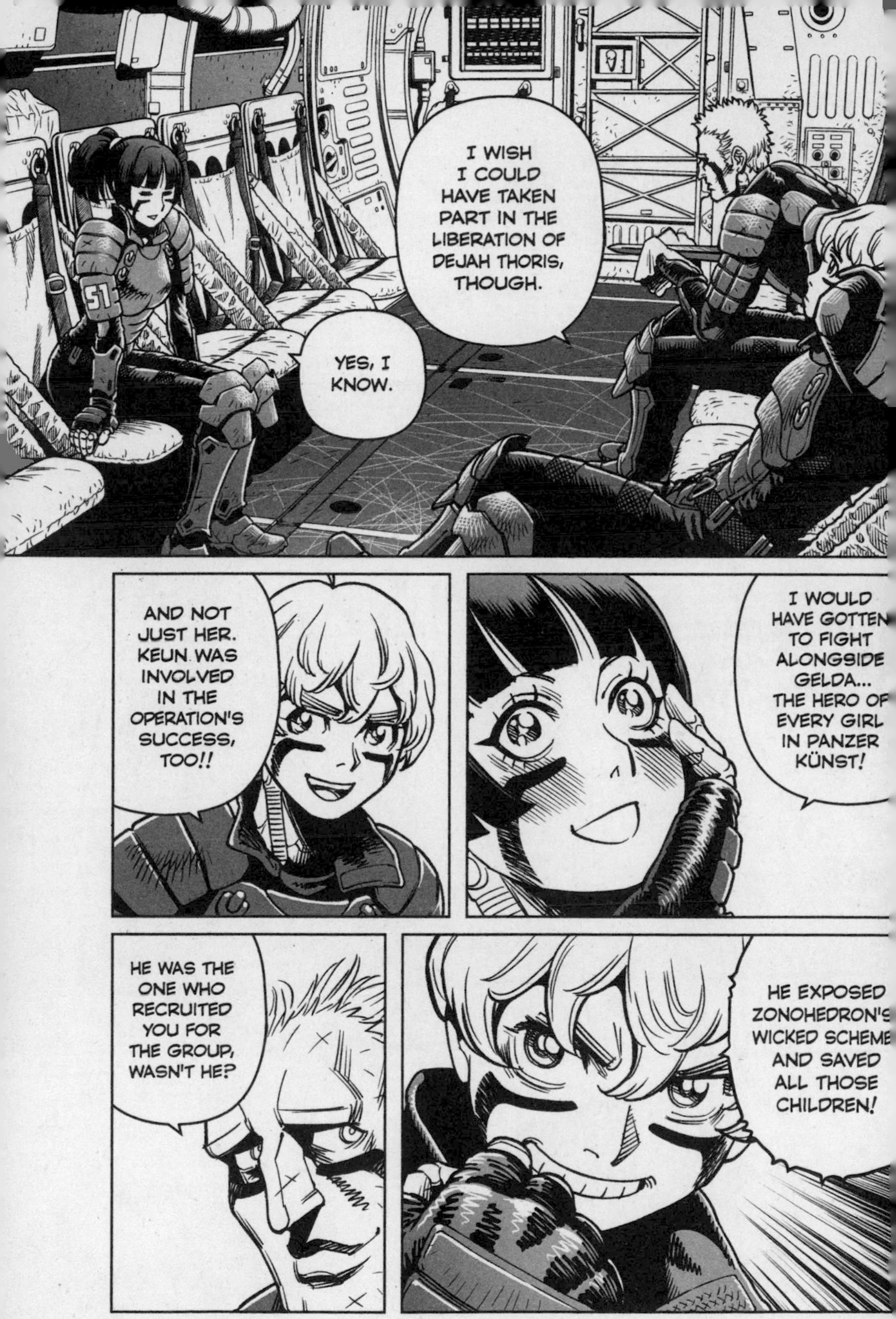
I WISH I COULD HAVE TAKEN PART IN THE LIBERATION OF DEJAH THORIS, THOUGH.
YES, I KNOW.
I WOULD HAVE GOTTEN TO FIGHT ALONGSIDE GELDA... THE HERO OF EVERY GIRL IN PANZER KÜNST!
AND NOT JUST HER. KEUN WAS INVOLVED IN THE OPERATION'S SUCCESS, TOO!!
HE EXPOSED ZONOHEDRON'S WICKED SCHEME AND SAVED ALL THOSE CHILDREN!
HE WAS THE ONE WHO RECRUITED YOU FOR THE GROUP, WASN'T HE?

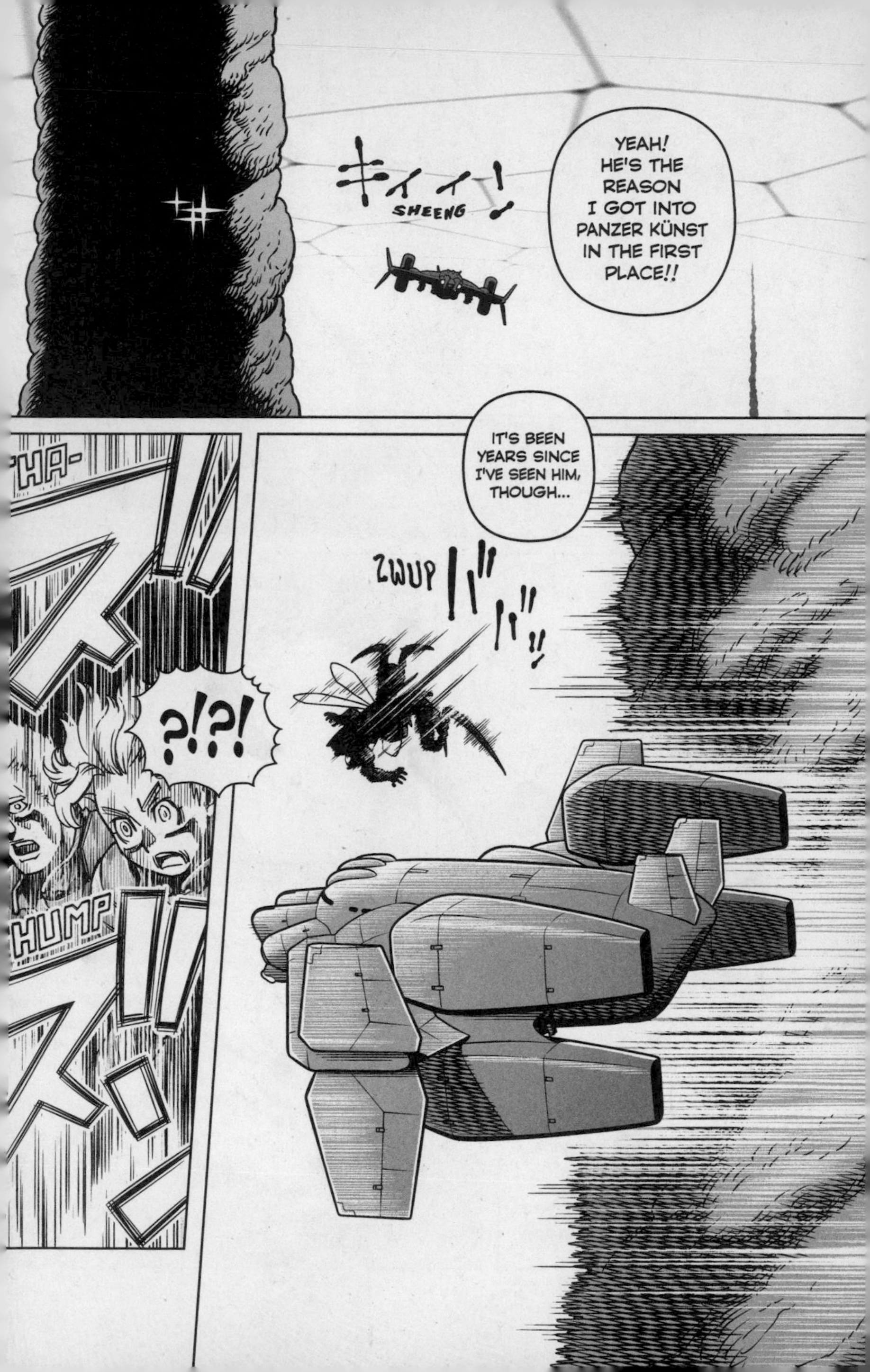
YEAH! HE'S THE REASON I GOT INTO PANZER KÜNST IN THE FIRST PLACE!!
SHEENG
IT'S BEEN YEARS SINCE I'VE SEEN HIM, THOUGH...
ZWUP
?!?!
PHA-
HUMP

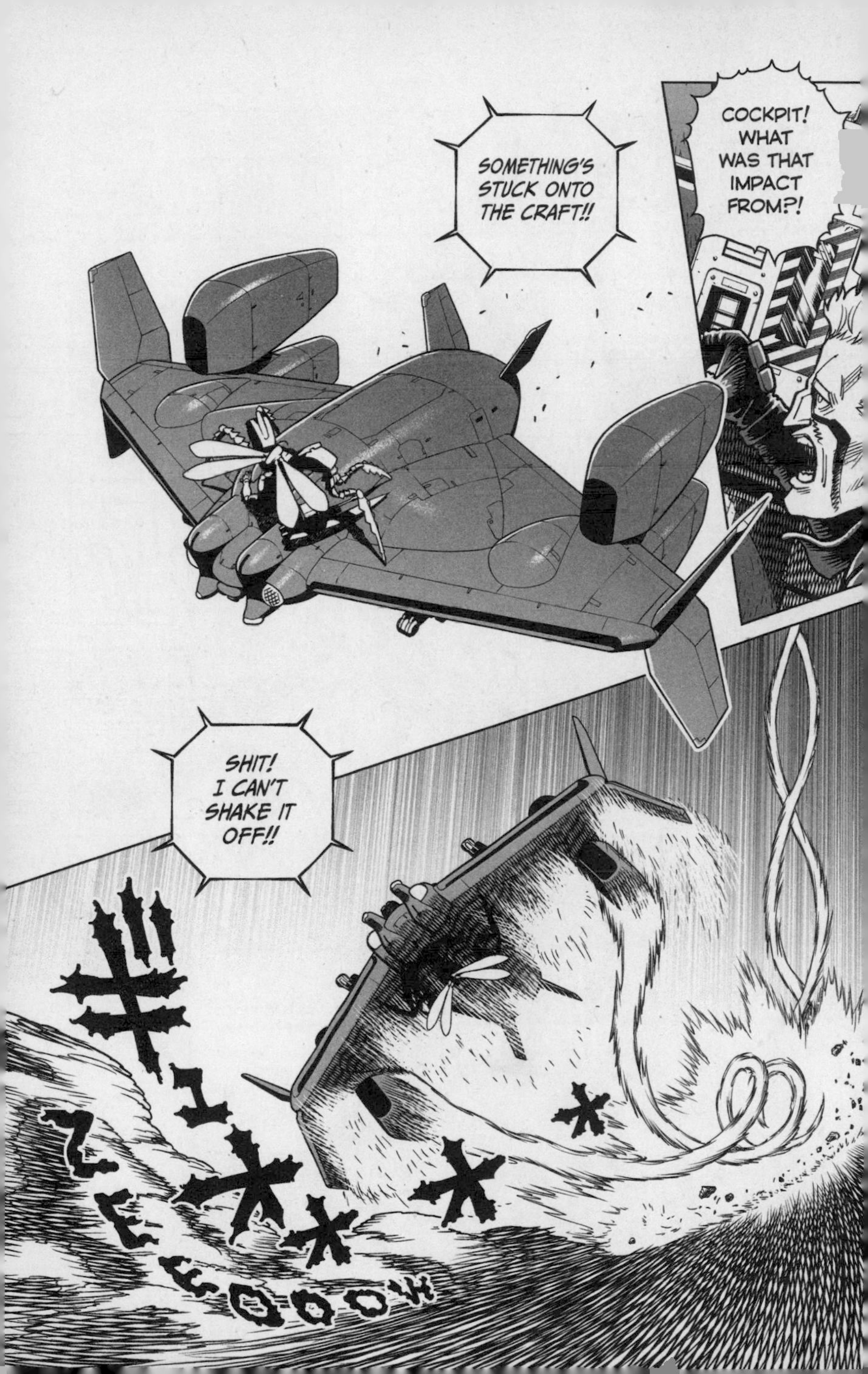
COCKPIT! WHAT WAS THAT IMPACT FROM?!
SOMETHING'S STUCK ONTO THE CRAFT!!
SHIT! I CAN'T SHAKE IT OFF!!

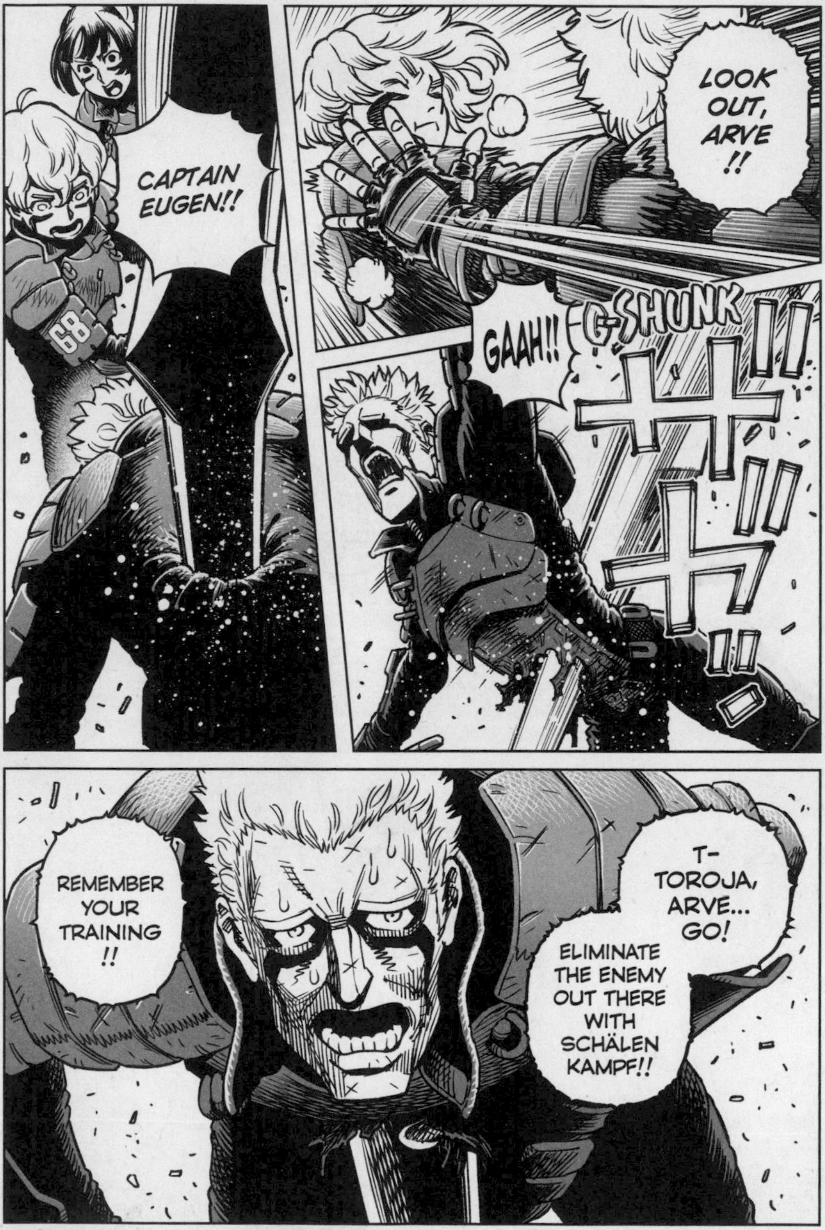
LOOK OUT, ARVE !!
GAAH!!
G-SHUNK
CAPTAIN EUGEN!!
T-TOROJA, ARVE... GO!
ELIMINATE THE ENEMY OUT THERE WITH SCHÄLEN KAMPF!!
REMEMBER YOUR TRAINING !!

***SCHÄLEN KAMPF:** A theoretical and practical application of Panzer Künst. A type of combat used when flat, solid ground is in short supply.

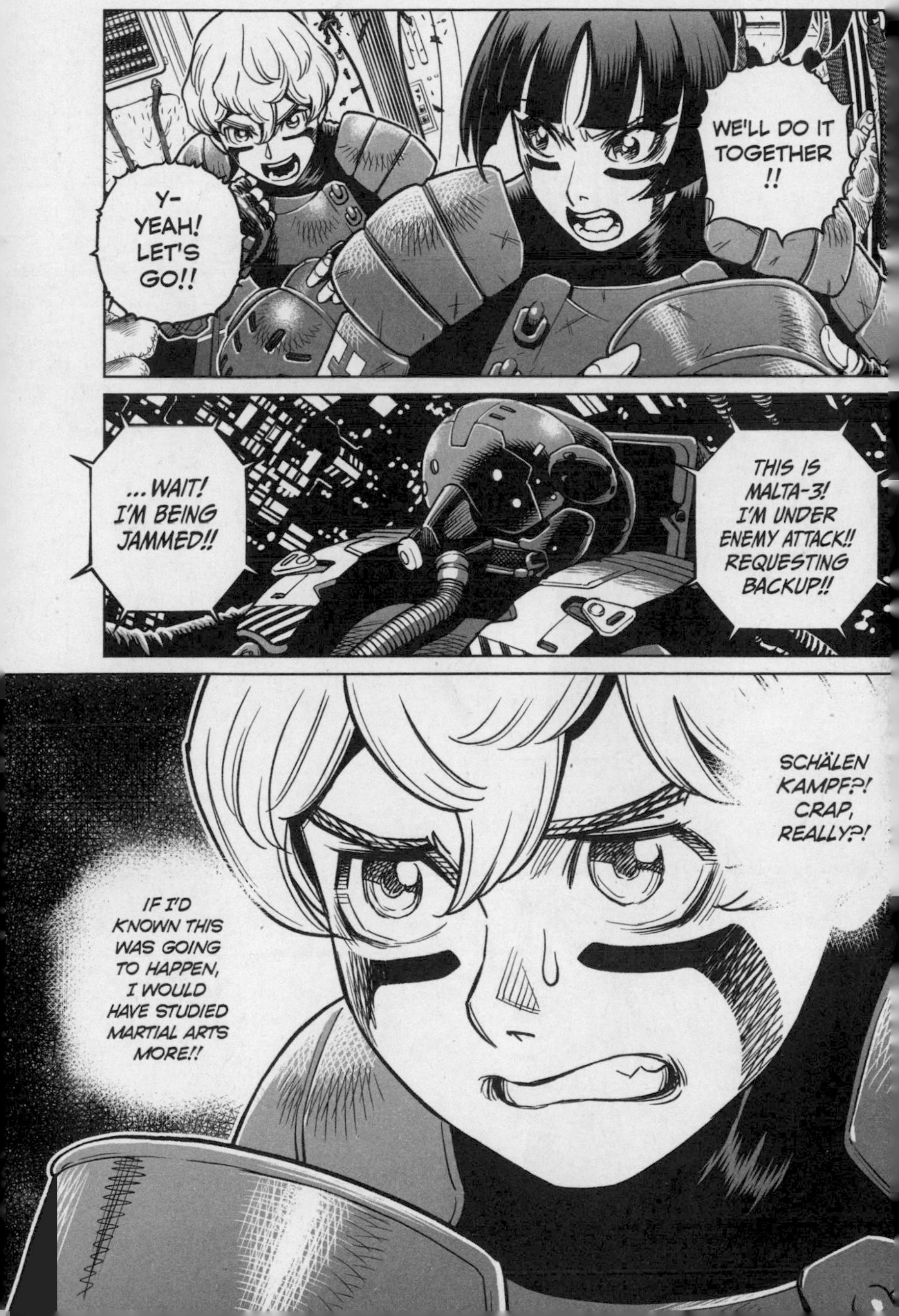
WE'LL DO IT TOGETHER !!
Y-YEAH! LET'S GO!!
THIS IS MALTA-3! I'M UNDER ENEMY ATTACK!! REQUESTING BACKUP!!
...WAIT! I'M BEING JAMMED!!
SCHÄLEN KAMPF?! CRAP, REALLY?!
IF I'D KNOWN THIS WAS GOING TO HAPPEN, I WOULD HAVE STUDIED MARTIAL ARTS MORE!!

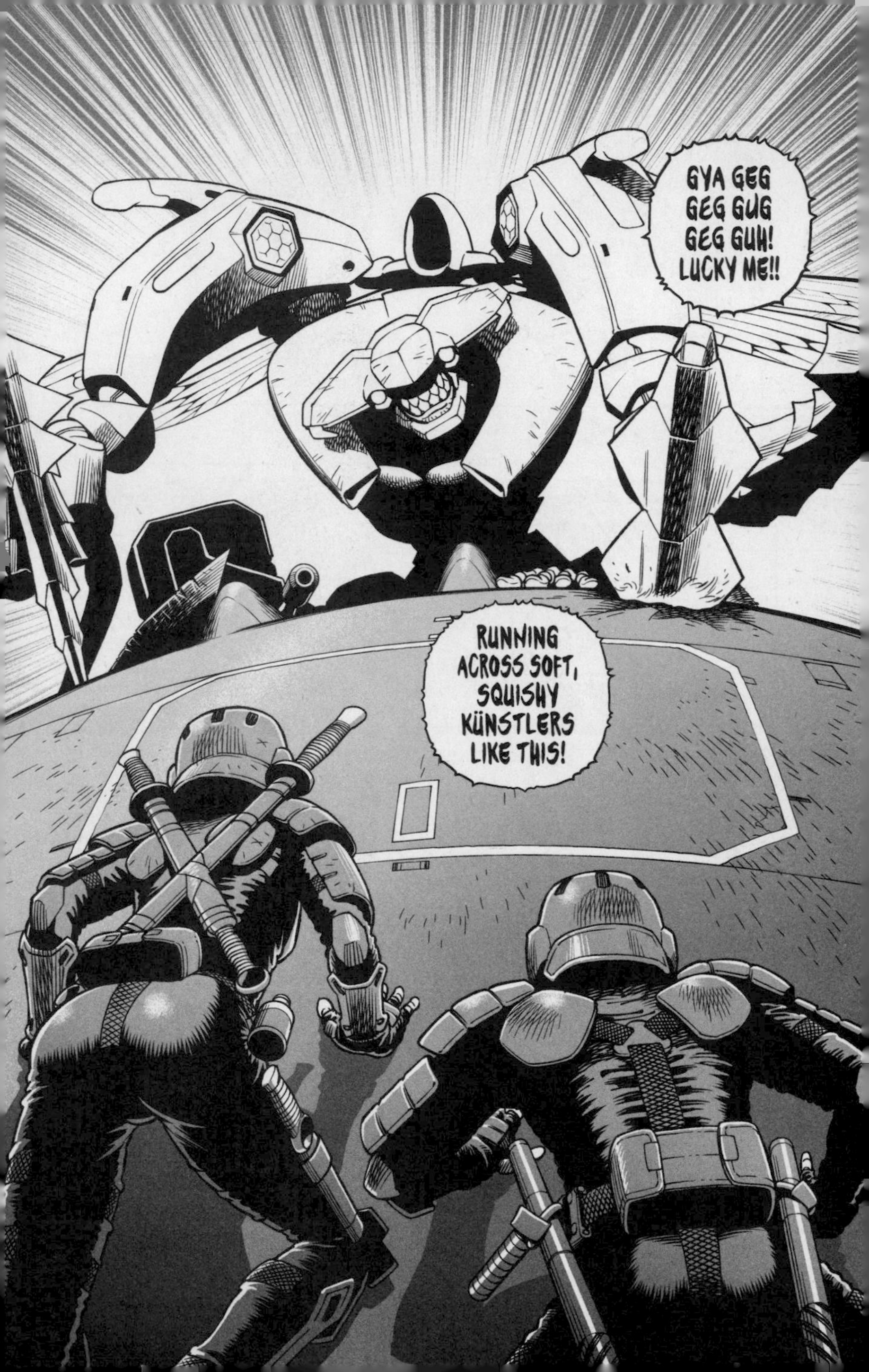
GYA GEG GEG GUG GEG GUH! LUCKY ME!!
RUNNING ACROSS SOFT, SQUISHY KÜNSTLERS LIKE THIS!

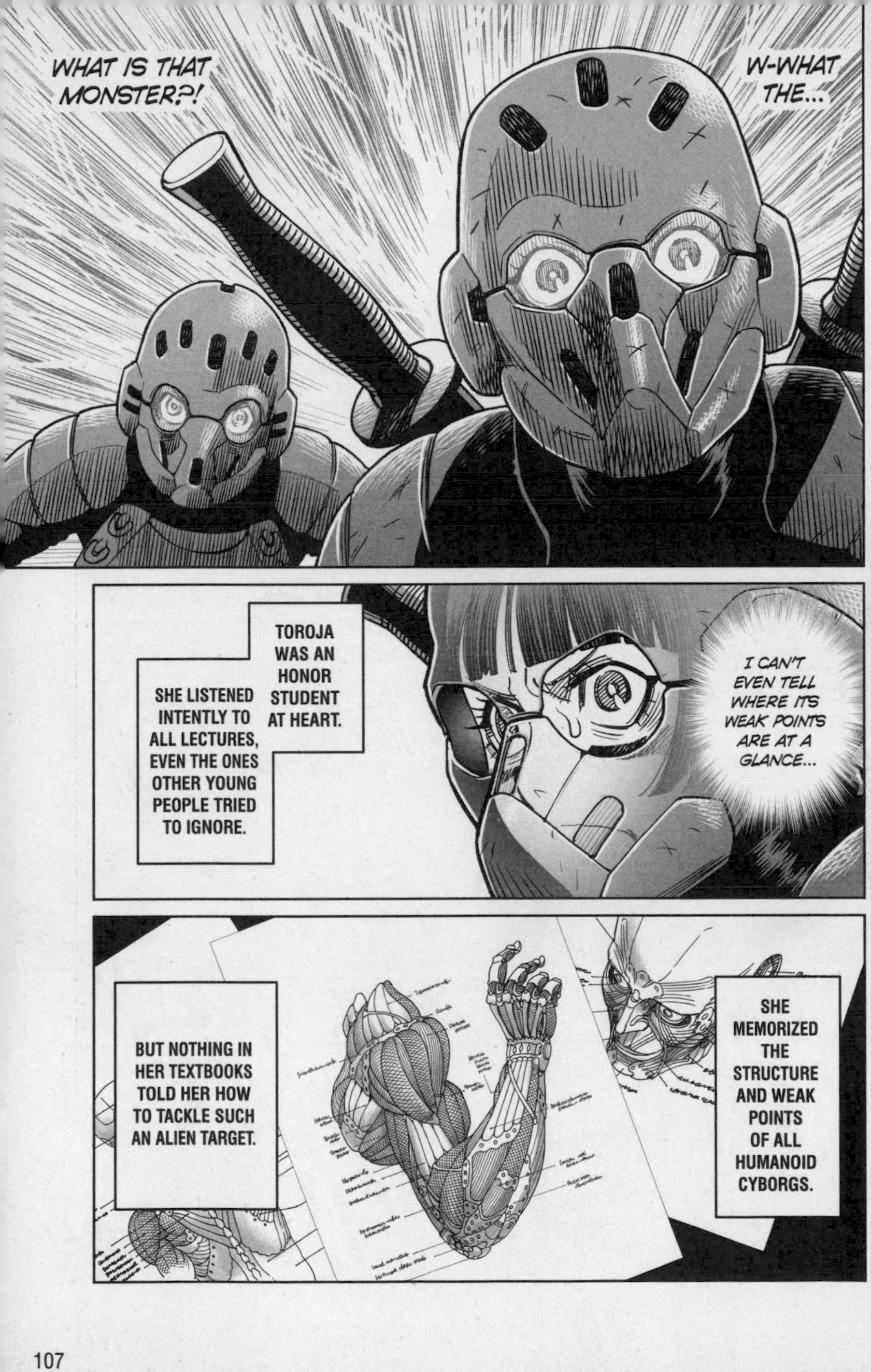
W-WHAT THE...
WHAT IS THAT MONSTER?!
I CAN'T EVEN TELL WHERE ITS WEAK POINTS ARE AT A GLANCE...
TOROJA WAS AN HONOR STUDENT AT HEART.
SHE LISTENED INTENTLY TO ALL LECTURES, EVEN THE ONES OTHER YOUNG PEOPLE TRIED TO IGNORE.
SHE MEMORIZED THE STRUCTURE AND WEAK POINTS OF ALL HUMANOID CYBORGS.
BUT NOTHING IN HER TEXTBOOKS TOLD HER HOW TO TACKLE SUCH AN ALIEN TARGET.

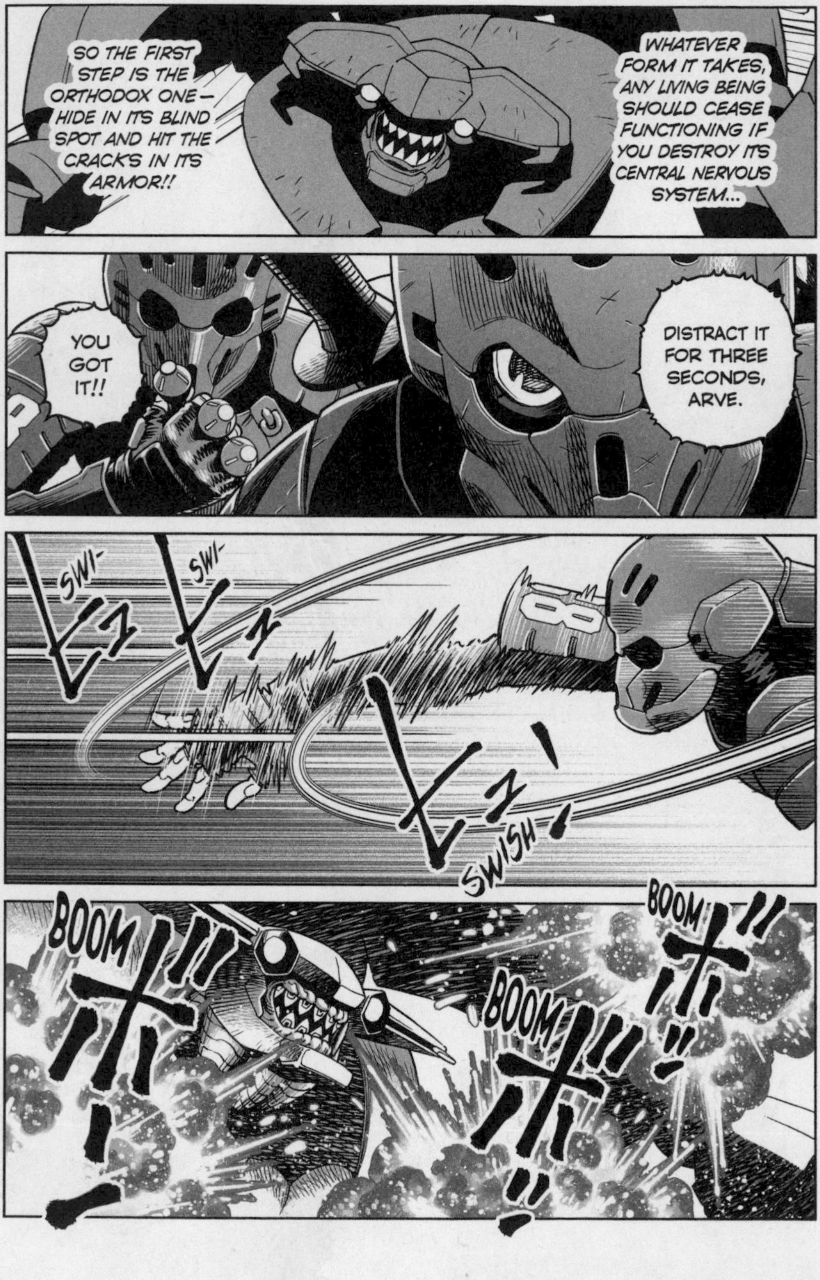
WHATEVER FORM IT TAKES, ANY LIVING BEING SHOULD CEASE FUNCTIONING IF YOU DESTROY ITS CENTRAL NERVOUS SYSTEM...
SO THE FIRST STEP IS THE ORTHODOX ONE— HIDE IN ITS BLIND SPOT AND HIT THE CRACKS IN ITS ARMOR!!
DISTRACT IT FOR THREE SECONDS, ARVE.
YOU GOT IT!!
SWI-
SWI-
SWISH
BOOM
BOOM
BOOM

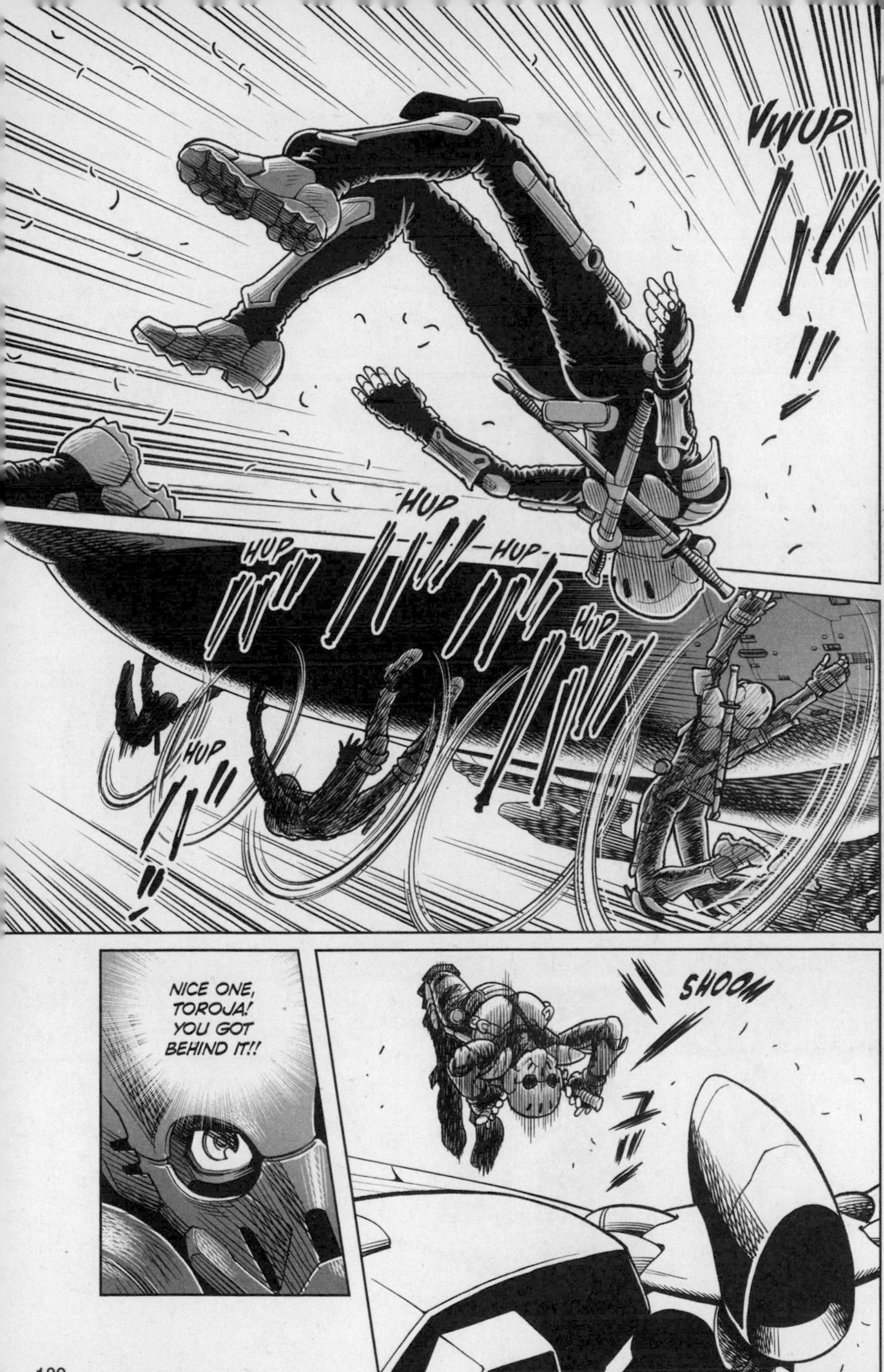
VWUP
HUP
HUP
HUP
HUP
HUP
SHOOM
NICE ONE, TOROJA! YOU GOT BEHIND IT!!

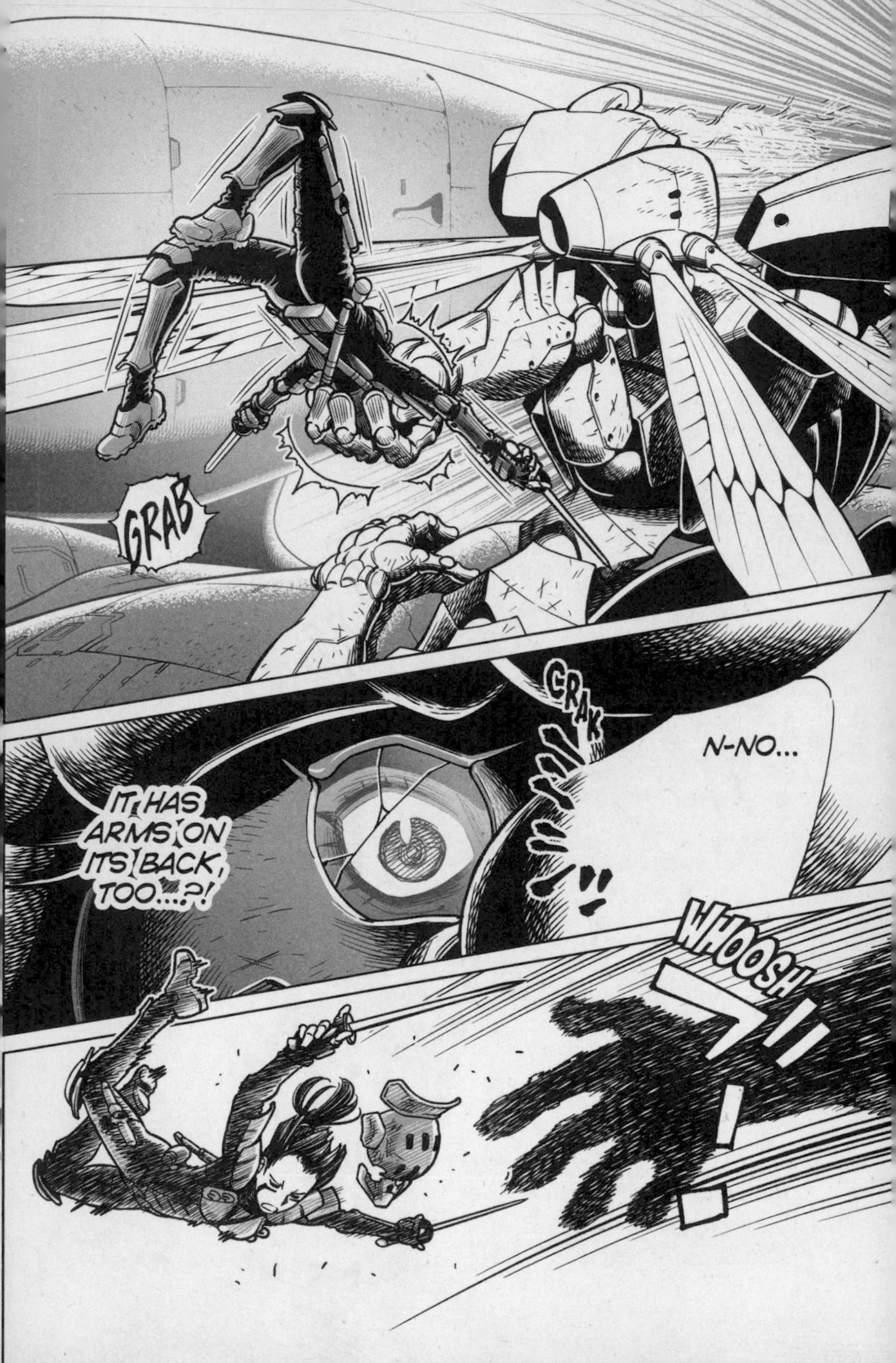
GRAB
CRAK
N-NO...
IT HAS ARMS ON ITS BACK, TOO...?!
WHOOSH

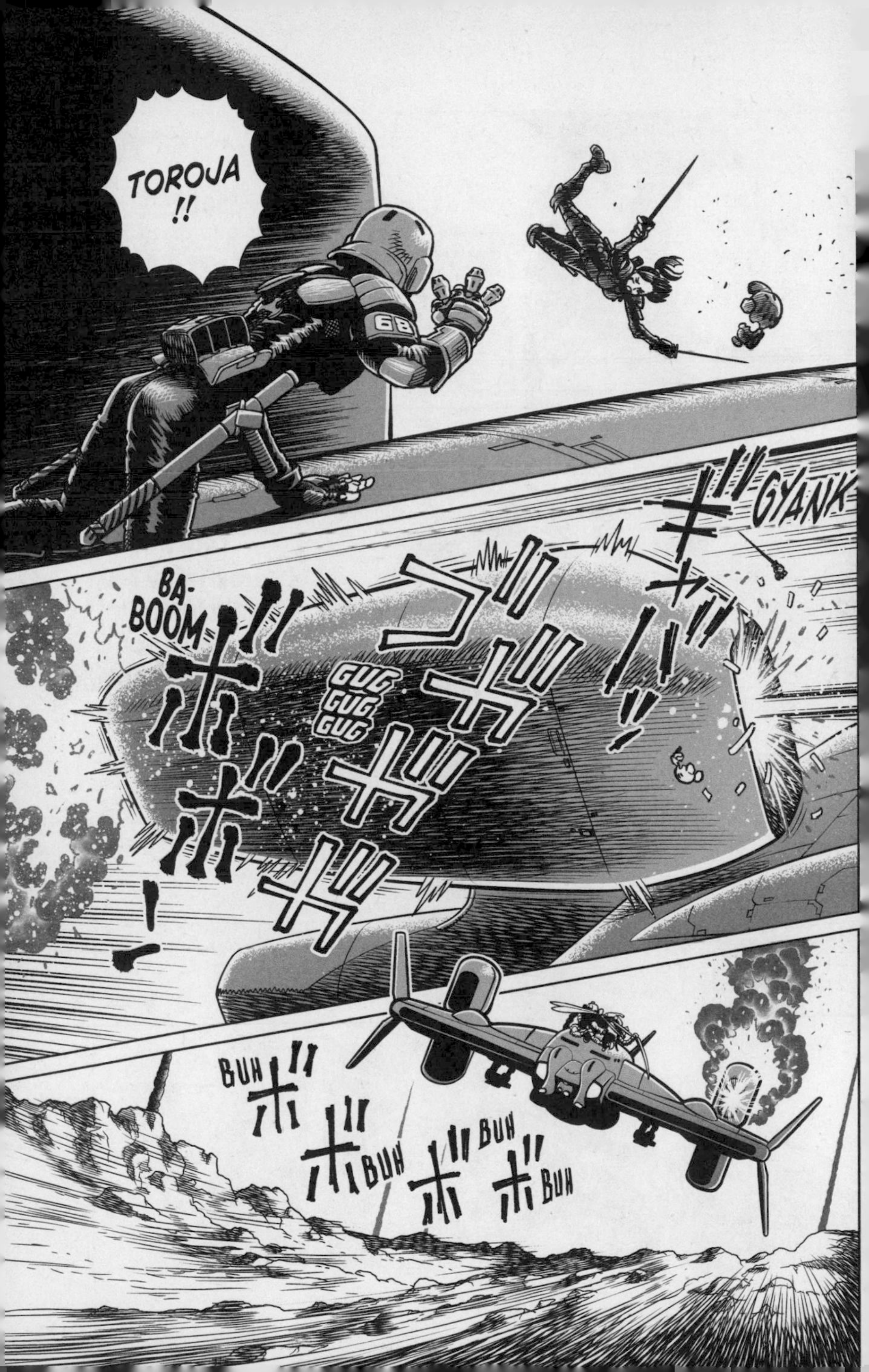
TOROJA !!
GYANK
GUG GUG GUG
BA-BOOM
BUH
BUH
BUH
BUH
BUH

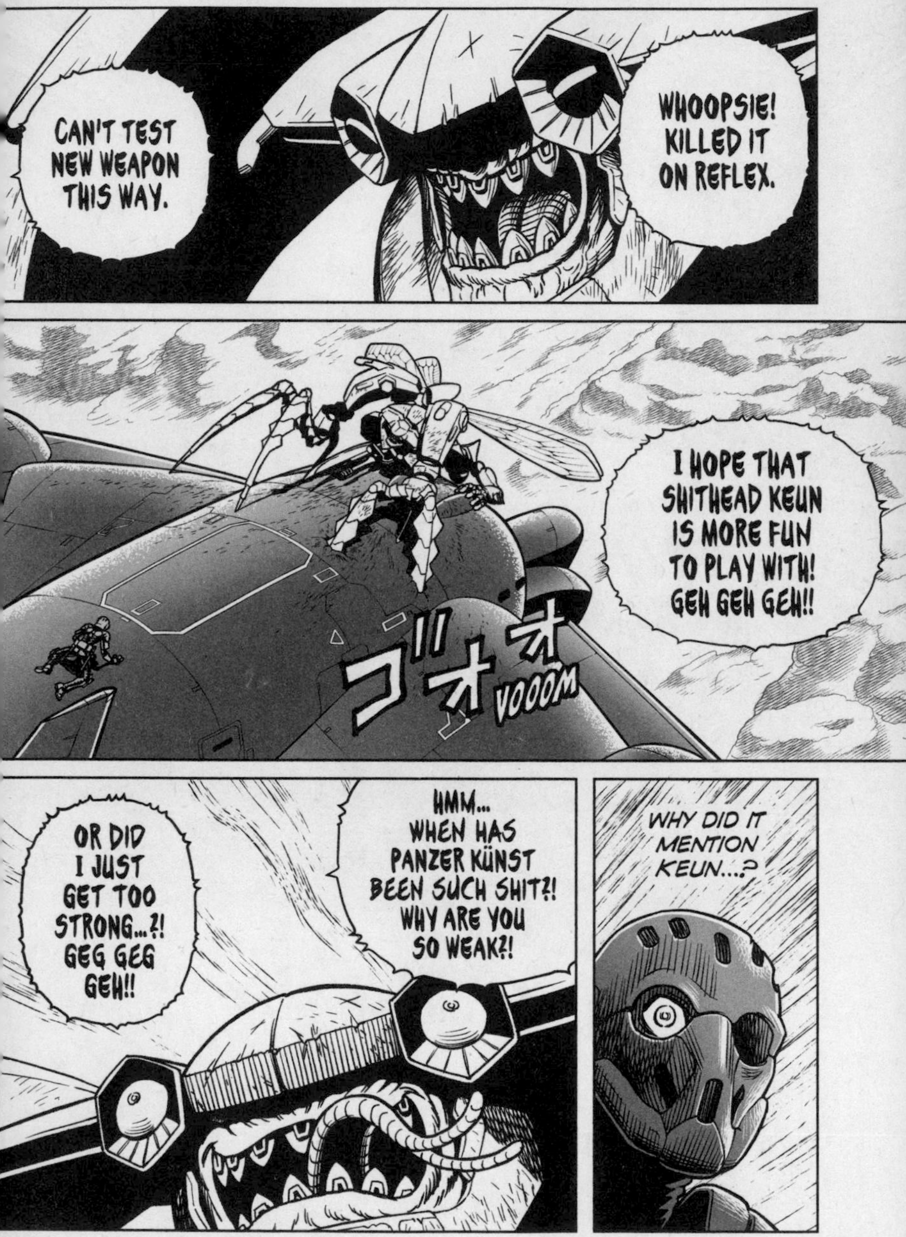
WHOOPSIE! KILLED IT ON REFLEX.
CAN'T TEST NEW WEAPON THIS WAY.
I HOPE THAT SHITHEAD KEUN IS MORE FUN TO PLAY WITH! GEH GEH GEH!!
ゴオオ
VOOOM
WHY DID IT MENTION KEUN...?
HMM... WHEN HAS PANZER KÜNST BEEN SUCH SHIT?! WHY ARE YOU SO WEAK?!
OR DID I JUST GET TOO STRONG...?! GEG GEG GEH!!

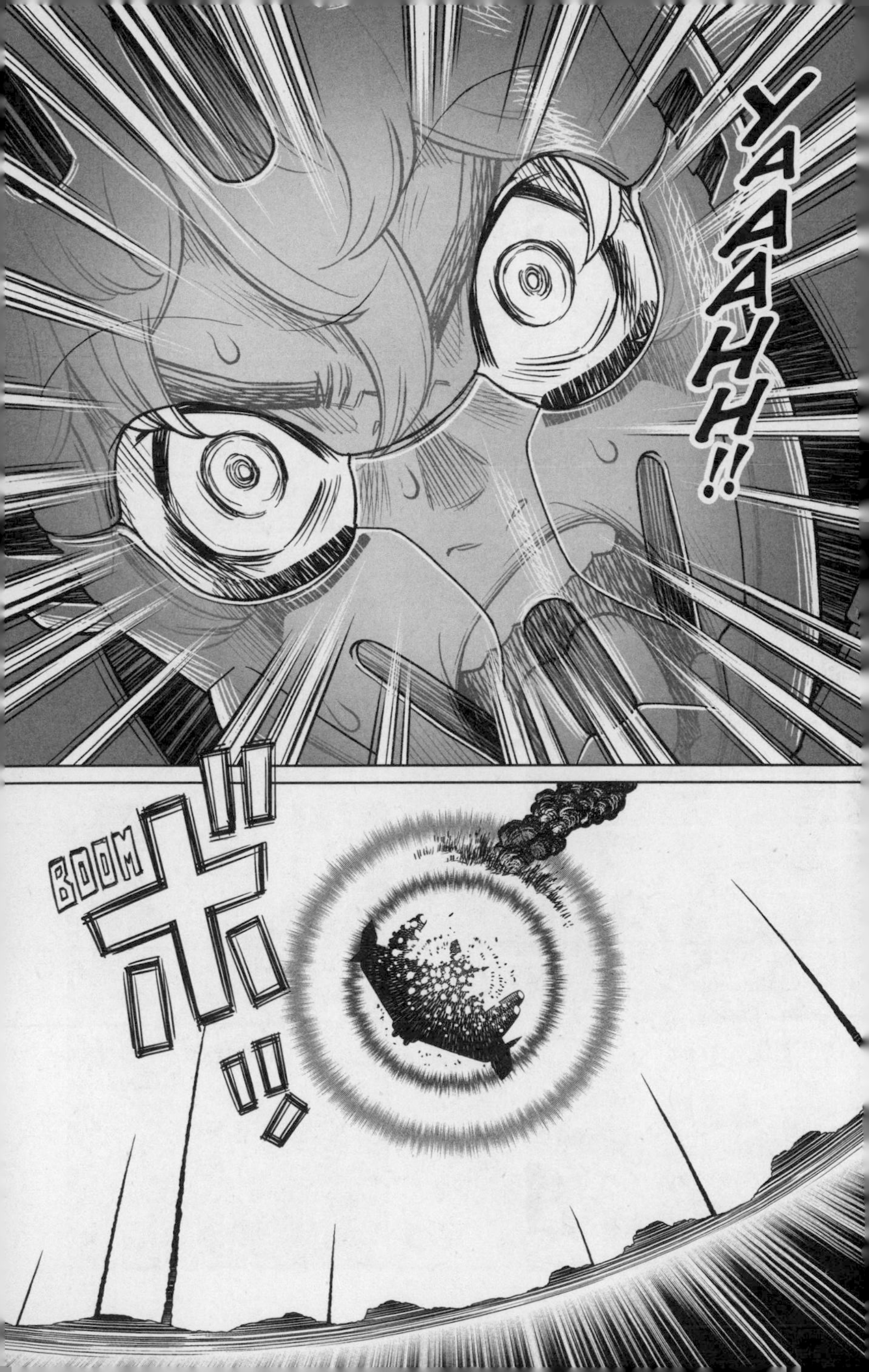
YAAAHH!!
BOOM

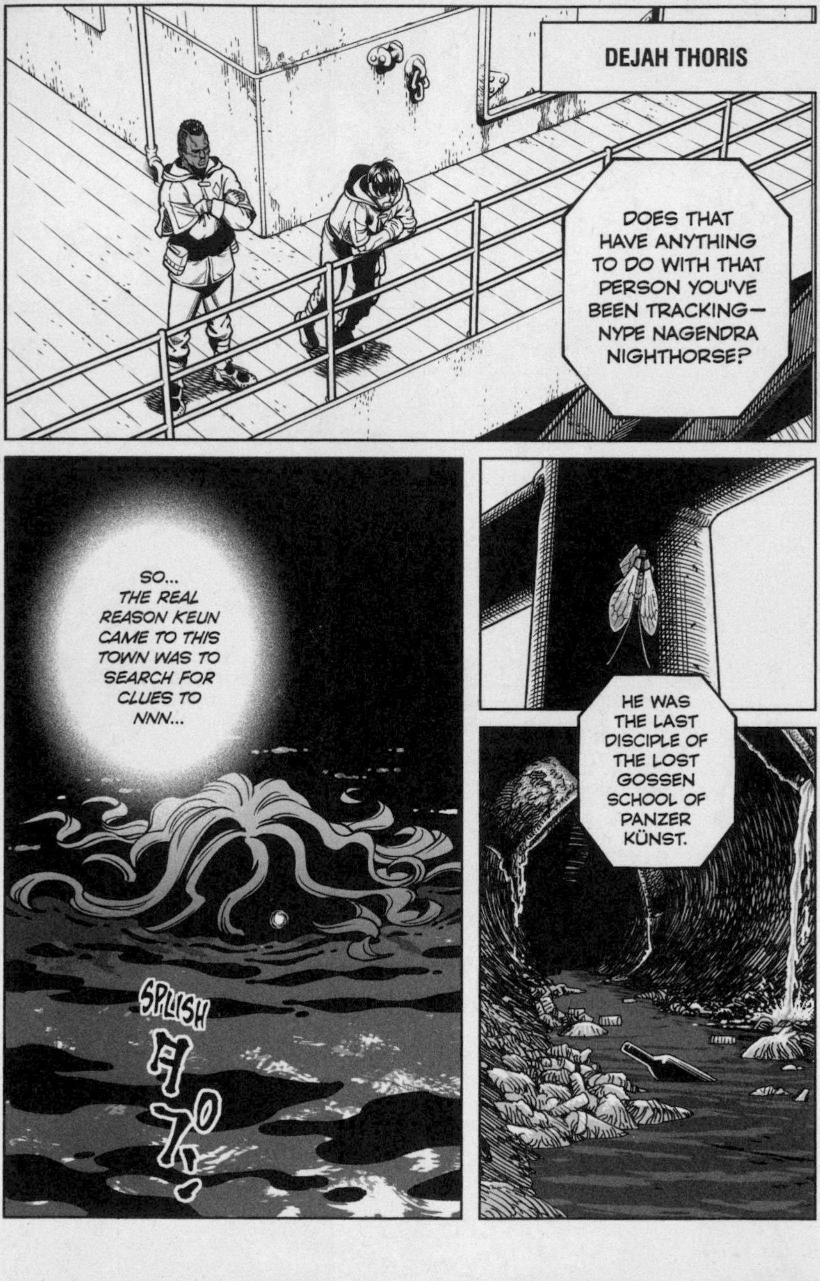
DEJAH THORIS
DOES THAT HAVE ANYTHING TO DO WITH THAT PERSON YOU'VE BEEN TRACKING— NYPE NAGENDRA NIGHTHORSE?
HE WAS THE LAST DISCIPLE OF THE LOST GOSSEN SCHOOL OF PANZER KÜNST.
SO... THE REAL REASON KEUN CAME TO THIS TOWN WAS TO SEARCH FOR CLUES TO NNN...
SPLISH

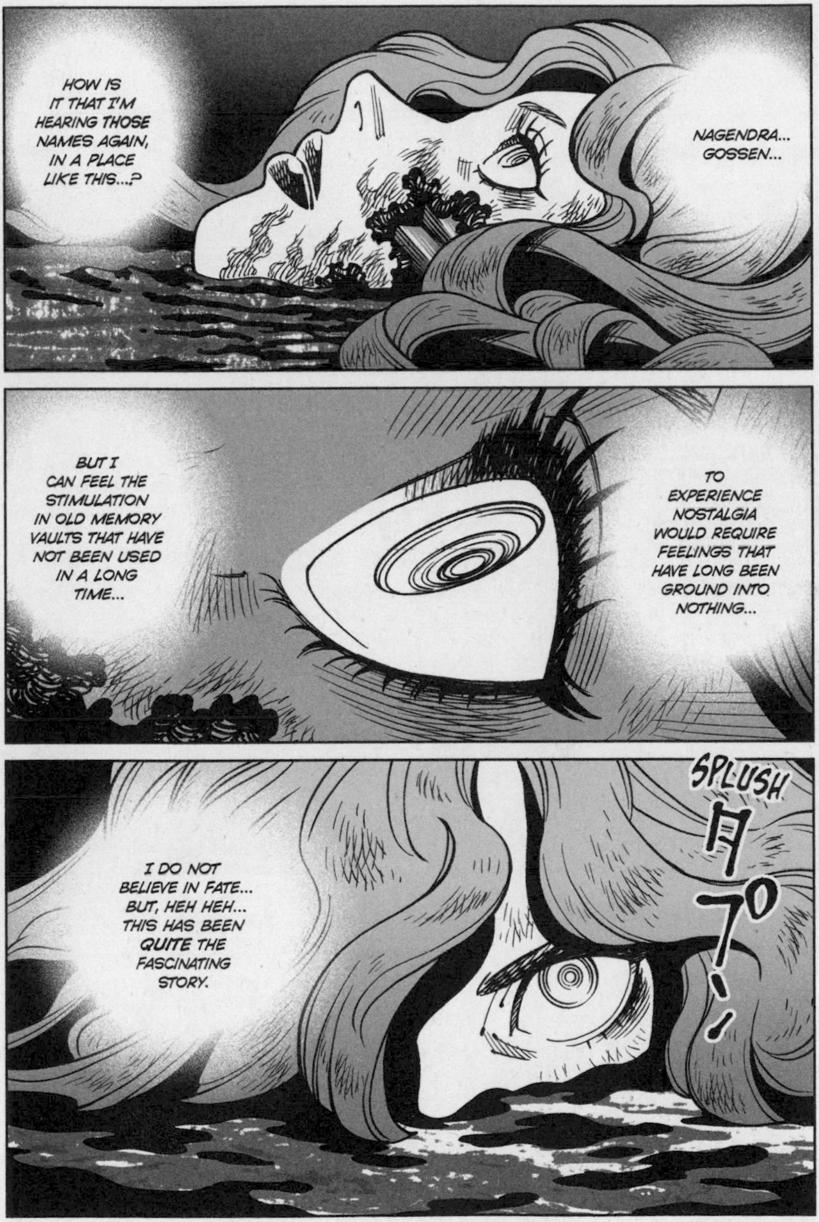
NAGENDRA... GOSSEN...
HOW IS IT THAT I'M HEARING THOSE NAMES AGAIN, IN A PLACE LIKE THIS...?
TO EXPERIENCE NOSTALGIA WOULD REQUIRE FEELINGS THAT HAVE LONG BEEN GROUND INTO NOTHING...
BUT I CAN FEEL THE STIMULATION IN OLD MEMORY VAULTS THAT HAVE NOT BEEN USED IN A LONG TIME...
SPLUSH
I DO NOT BELIEVE IN FATE... BUT, HEH HEH... THIS HAS BEEN QUITE THE FASCINATING STORY.

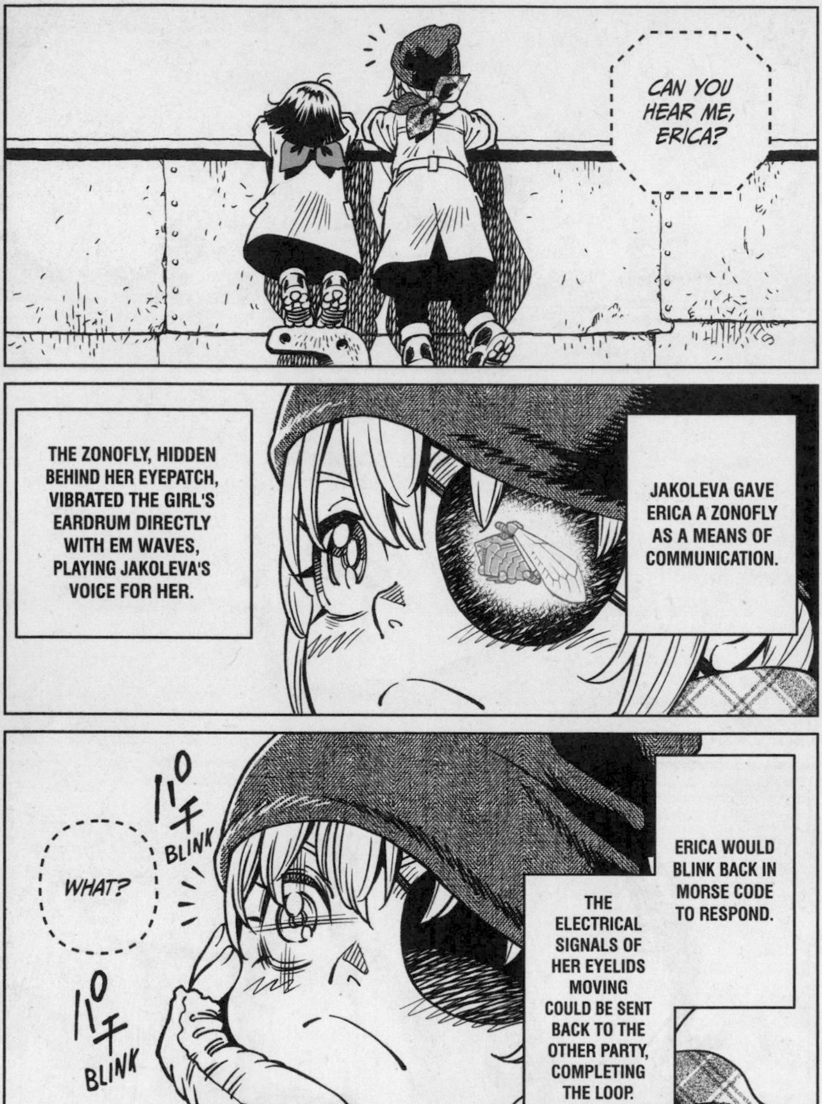
CAN YOU HEAR ME, ERICA?
JAKOLEVA GAVE ERICA A ZONOFLY AS A MEANS OF COMMUNICATION.
THE ZONOFLY, HIDDEN BEHIND HER EYEPATCH, VIBRATED THE GIRL'S EARDRUM DIRECTLY WITH EM WAVES, PLAYING JAKOLEVA'S VOICE FOR HER.
ERICA WOULD BLINK BACK IN MORSE CODE TO RESPOND.
THE ELECTRICAL SIGNALS OF HER EYELIDS MOVING COULD BE SENT BACK TO THE OTHER PARTY, COMPLETING THE LOOP.
パチ BLINK
WHAT?
パチ BLINK

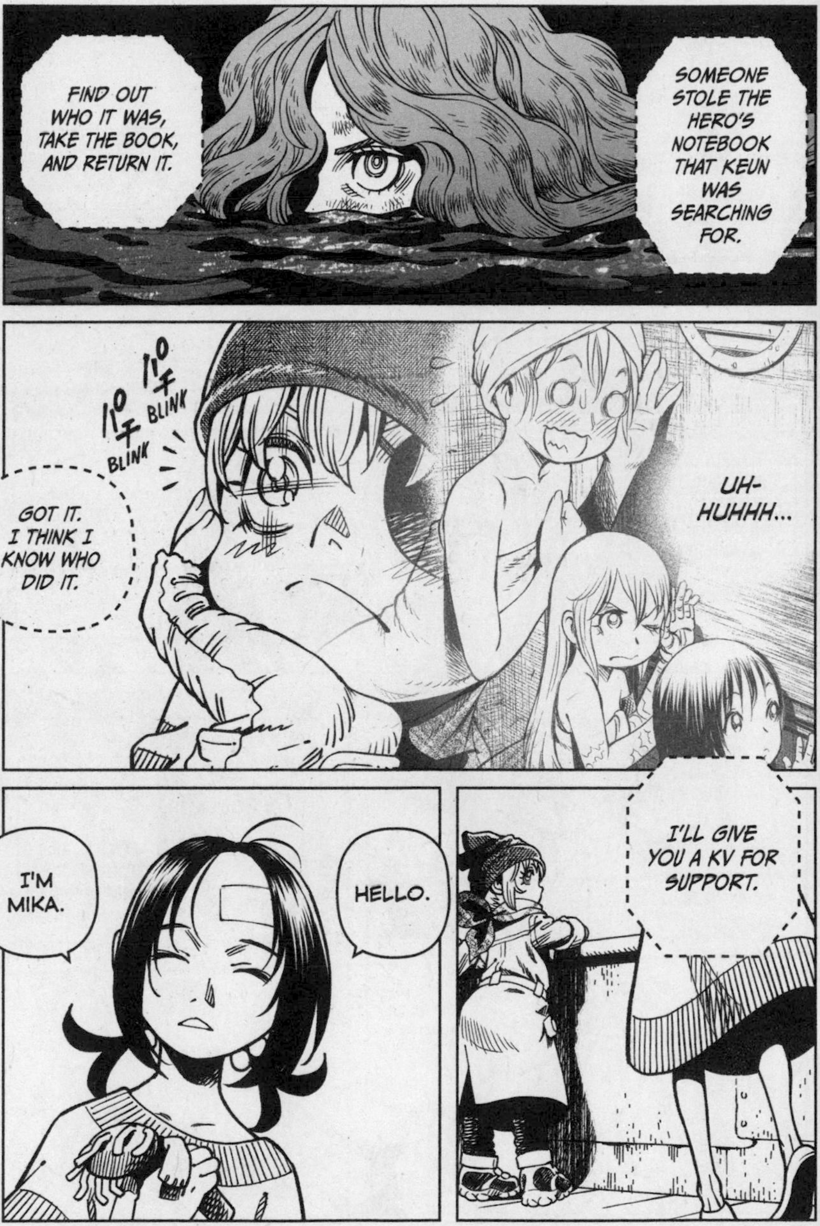
SOMEONE STOLE THE HERO'S NOTEBOOK THAT KEUN WAS SEARCHING FOR.
FIND OUT WHO IT WAS, TAKE THE BOOK, AND RETURN IT.
UH-HUHHH...
パチ BLINK
パチ BLINK
GOT IT. I THINK I KNOW WHO DID IT.
I'LL GIVE YOU A KV FOR SUPPORT.
HELLO.
I'M MIKA.

***KV (KINDER VERSUCHSKANINCHEN):** Children who underwent brain augmentation in Zonohedron's TGIV project. "Child guinea pigs."

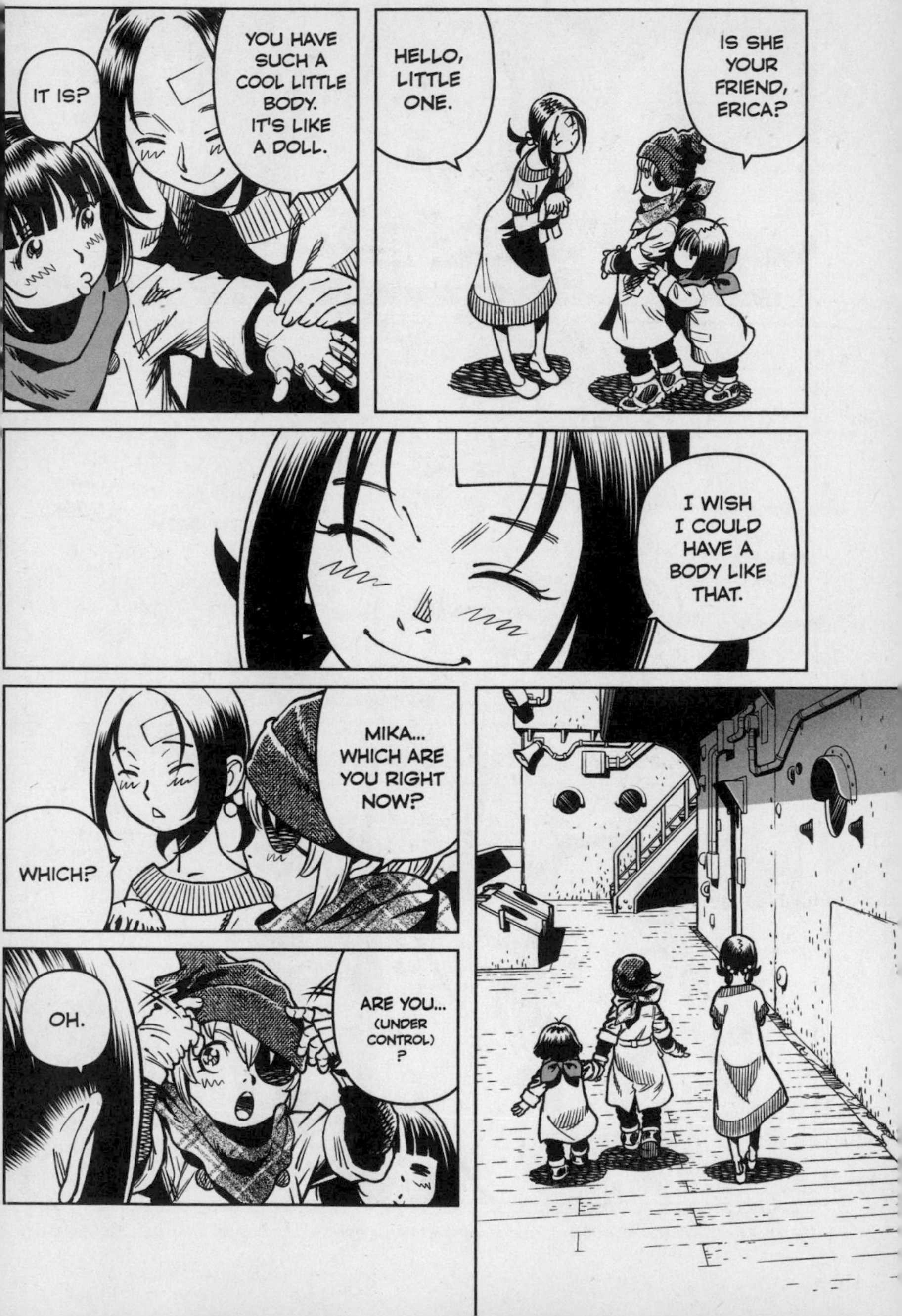
IS SHE YOUR FRIEND, ERICA?
HELLO, LITTLE ONE.
YOU HAVE SUCH A COOL LITTLE BODY. IT'S LIKE A DOLL.
IT IS?
I WISH I COULD HAVE A BODY LIKE THAT.
MIKA... WHICH ARE YOU RIGHT NOW?
WHICH?
ARE YOU... (UNDER CONTROL) ?
OH.

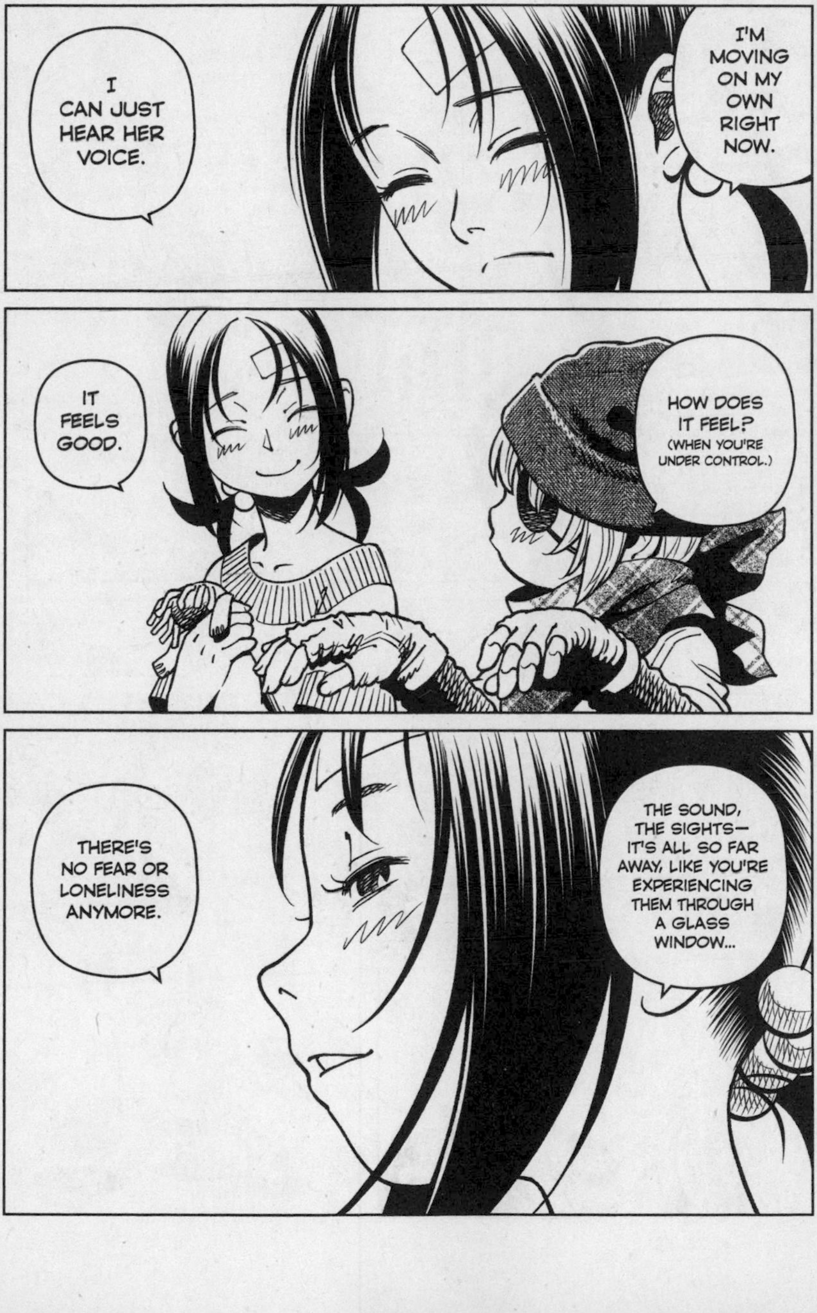
I'M MOVING ON MY OWN RIGHT NOW.
I CAN JUST HEAR HER VOICE.
HOW DOES IT FEEL? (WHEN YOU'RE UNDER CONTROL.)
IT FEELS GOOD.
THE SOUND, THE SIGHTS— IT'S ALL SO FAR AWAY, LIKE YOU'RE EXPERIENCING THEM THROUGH A GLASS WINDOW...
THERE'S NO FEAR OR LONELINESS ANYMORE.

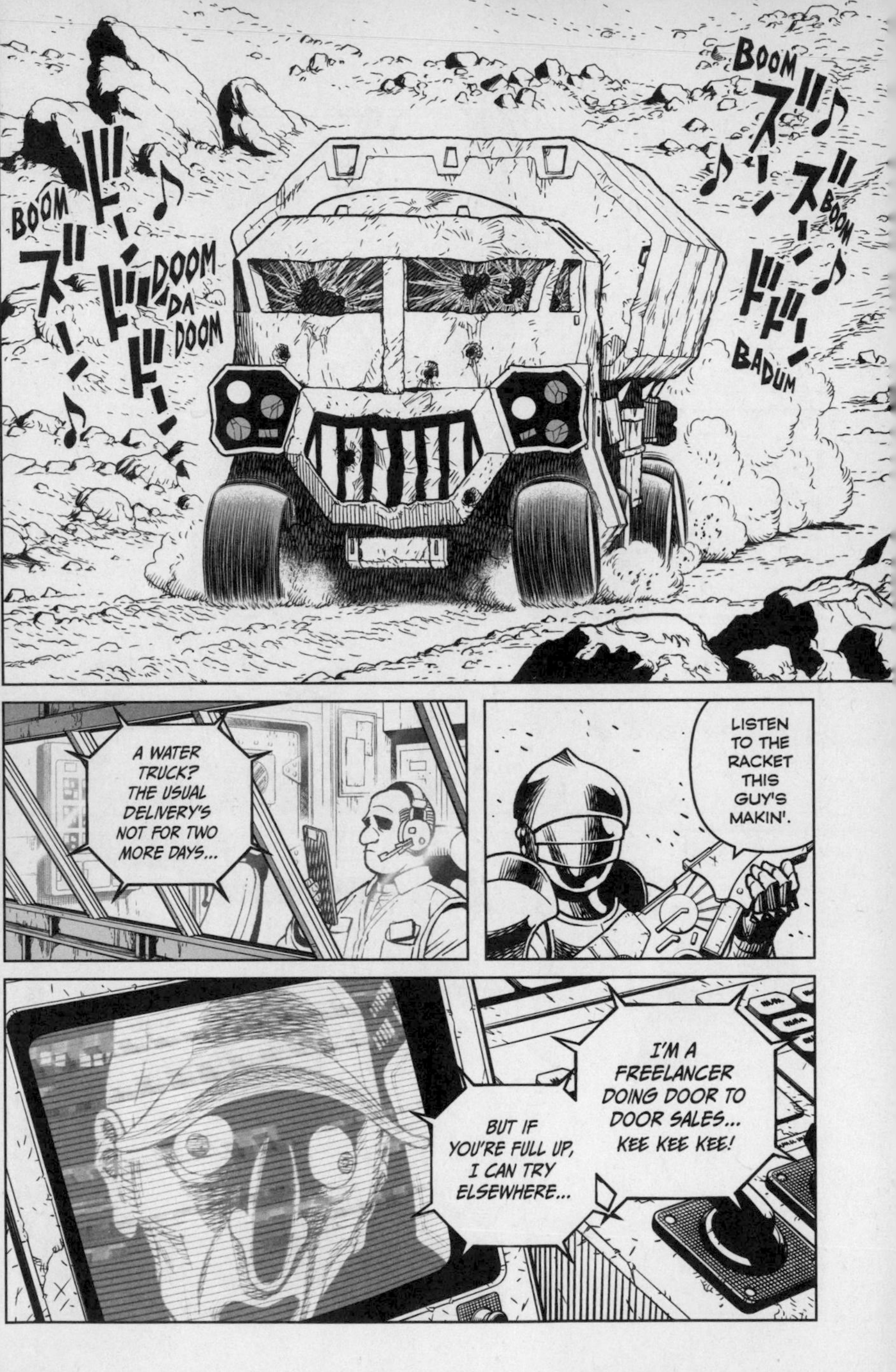
BOOM
ズン♪
ズン
BOOM♪
ドドン
BADUM
BOOM
ドン
ドドン
DOOM DA DOOM
ズーン♪
LISTEN TO THE RACKET THIS GUY'S MAKIN'.
A WATER TRUCK? THE USUAL DELIVERY'S NOT FOR TWO MORE DAYS...
I'M A FREELANCER DOING DOOR TO DOOR SALES... KEE KEE KEE!
BUT IF YOU'RE FULL UP, I CAN TRY ELSEWHERE...

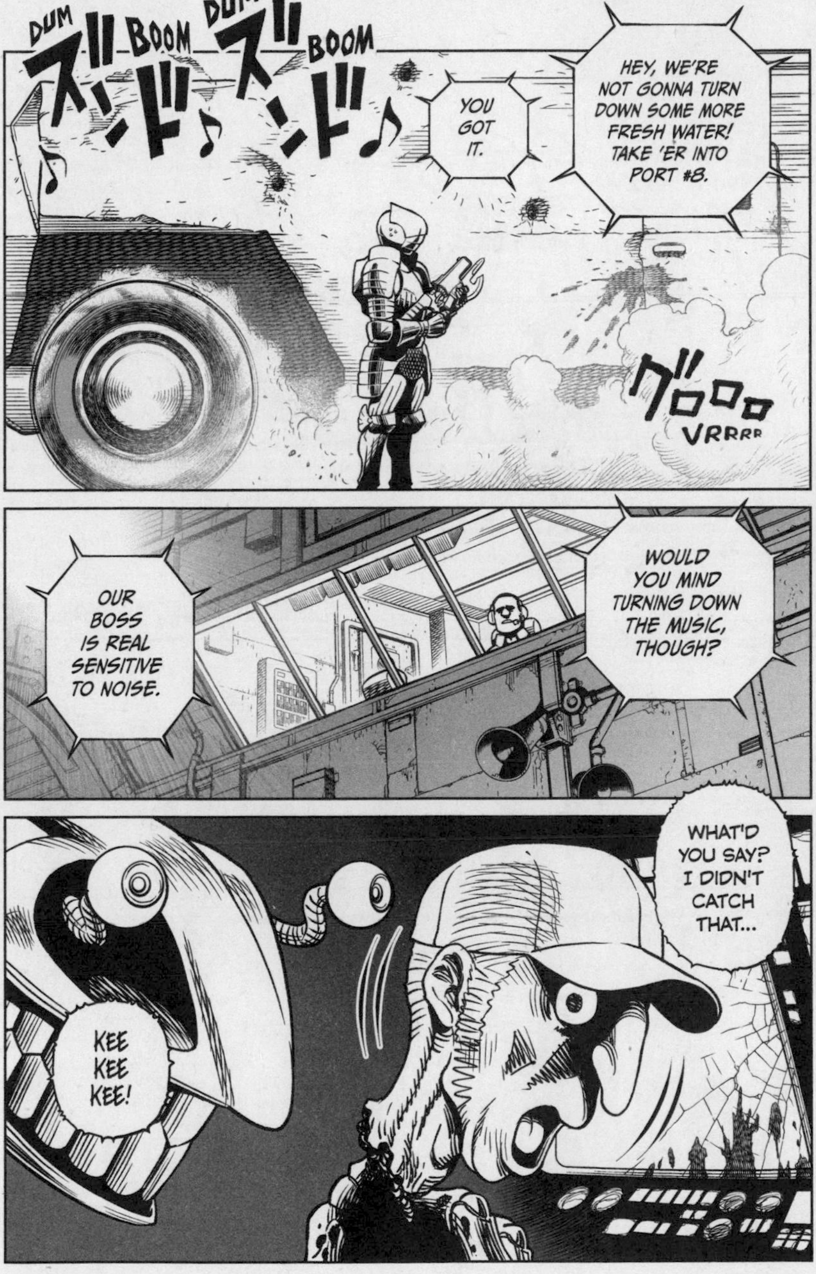
HEY, WE'RE NOT GONNA TURN DOWN SOME MORE FRESH WATER! TAKE 'ER INTO PORT #8.
YOU GOT IT.
ズンド♪ズンド♪
DUM BOOM DUM BOOM
グロロロ
VRRRR
WOULD YOU MIND TURNING DOWN THE MUSIC, THOUGH?
OUR BOSS IS REAL SENSITIVE TO NOISE.
WHAT'D YOU SAY? I DIDN'T CATCH THAT...
KEE KEE KEE!

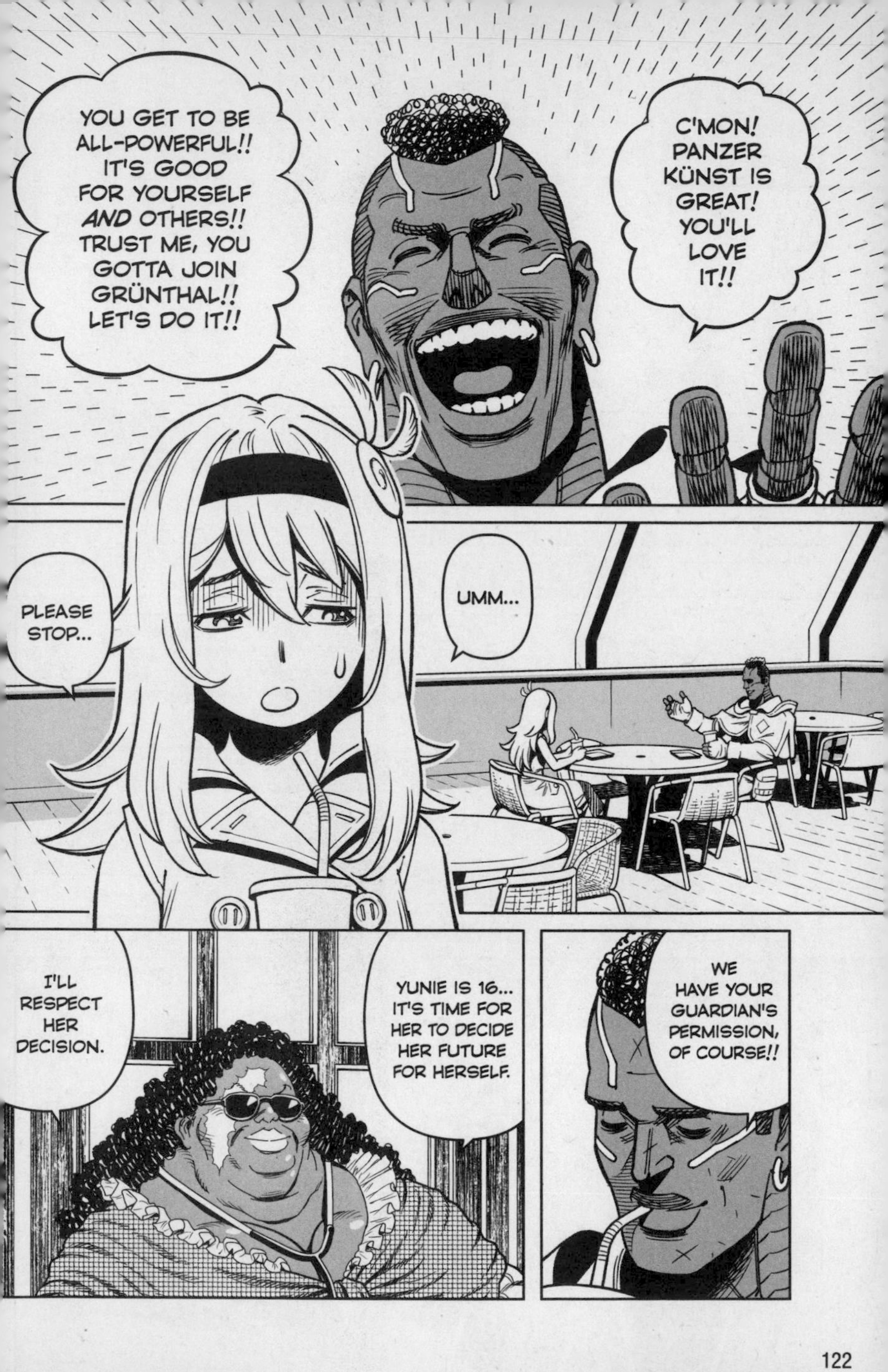
C'MON! PANZER KÜNST IS GREAT! YOU'LL LOVE IT!!
YOU GET TO BE ALL-POWERFUL!! IT'S GOOD FOR YOURSELF *AND* OTHERS!! TRUST ME, YOU GOTTA JOIN GRÜNTHAL!! LET'S DO IT!!
UMM...
PLEASE STOP...
WE HAVE YOUR GUARDIAN'S PERMISSION, OF COURSE!!
YUNIE IS 16... IT'S TIME FOR HER TO DECIDE HER FUTURE FOR HERSELF.
I'LL RESPECT HER DECISION.

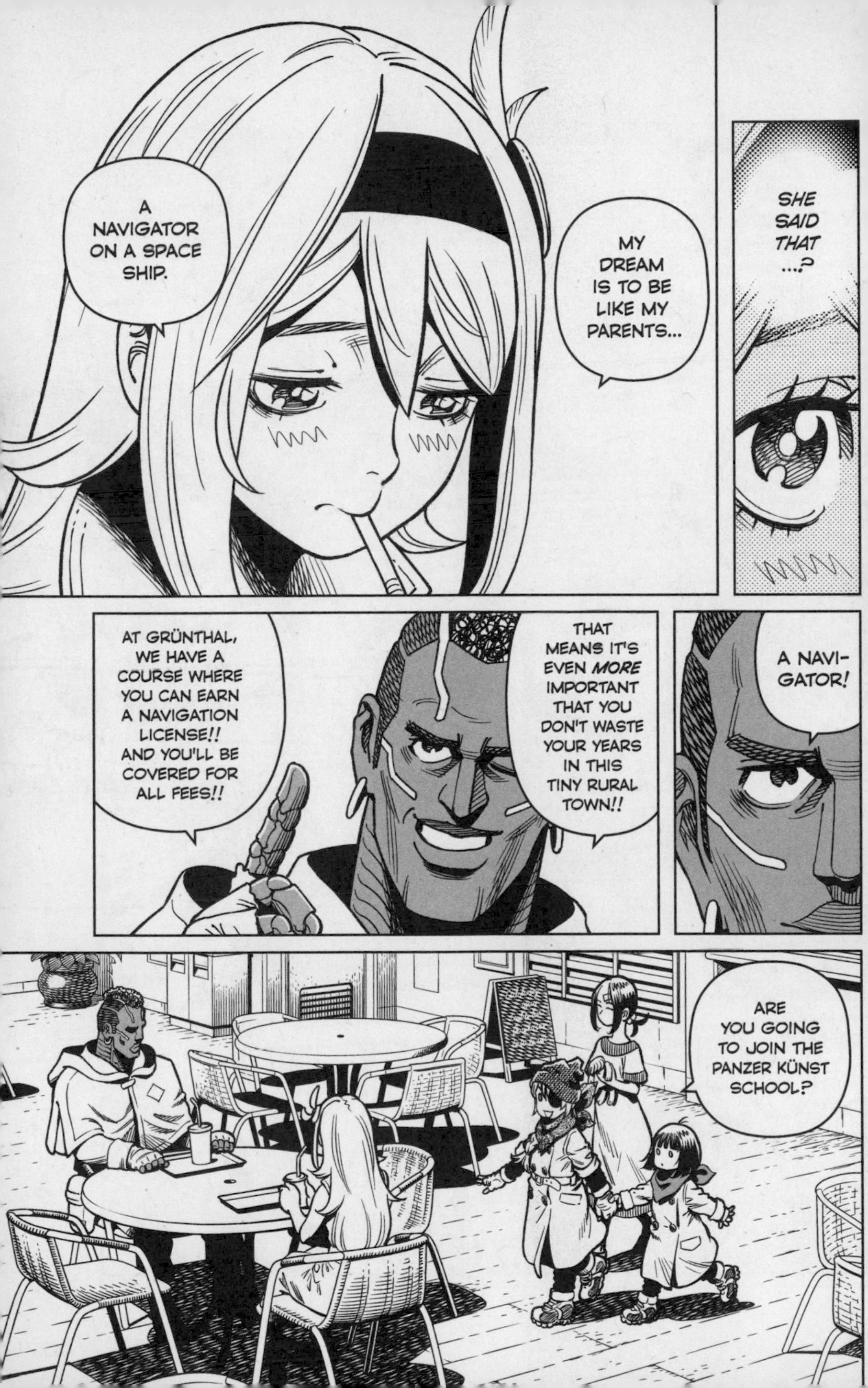
SHE SAID THAT ...?
MY DREAM IS TO BE LIKE MY PARENTS...
A NAVIGATOR ON A SPACE SHIP.
A NAVI-GATOR!
THAT MEANS IT'S EVEN *MORE* IMPORTANT THAT YOU DON'T WASTE YOUR YEARS IN THIS TINY RURAL TOWN!!
AT GRÜNTHAL, WE HAVE A COURSE WHERE YOU CAN EARN A NAVIGATION LICENSE!! AND YOU'LL BE COVERED FOR ALL FEES!!
ARE YOU GOING TO JOIN THE PANZER KÜNST SCHOOL?

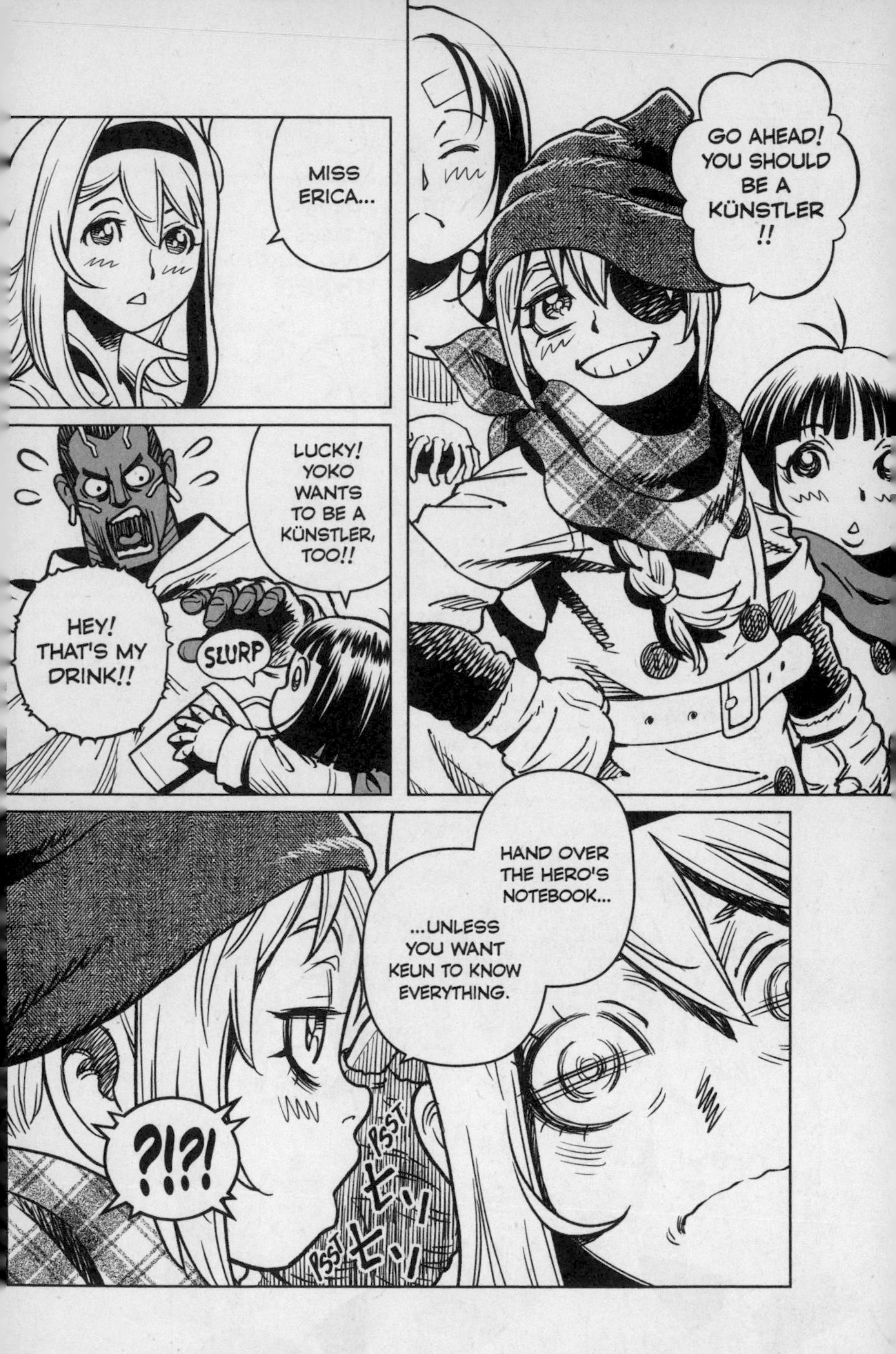
GO AHEAD! YOU SHOULD BE A KÜNSTLER!!
MISS ERICA...
LUCKY! YOKO WANTS TO BE A KÜNSTLER, TOO!!
SLURP
HEY! THAT'S MY DRINK!!
HAND OVER THE HERO'S NOTEBOOK...
...UNLESS YOU WANT KEUN TO KNOW EVERYTHING.
?!?!
PSST
PSST

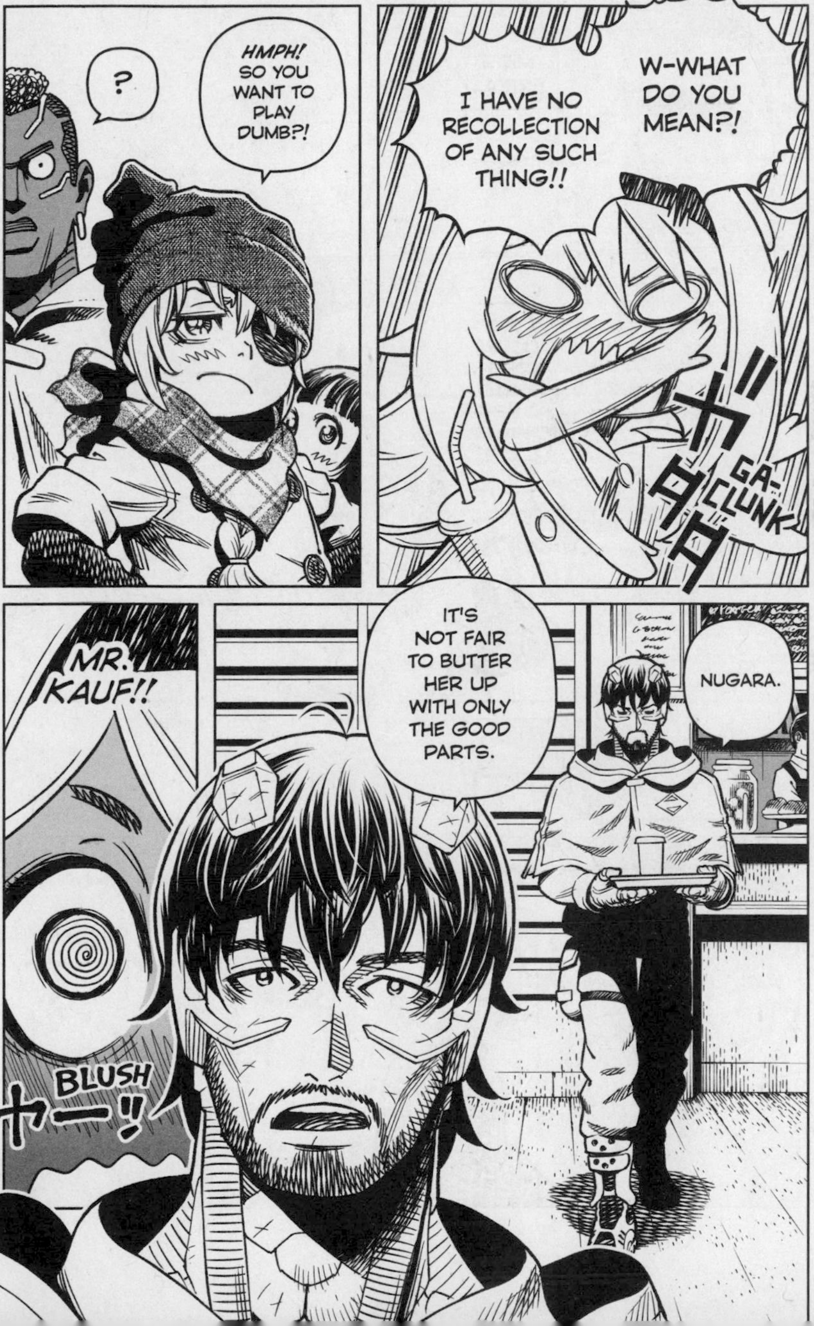
W-WHAT DO YOU MEAN?!
I HAVE NO RECOLLECTION OF ANY SUCH THING!!
GA-CLUNK
HMPH! SO YOU WANT TO PLAY DUMB?!
?
NUGARA.
IT'S NOT FAIR TO BUTTER HER UP WITH ONLY THE GOOD PARTS.
MR. KAUF!!
BLUSH

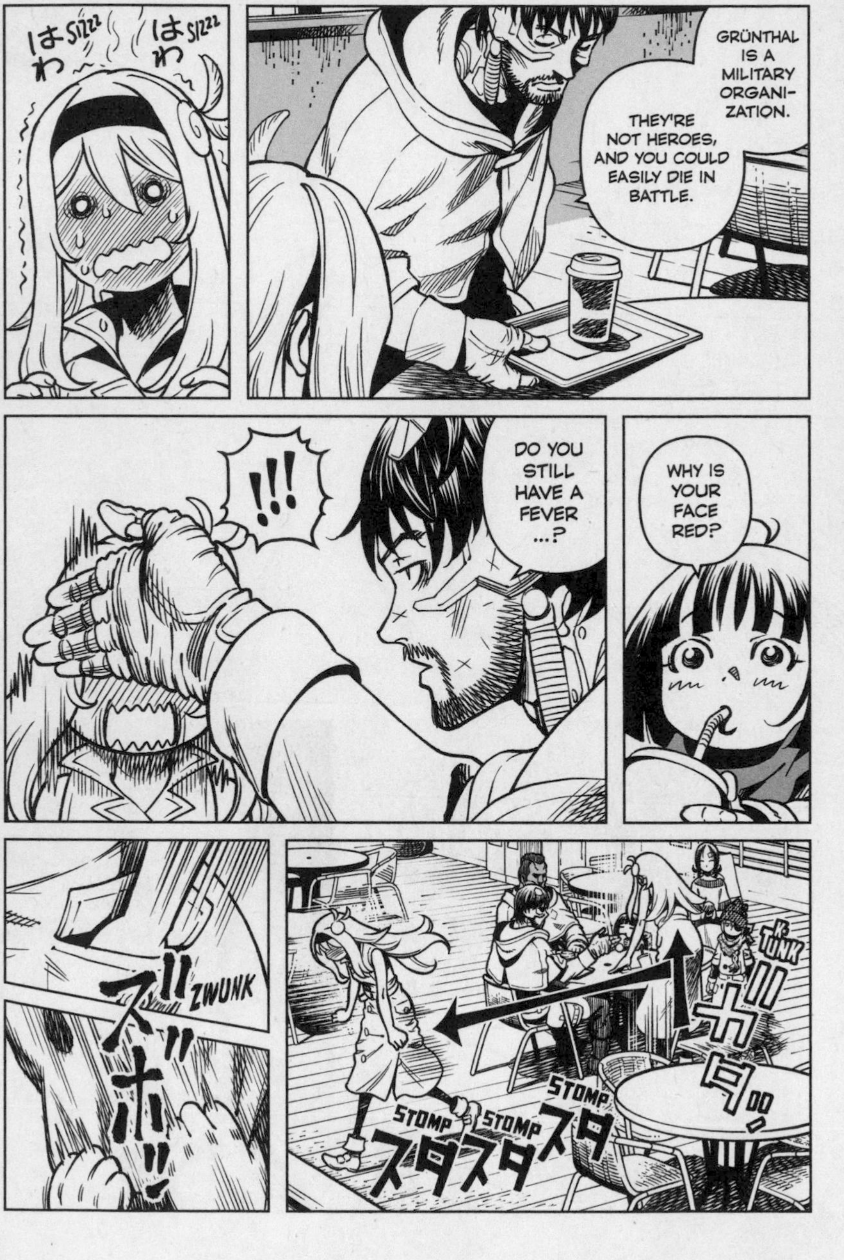
GRÜNTHAL IS A MILITARY ORGANIZATION.
THEY'RE NOT HEROES, AND YOU COULD EASILY DIE IN BATTLE.
はわ~ SIZZZ
はわ SIZZZ
WHY IS YOUR FACE RED?
DO YOU STILL HAVE A FEVER ...?
!!!
K-TUNK
STOMP STOMP STOMP
ZWUNK

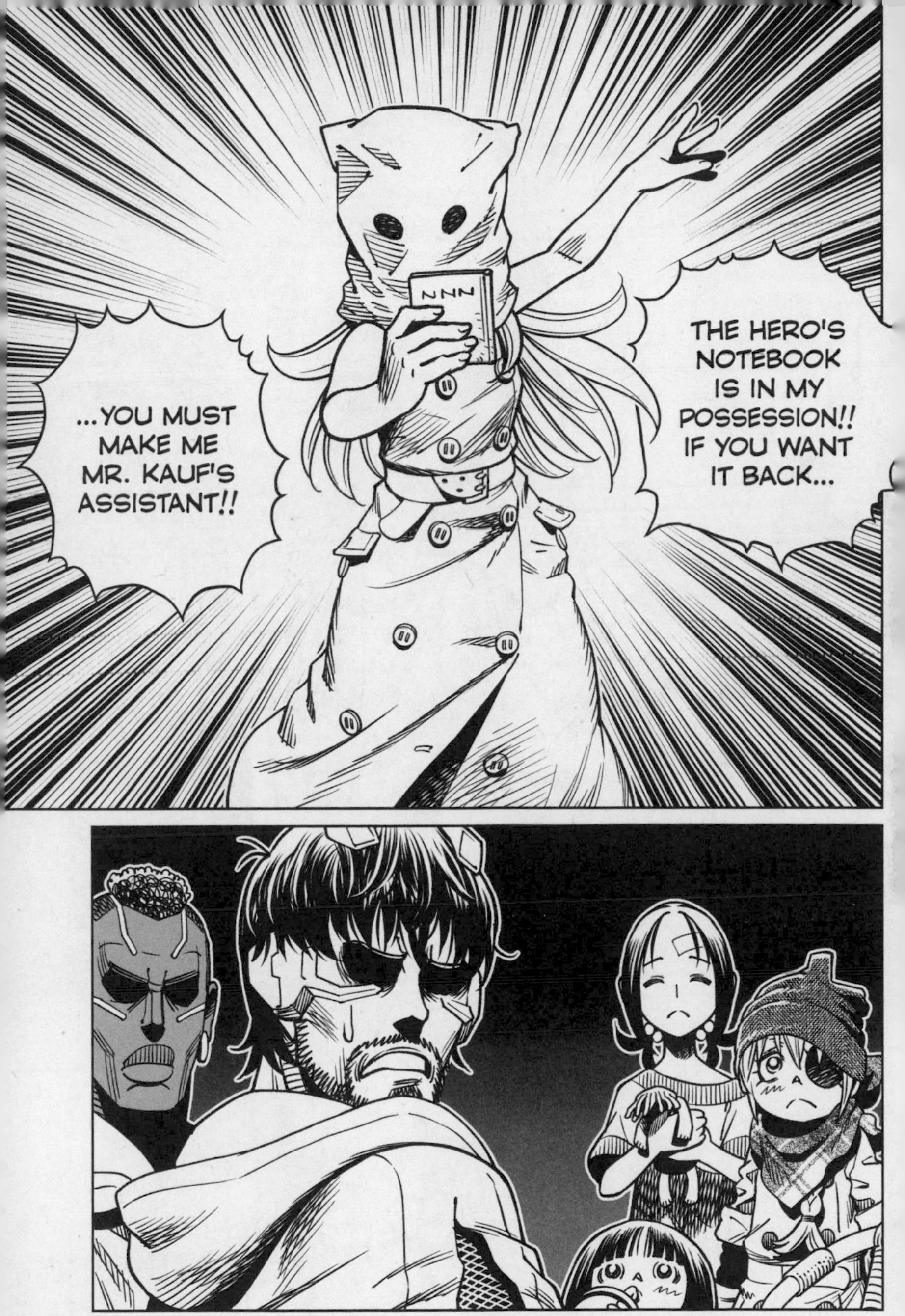
THE HERO'S NOTEBOOK IS IN MY POSSESSION!! IF YOU WANT IT BACK...
...YOU MUST MAKE ME MR. KAUF'S ASSISTANT!!

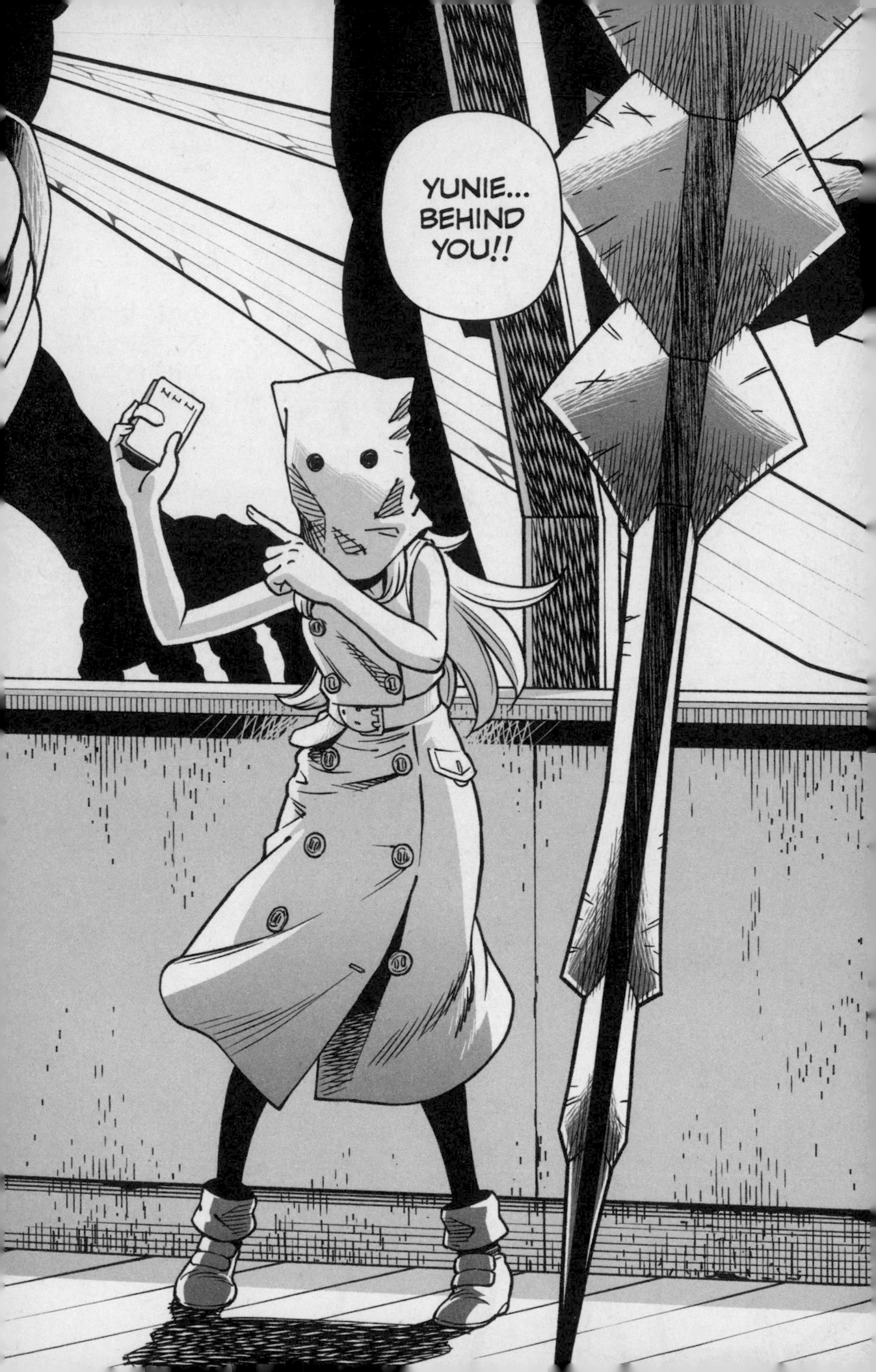
YUNIE... BEHIND YOU!!

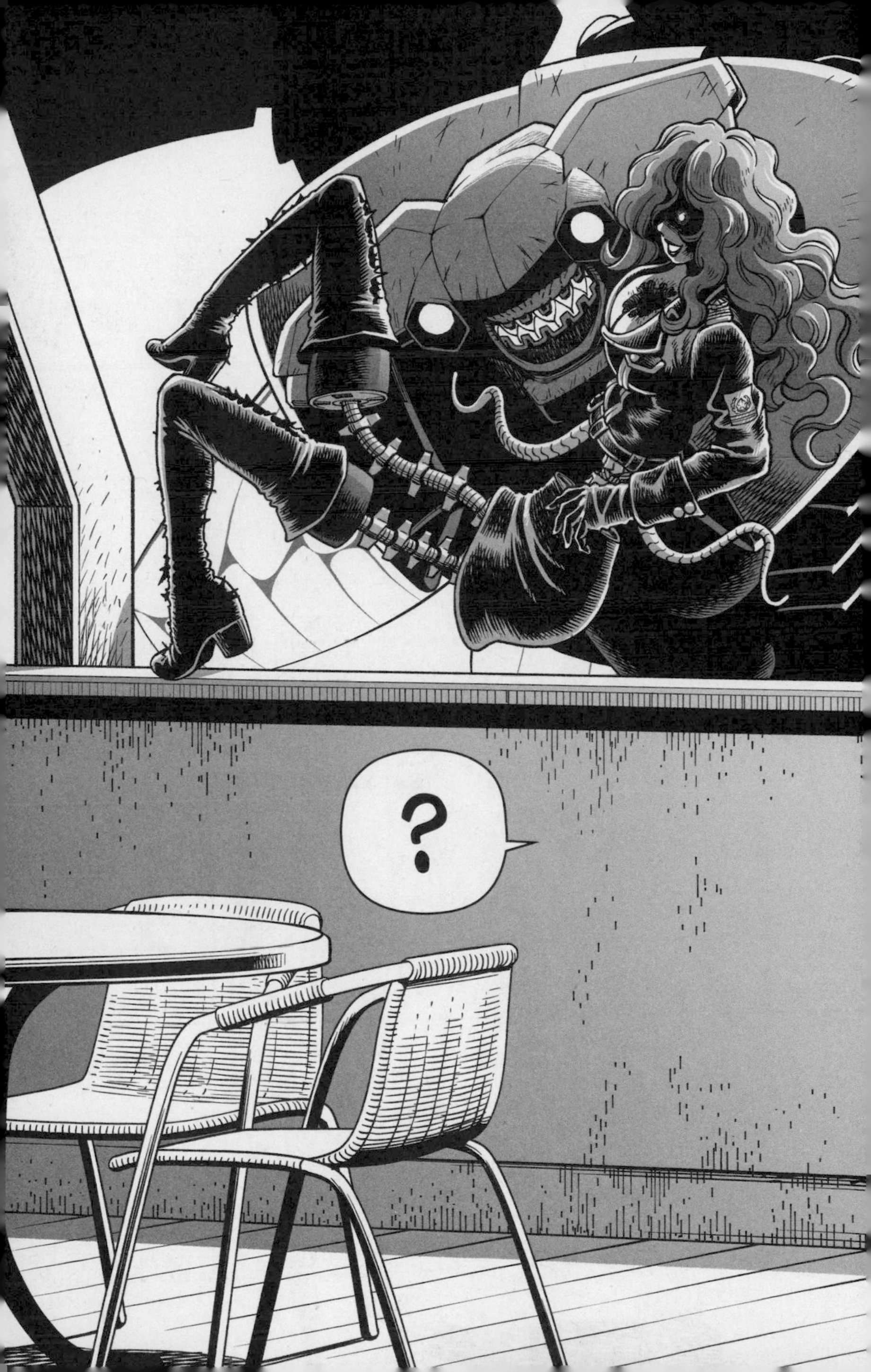
?

LOG:041

JAKOLEVA'S COUNTERATTACK

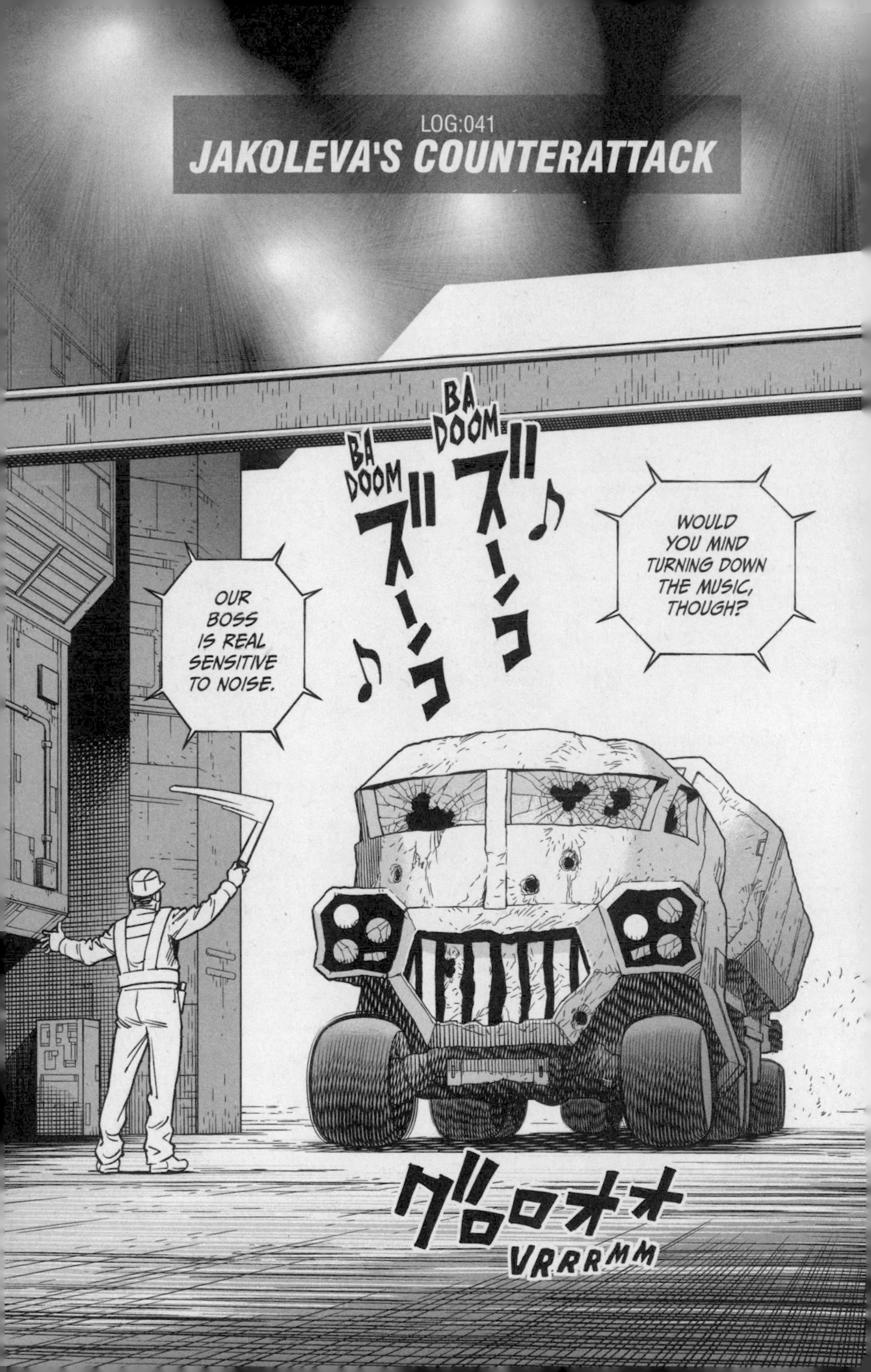
BA DOOM
ズンッ
BA DOOM
ズンッ
WOULD YOU MIND TURNING DOWN THE MUSIC, THOUGH?
OUR BOSS IS REAL SENSITIVE TO NOISE.
グロオオ
VRRRRMM

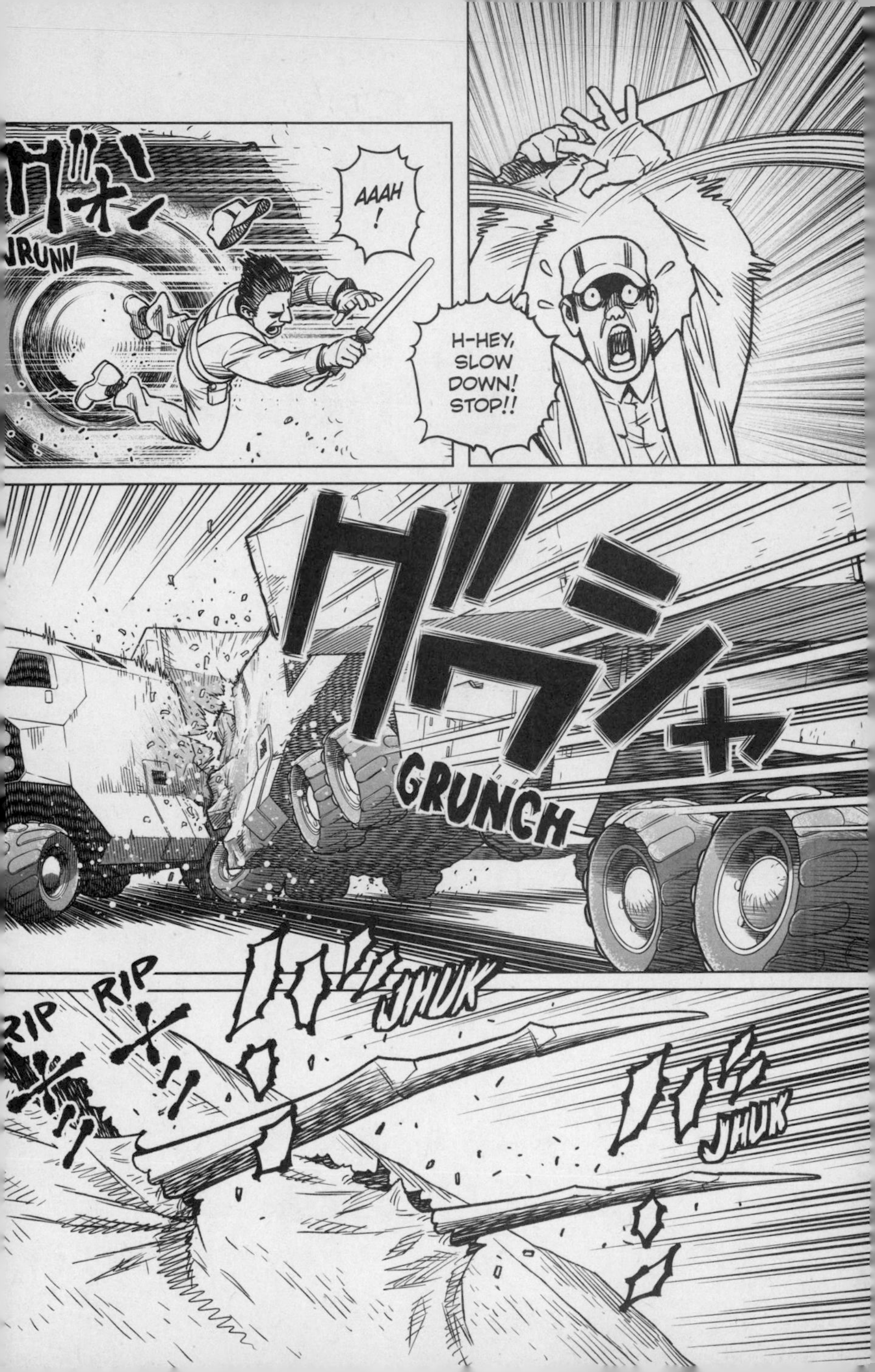
H-HEY, SLOW DOWN! STOP!!
AAAH!
GRUNCH
JHUK
JHUK
RIP
RIP

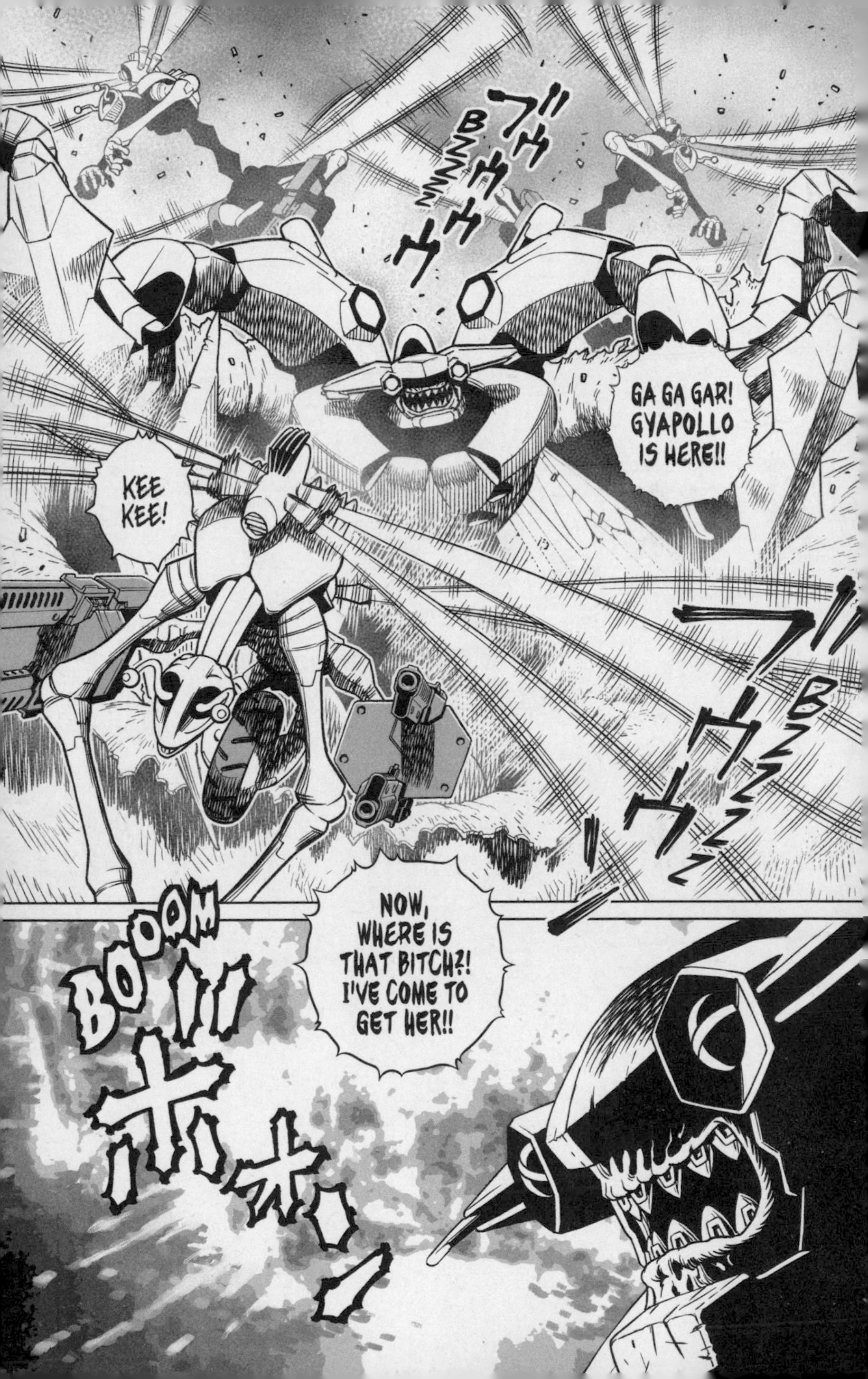
BZZZZZ
GA GA GAR! GYAPOLLO IS HERE!!
KEE KEE!
BZZZZZZ
NOW, WHERE IS THAT BITCH?! I'VE COME TO GET HER!!
BOOOM

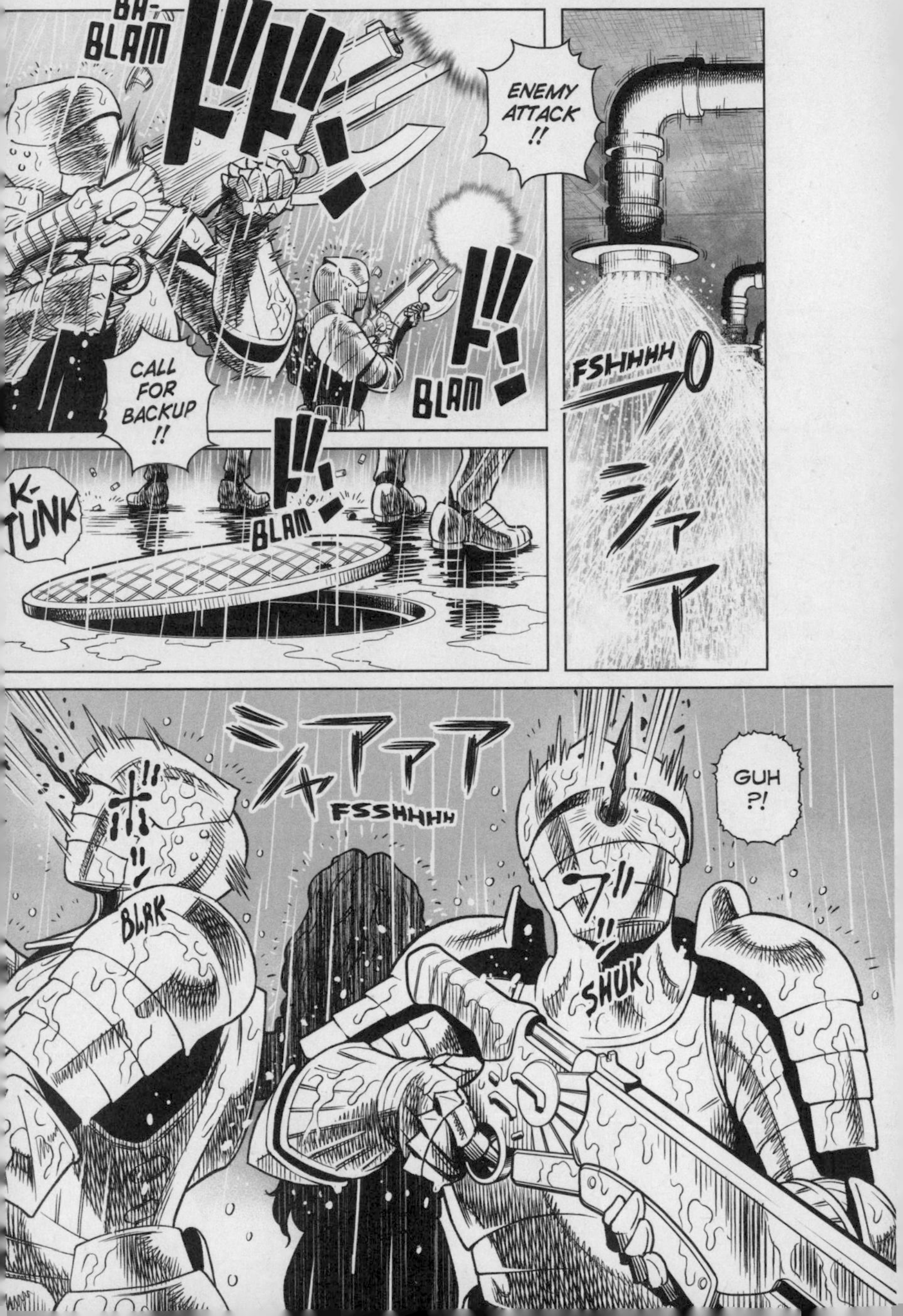

FSHHHH
シァァ
ENEMY ATTACK !!
ド!
BLAM
BA-BLAM
ドドド
CALL FOR BACKUP !!
ド
BLAM
K-TUNK
GUH ?!
ッ!!
SHUK
シャァァァ
FSSHHHH
!!
BLRK

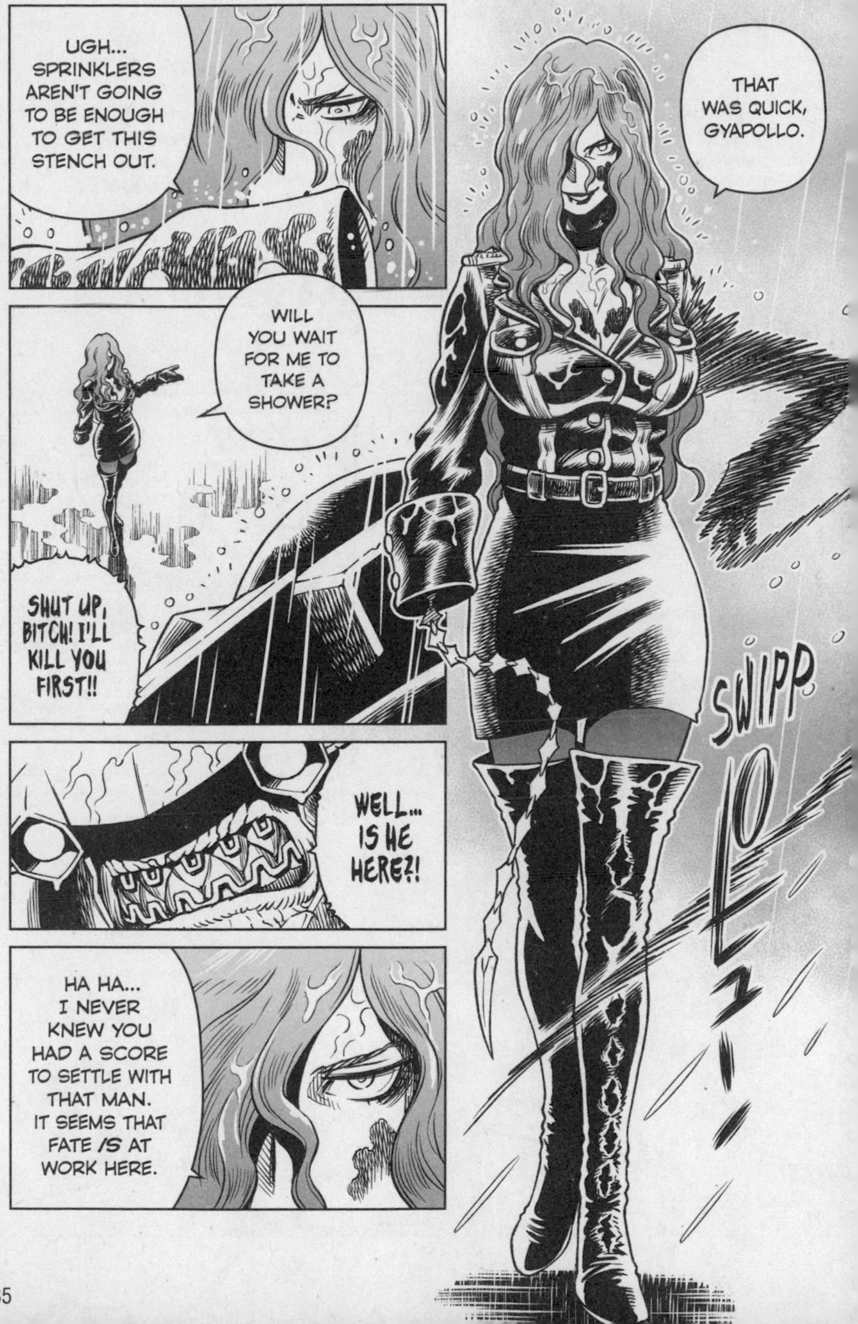
THAT WAS QUICK, GYAPOLLO.
SWIPP
UGH... SPRINKLERS AREN'T GOING TO BE ENOUGH TO GET THIS STENCH OUT.
WILL YOU WAIT FOR ME TO TAKE A SHOWER?
SHUT UP, BITCH! I'LL KILL YOU FIRST!!
WELL... IS HE HERE?!
HA HA... I NEVER KNEW YOU HAD A SCORE TO SETTLE WITH THAT MAN. IT SEEMS THAT FATE *IS* AT WORK HERE.

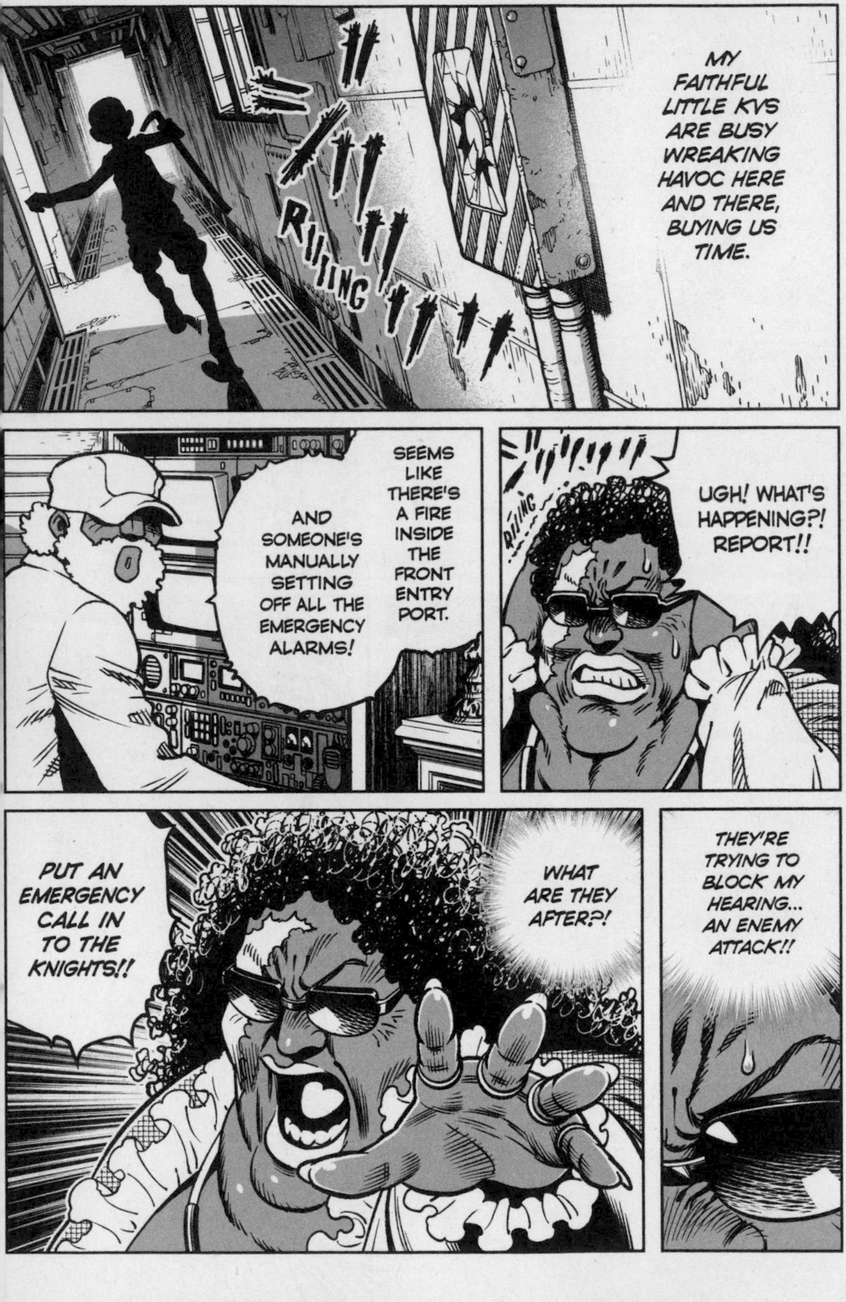
RIIING
MY FAITHFUL LITTLE KVS ARE BUSY WREAKING HAVOC HERE AND THERE, BUYING US TIME.
UGH! WHAT'S HAPPENING?! REPORT!!
SEEMS LIKE THERE'S A FIRE INSIDE THE FRONT ENTRY PORT.
AND SOMEONE'S MANUALLY SETTING OFF ALL THE EMERGENCY ALARMS!
THEY'RE TRYING TO BLOCK MY HEARING... AN ENEMY ATTACK!!
WHAT ARE THEY AFTER?!
PUT AN EMERGENCY CALL IN TO THE KNIGHTS!!

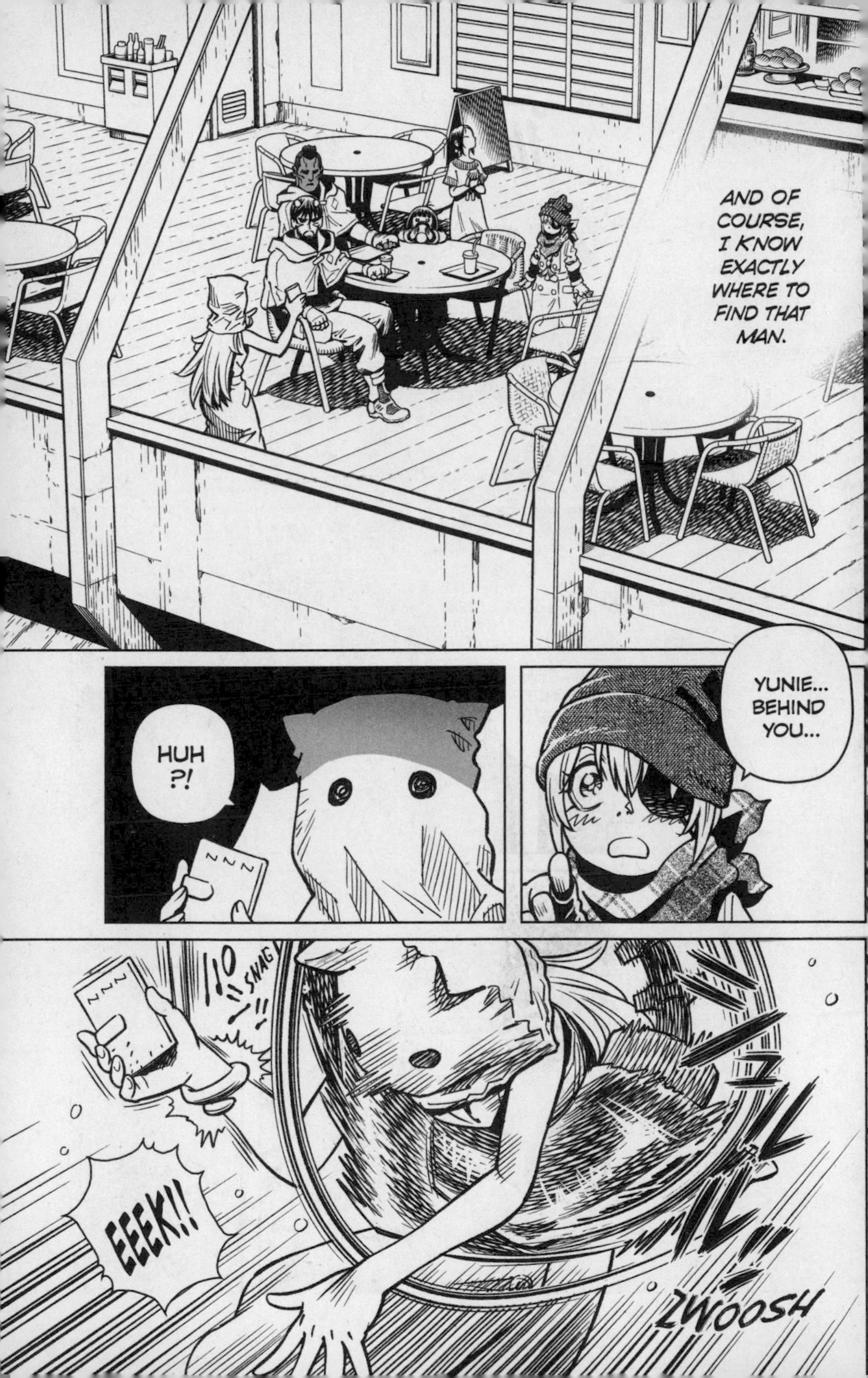
AND OF COURSE, I KNOW EXACTLY WHERE TO FIND THAT MAN.
YUNIE... BEHIND YOU...
HUH ?!
SNAG
ZWOOSH
EEEK!!

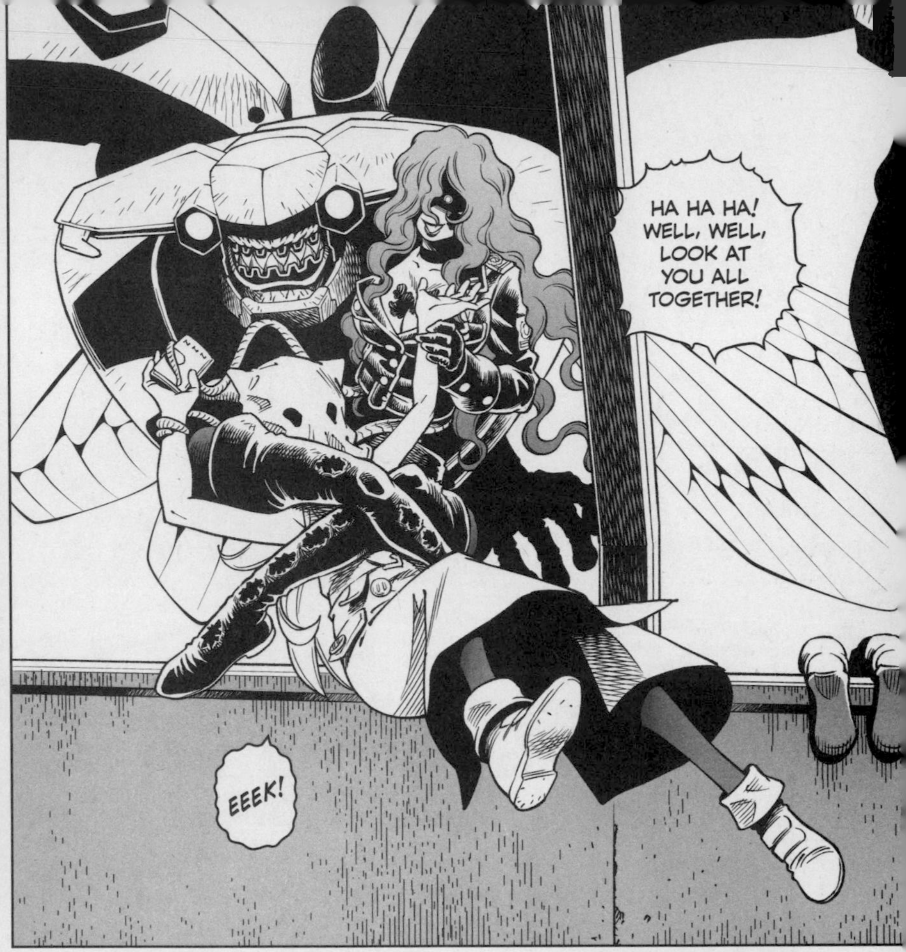
HA HA HA! WELL, WELL, LOOK AT YOU ALL TOGETHER!
EEEK!
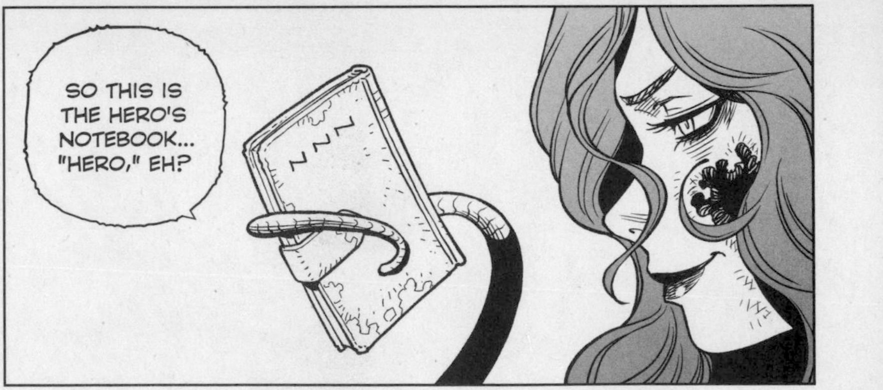
SO THIS IS THE HERO'S NOTEBOOK... "HERO," EH?

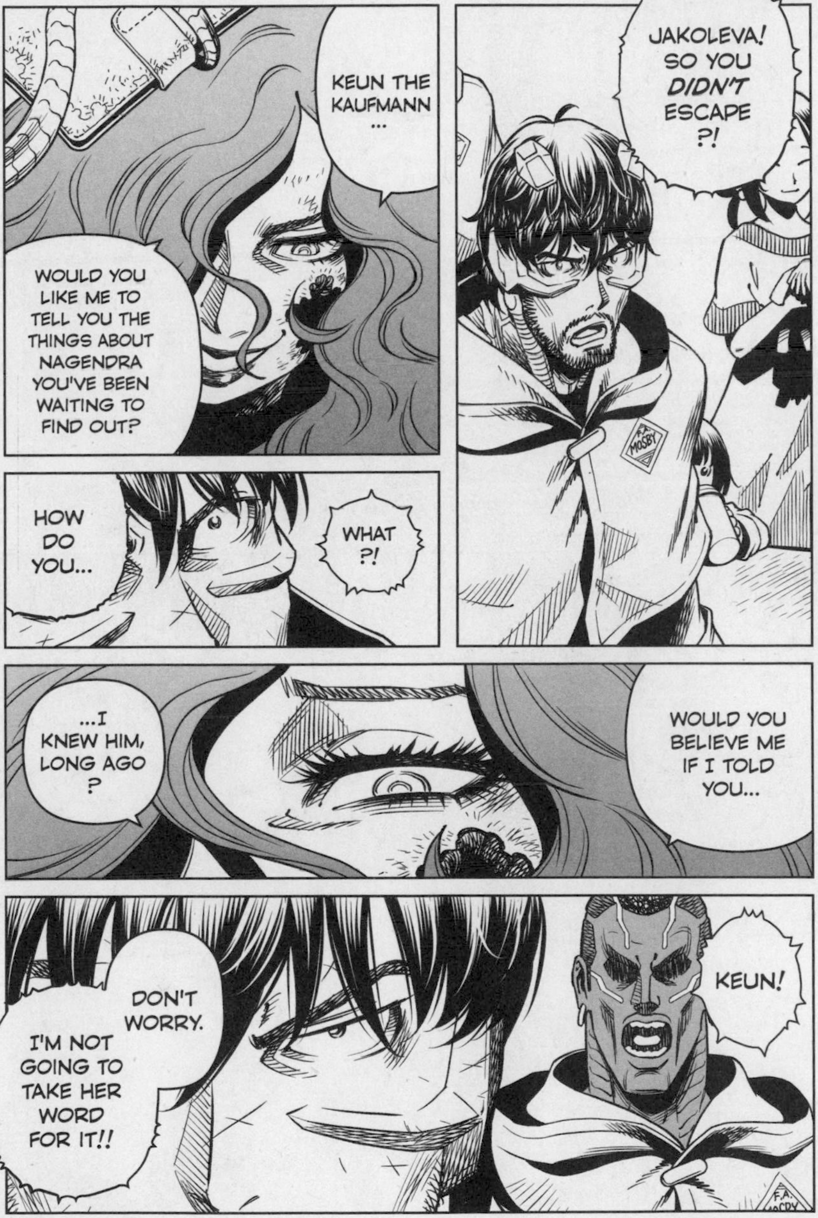
JAKOLEVA! SO YOU *DIDN'T* ESCAPE?!
KEUN THE KAUFMANN...
WOULD YOU LIKE ME TO TELL YOU THE THINGS ABOUT NAGENDRA YOU'VE BEEN WAITING TO FIND OUT?
WHAT?!
HOW DO YOU...
WOULD YOU BELIEVE ME IF I TOLD YOU...
...I KNEW HIM, LONG AGO?
KEUN!
DON'T WORRY.
I'M NOT GOING TO TAKE HER WORD FOR IT!!

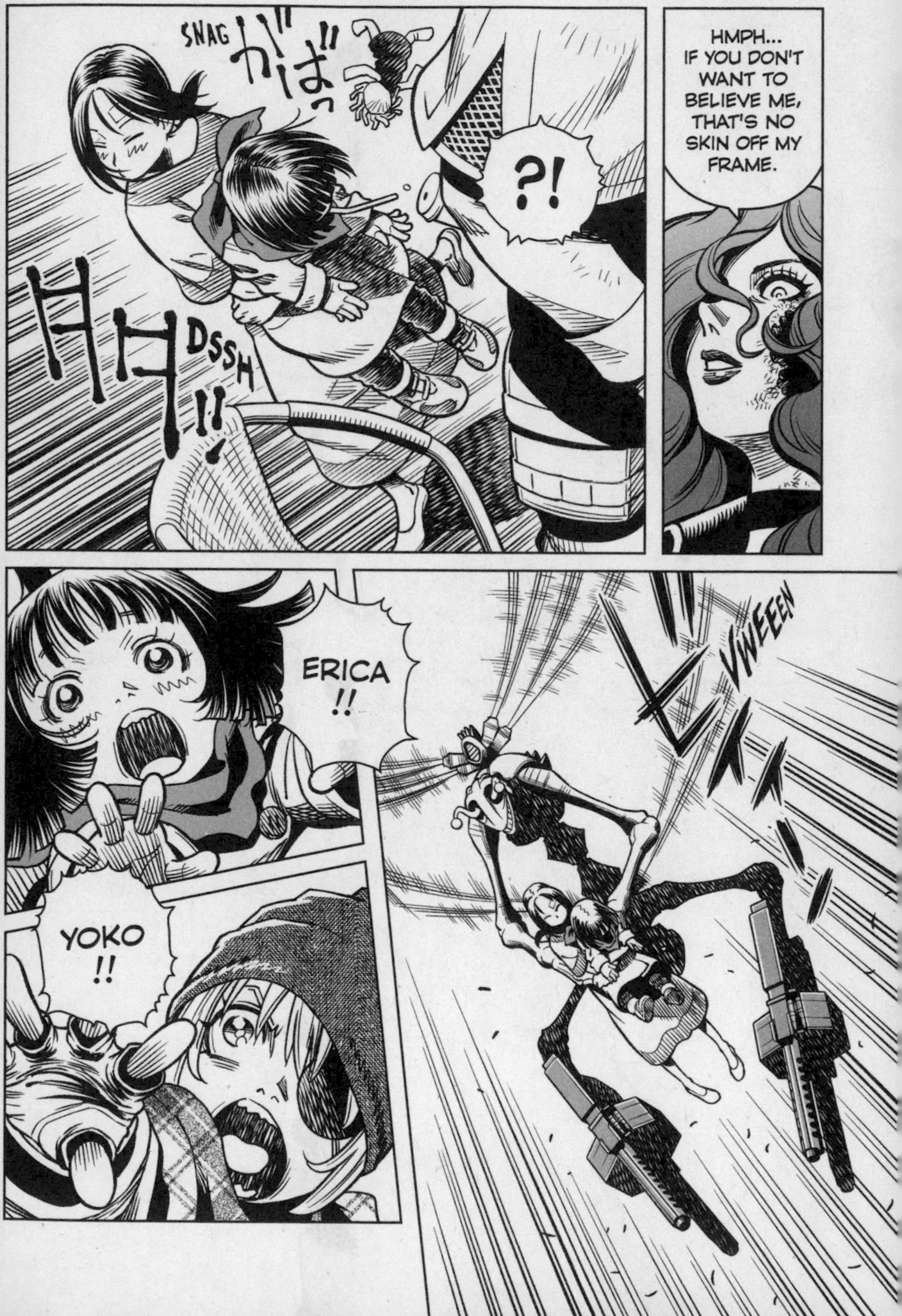
HMPH... IF YOU DON'T WANT TO BELIEVE ME, THAT'S NO SKIN OFF MY FRAME.
SNAG かばっ!!
?!
DSSH!!
VWEEEN
ERICA!!
YOKO!!

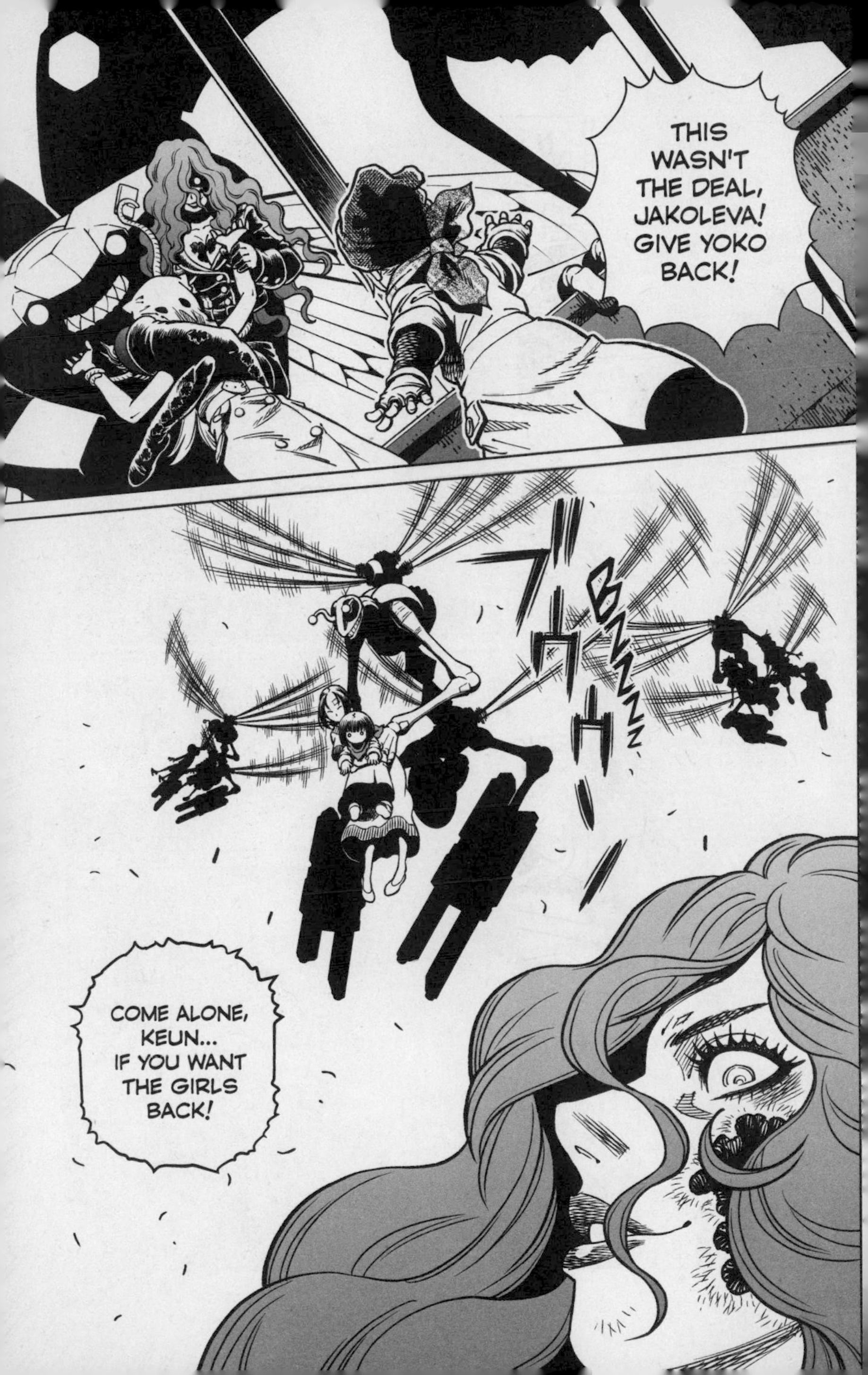
THIS WASN'T THE DEAL, JAKOLEVA! GIVE YOKO BACK!
BZZZZZ
COME ALONE, KEUN... IF YOU WANT THE GIRLS BACK!

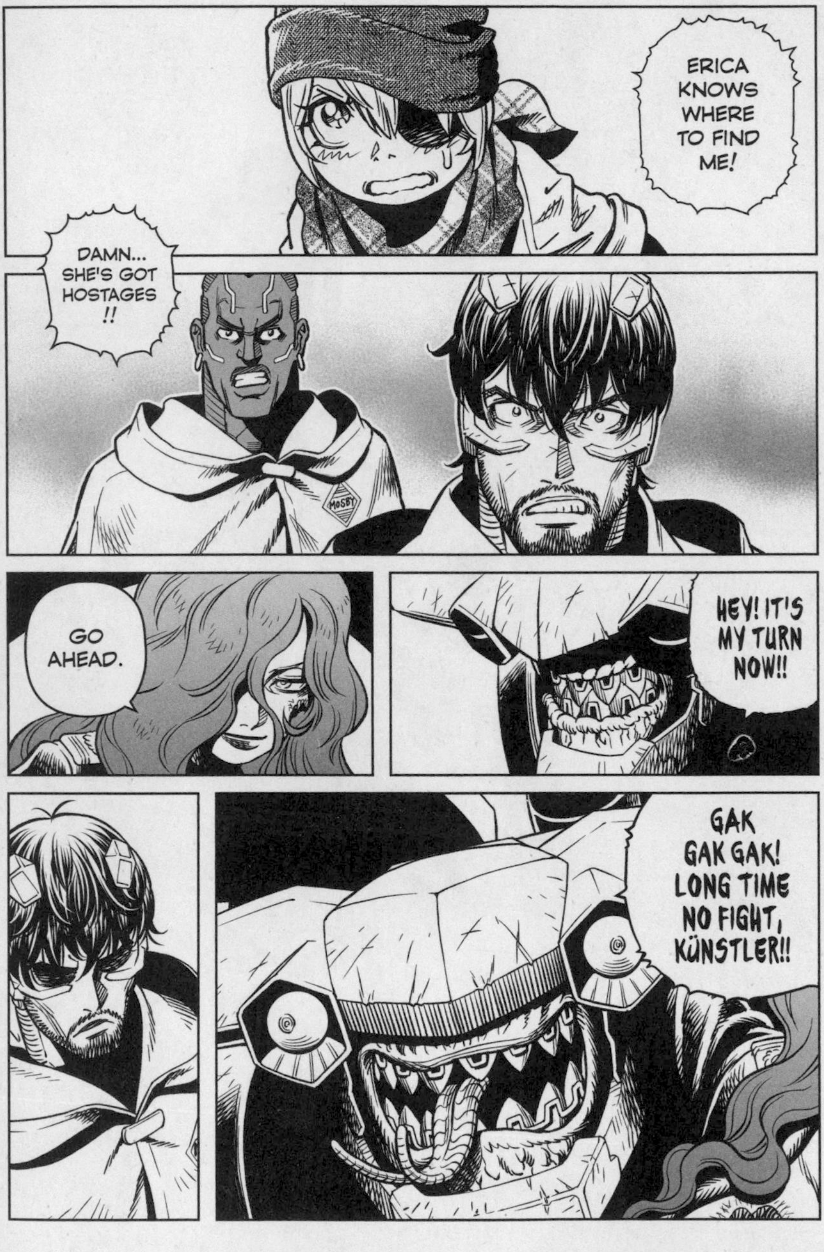
ERICA KNOWS WHERE TO FIND ME!
DAMN... SHE'S GOT HOSTAGES !!
MOSBY
HEY! IT'S MY TURN NOW!!
GO AHEAD.
GAK GAK GAK! LONG TIME NO FIGHT, KÜNSTLER!!

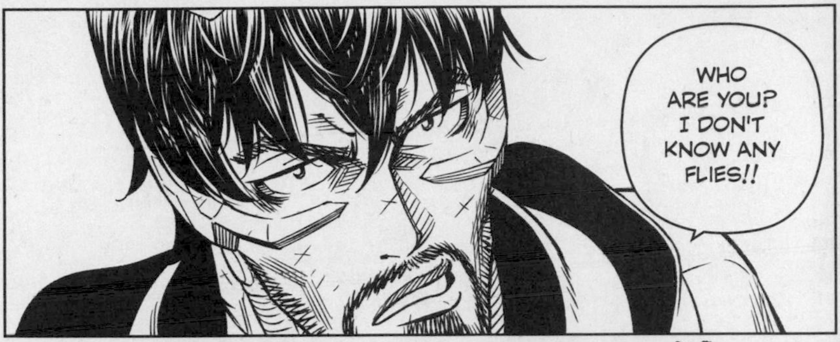
WHO ARE YOU? I DON'T KNOW ANY FLIES!!

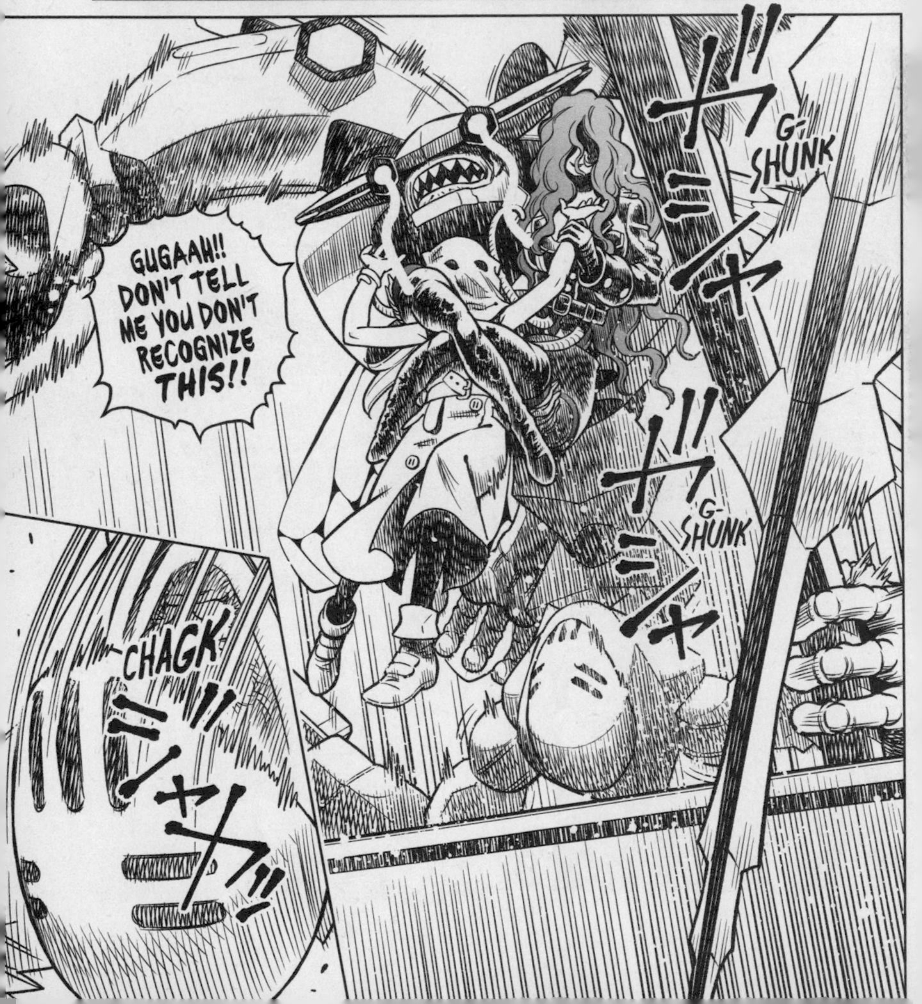
G-SHUNK
GUGAAH!! DON'T TELL ME YOU DON'T RECOGNIZE THIS!!
G-SHUNK
CHAGK

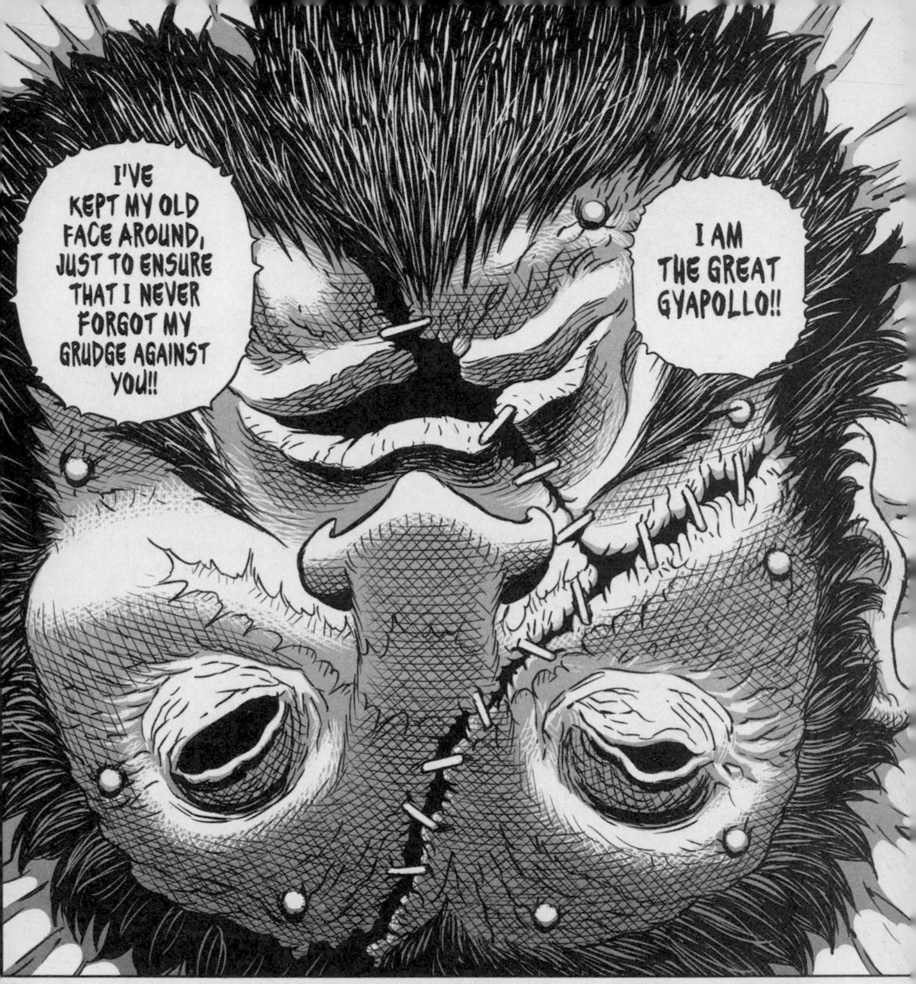
I AM THE GREAT GYAPOLLO!!
I'VE KEPT MY OLD FACE AROUND, JUST TO ENSURE THAT I NEVER FORGOT MY GRUDGE AGAINST YOU!!

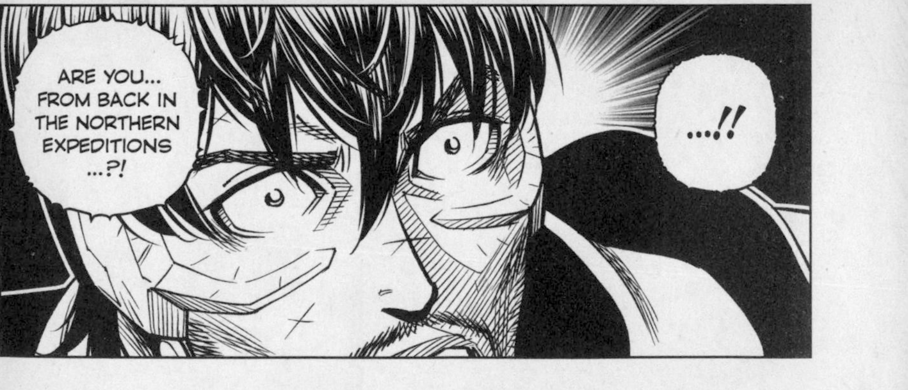
...!!
ARE YOU... FROM BACK IN THE NORTHERN EXPEDITIONS ...?!

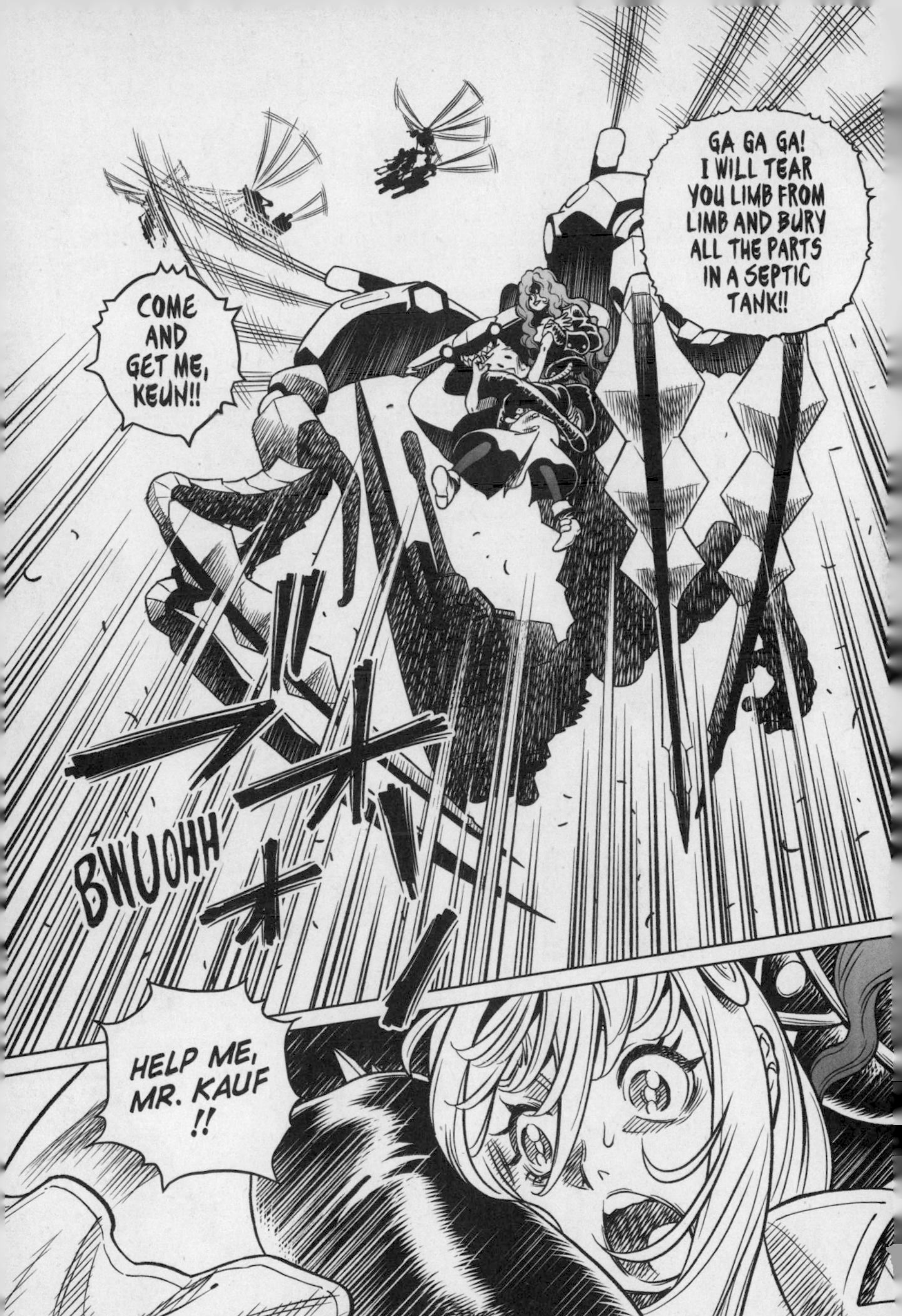
GA GA GA! I WILL TEAR YOU LIMB FROM LIMB AND BURY ALL THE PARTS IN A SEPTIC TANK!!
COME AND GET ME, KEUN!!
BWUOHH
HELP ME, MR. KAUF !!

AROUND THE WORLD

COMMENTS FROM VARIOUS COUNTRIES

The *Alita* series continues to be successful all around the world. How does Japan's crowning sci-fi achievement keep enthralling readers all over? We heard from the series' international publishers! See what they have to say, along with their book designs!

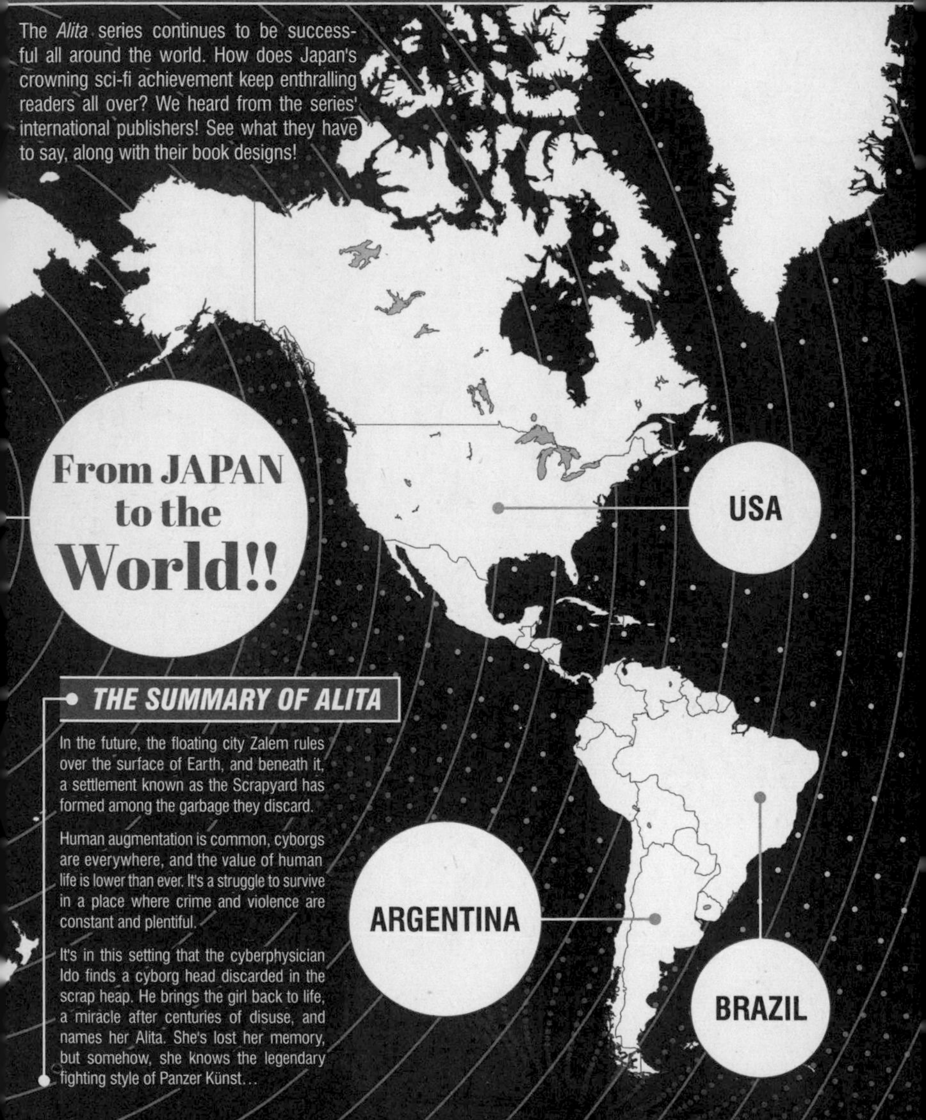
From JAPAN to the World!!
USA
ARGENTINA
BRAZIL

THE SUMMARY OF ALITA

In the future, the floating city Zalem rules over the surface of Earth, and beneath it, a settlement known as the Scrapyard has formed among the garbage they discard.

Human augmentation is common, cyborgs are everywhere, and the value of human life is lower than ever. It's a struggle to survive in a place where crime and violence are constant and plentiful.

It's in this setting that the cyberphysician Ido finds a cyborg head discarded in the scrap heap. He brings the girl back to life, a miracle after centuries of disuse, and names her Alita. She's lost her memory, but somehow, she knows the legendary fighting style of Panzer Künst…

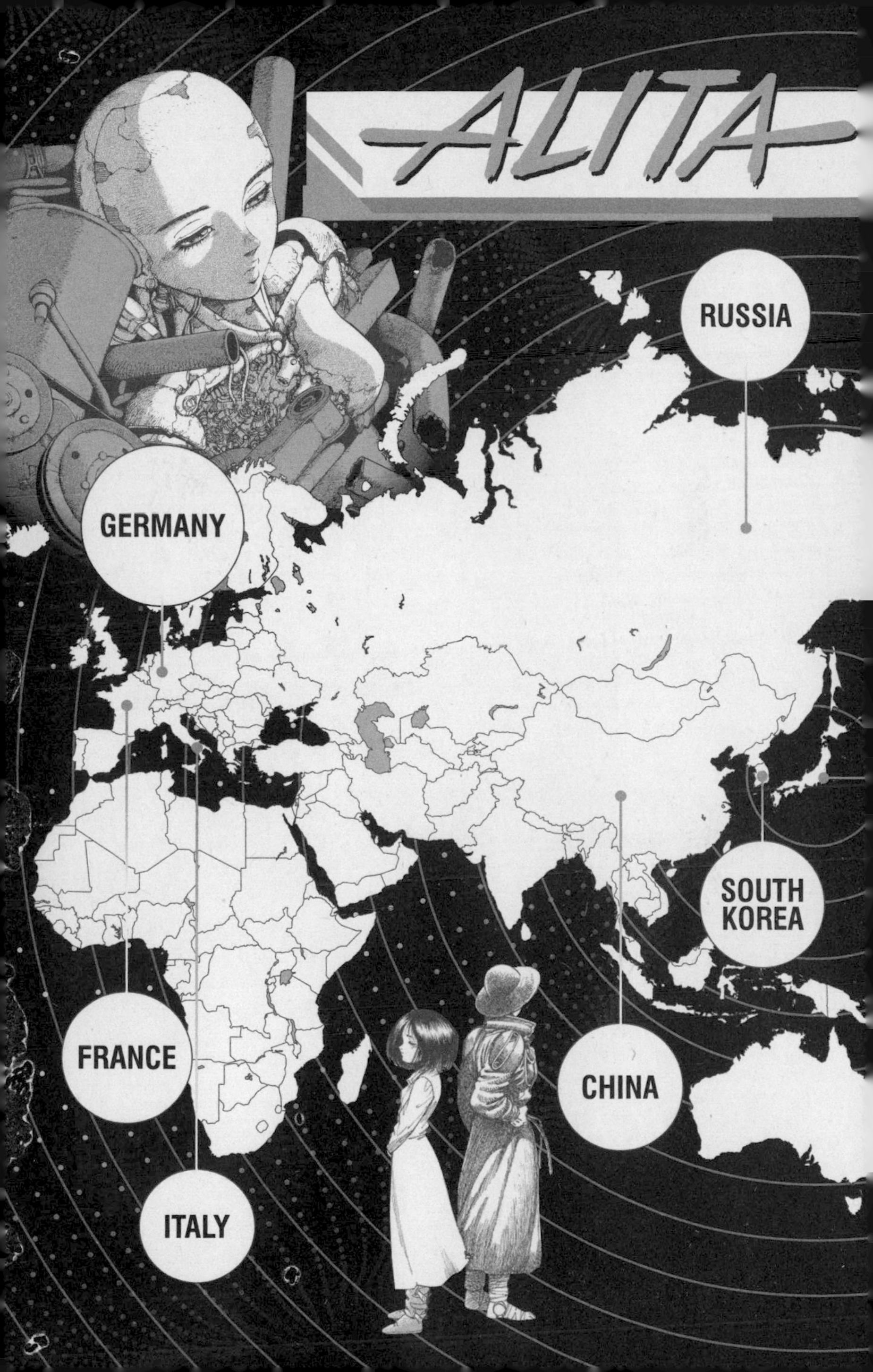
ALITA
RUSSIA
GERMANY
SOUTH KOREA
FRANCE
CHINA
ITALY

ALITA AROUND THE WORLD

UNITED STATES

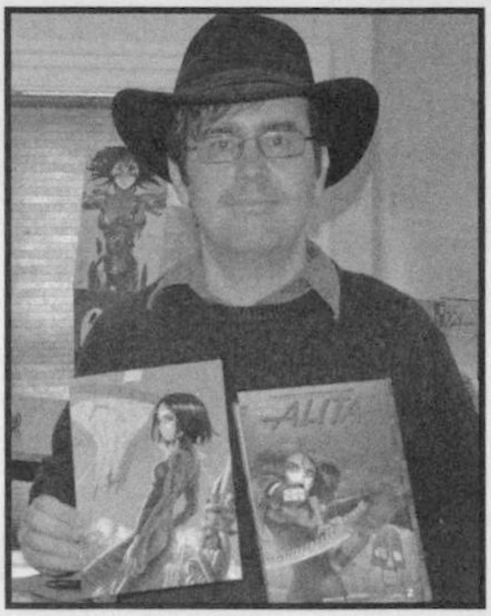
ALITA

KODANSHA USA PUBLISHING, LLC

BEN APPLEGATE

When the manga *Gunnm* was first published in English in 1992, Japanese comics were totally unknown to most North American readers. The manga had to be "flipped" to read left-to-right, American style, and it was published not in tankobon, but one chapter at a time, in glossy comic books. It was an immediate hit. A generation of comics readers were instantly addicted to its masterful sequential art, story of desperation and hope, unforgettable post-apocalyptic setting, and at once pure-heartedand deadly heroine. *Alita* helped teach America the word "manga." Twenty-nine years later, the series is recognized in the English-speaking world as one of the greatest action comics of all time, with a deluxe hardcover edition that features the original Japanese sound effects and right-to-left page order. And, of course, there's the big-budget American film adaptation from director Robert Rodriguez. *Alita* takes place in a unique world that carries strands of DNA from every corner of global genre fiction, from gothic and slasher horror to wuxia novels and transhumanist fiction. Its wide appeal around the world must derive in part from this diversity of influence. Another key element to *Alita's* appeal is its pace. The story moves at an exhilarating speed, driven forward along with its main character's unstoppable, existential desires, desires anyone can understand—for life, love, revenge, survival, understanding.

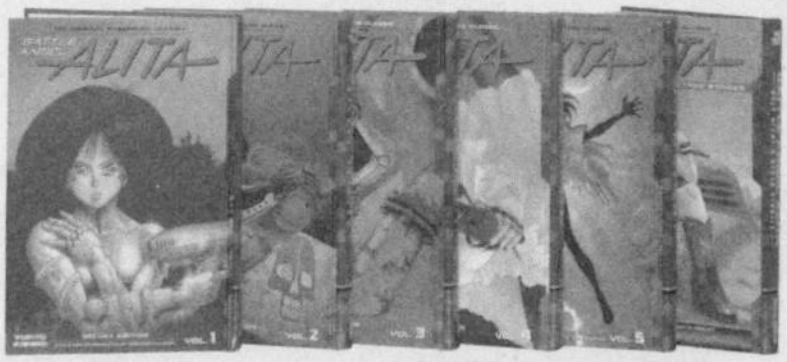
ALITA

ARGENTINA

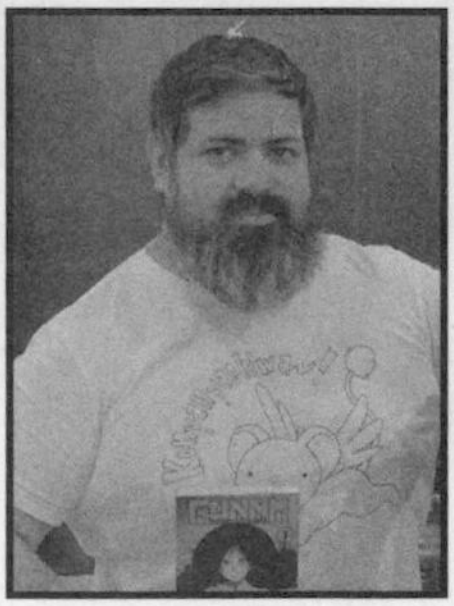

EDITORIAL IVREA S.L.

JAVIER HEREDIA

Alita became an iconic part of 90s culture in Argentina after the release of its 1993 anime OVA. In the nearly thirty years since, it's become a beloved staple for a wide selection of demographics. With the release of the *Alita: Battle Angel* movie, we at Ivrea pulled out all the stops to promote the original manga, placing *Alita* ads in all of our other manga releases, distributing promotional posters, and holding preview events for the film.

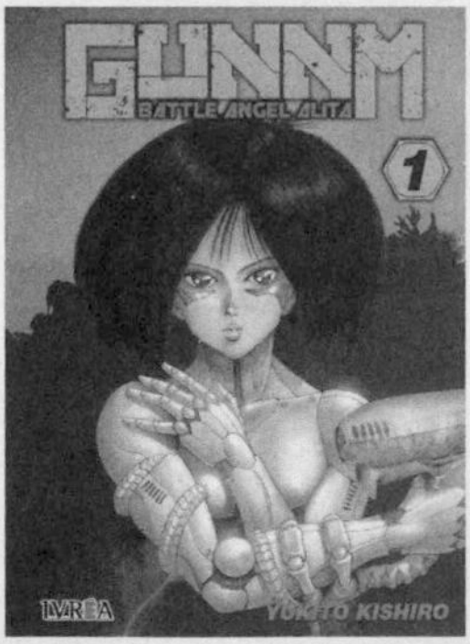
GUNNM
BATTLE ANGEL ALITA
1
IVREA
YUKITO KISHIRO

Gunnm o Alita, impactó en los 90's en Argentina gracias a la llegada de la OVA animada de 1993. Desde entonces se convirtió en una amada serie de culto que sigue sumando fans de todas las edades incluso hasta el día de hoy, casi 30 años después. Publicitamos la serie con avisos en todos nuestros mangas, hemos regalado poster promocionales en eventos y organizamos un preestreno de la película live action promoviendo el manga.

ITALY

PANINI S.P.A.

ALESSANDRA MARCHIONI, ENRICO FERRARESI, FRANCESCA ROMANA GUARRACINO (L-R)

It is such an honor and joy to publish *Alita* through Panini. Publishing began here a few years after the series started in Japan, and ever since, it has continued to be a bestseller. When the film *Alita: Battle Angel* came out, we issued a deluxe box set edition, which we've reprinted several times. Alita fans went wild for it! We're so grateful to Kishiro-sensei and Kodansha to be involved in such a wonderful series!

Alita is considered one of the crown jewels of manga among Italian fans. We've collected some of their comments for you. "The heroine of *Alita* is both grounded and fantastical. It's a masterpiece that always goes beyond our expectations." "I love that you can see her grow from a child into an adult." "*Alita* is both a grand, epic tale, and also very poetic." "It was the first manga I ever read. It's still my favorite, and it was my gateway into other manga in this genre." "The first cyberpunk manga I read. A true masterpiece!"

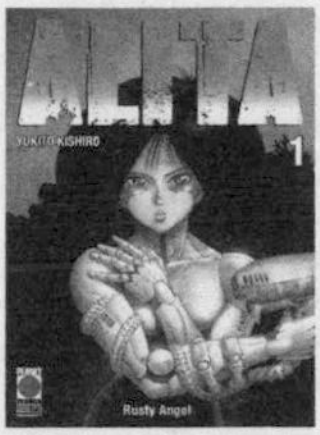
ALITA
YUKITO KISHIRO
1
Rusty Angel

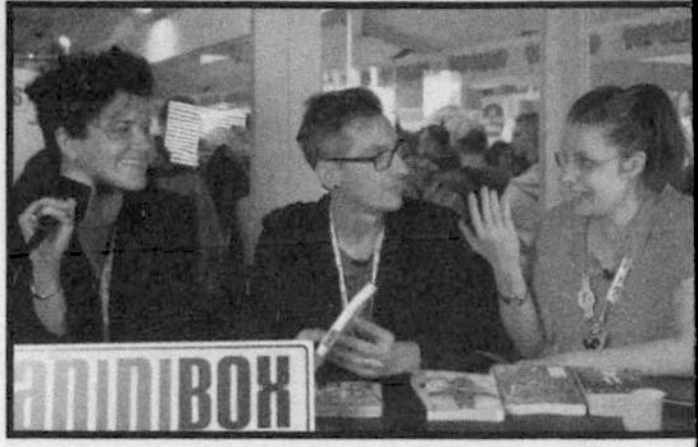
aniniBOX

Essere l'editore di ALITA in Italia ci rende molto felici e orgogliosi. Abbiamo cominciato a pubblicare questo capolavoro per la prima volta pochi anni dopo il suo successo in patria e da allora è sempre stato uno dei nostri bestseller, fino alla recente edizione celebrativa per il film ALITA – BATTLE ANGEL, la COMPLETE DELUXE EDITION in grande formato con speciale cofanetto, che abbiamo ristampato varie volte: possiamo dire che ha fatto veramente impazzire i lettori! Grazie Kishiro Sensei e Kodansha per averci permesso di essere parte di questo successo! ~~~~~~~~~~ La community di lettori italiani considera ALITA uno dei migliori manga mai pubblicati, come si può vedere dagli affettuosi commenti che abbiamo ricevuto. "i protagonisti di ALITA sono sia realistici sia fantastici allo stesso tempo, è un capolavoro oltre ogni aspettativa" "amo ALITA per il modo in cui racconta la crescita personale dei protagonisti dalla giovane età fino all'età adulta" "la trama di ALITA è molto dura, ma anche così poetica." "ALITA è stato il mio primo manga, assolutamente il mio preferito, il manga che mi ha fatto amare questo genere di opere." "ALITA...uno dei primi manga cyberpunk che abbia mai letto. Fantastico!"

SOUTH KOREA

ANIBOOKS

MUNHAKDONGNE MANGA EDITORIAL STAFF

With the release of the film *Alita: Battle Angel* in Korea, many people were looking to read the Korean edition of the original manga. It had already been in print for many years, but this was a fresh new wave of interest. You could feel the enthusiasm—before we published our *Alita Perfect Edition*, used copies of the original edition were going for several times their previous price. Reader reaction to the new edition was extremely intense; each new volume to come out became a bestseller, and immediately went into reprints. There was equal demand for digital editions. There was also a great response on *Alita* merchandise from Korean fans. In fact, when a well-known artist visited the office, he was delighted when we presented him with some *Alita* merch, and it helped us sign a deal with him. Many fans gathered to see an airing of *Alita: Battle Angel* promoting the Perfect Edition release of the manga, and there was a deep discussion about the Korean edition of the series afterward. It was a day that really impressed upon us the enthusiasm of the fans toward a series they've followed for over twenty years, and the greatness of the story that inspired them.

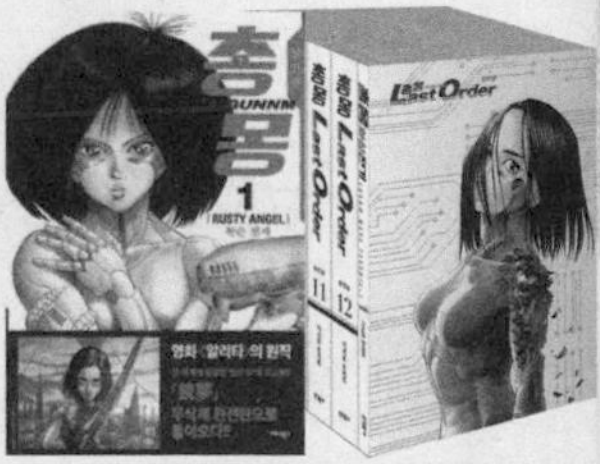
총몽
GUNNM
1
RUSTY ANGEL
Last Order
영화 '알리타'의 원작

총몽 완전판」이 출간되기 전, 중고책이 정가의 몇 배로 거래된 것만 봐도 작품을 향한 뜨거운 인기를 느낄 수 있다. 『총몽 완전판」이 출간되면서 독자들의 반응은 매우 뜨거웠고, 후속권이 출간될 때마다 만화 베스트셀러에 오르며 중쇄에 돌입했다. 이 인기는 전자책 출간에 대한 문의로 이어졌다. 한국어판 출간에 목말랐던 독자들은 새로운 굿즈에도 반응이 뜨겁다. 실제로 편집부 사무실을 방문한 어느 작가님께 총몽 굿즈를 선물해드렸더니 매우 감격하셨고, 작가님의 작품을 순조롭게 계약할 수 있었던 에피소드가 있다. 『총몽 완전판』 출간을 기념하기 위해 열린 영화 〈알리타: 배틀 엔젤〉의 상영회에는 수많은 독자들이 모여 작품에 대해 보다 심도 있는 질의를 나누었다. 약 20년간 재출간을 기다려온 독자들의 폭발적인 반응과 함께 그것을 가능하게 한 명작의 위엄을 실감한 날이었다. 문학동네 만화편집부

CHINA

BILIBILI

JIMMY BILIBILI MANGA CONTENT OVERSEER

With the release of the film in China, there was a huge increase of interest in the *Alita* manga, which was placed in the recommended section of China's Apple Store. It also brought about greater attention to cyberpunk and sci-fi manga in China.

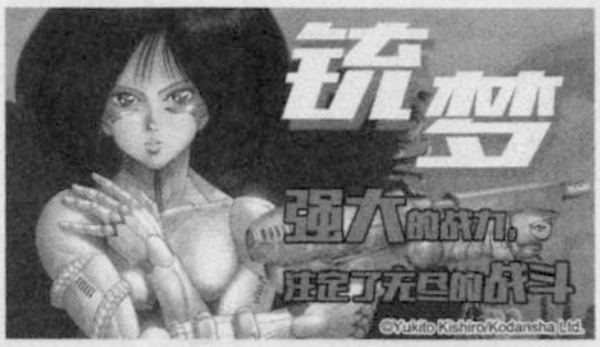
铳梦
©Yukito Kishiro/Kodansha Ltd.

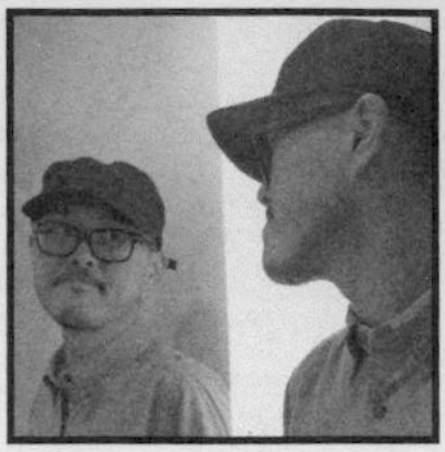

随着电影的上映，《铳梦》的漫画被国内的读者们高度关注。漫画内容还登上中国区苹果商店推荐，也同时带动了中国读者对于赛博朋克与科幻漫画的喜好与认知。

GERMANY

CARLSEN VERLAG GMBH

PETRA LOHMANN EDITOR, CARLSEN MANGA

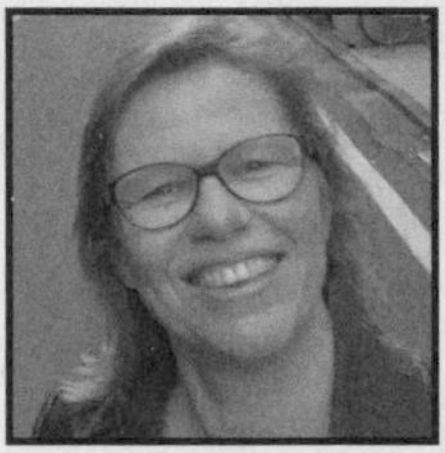

Ever since Carlsen began publishing the German edition of the *Alita* series in the 1990s, it's been considered a masterpiece that appeals to multiple generations of readers. We had fantastic sales after the release of the live action movie in 2019. It just keeps rockin' after 25 years. From Germany, with love and respect!

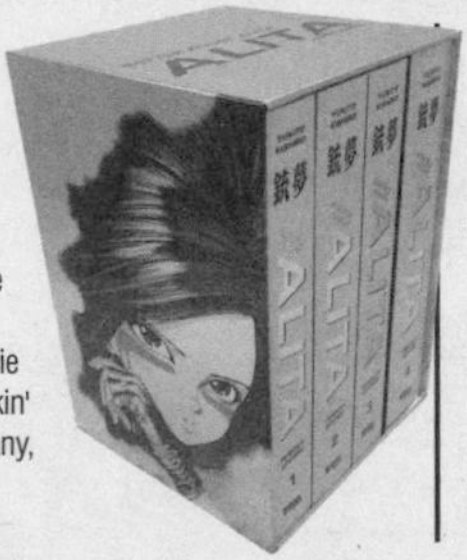
ALITA

GUNNM gehörte zu den ersten japanischen Mangas, die seit den 1990er Jahren in Deutschland im Carlsen Verlag erschienen sind und wurde zu einem sofortigen Klassiker, als er 1996 unter dem Titel BATTLE ANGEL ALITA bei uns erschien, gefolgt von LAST ORDER und KASEI SENKI (MARS CHRONICLES). Seitdem hat das Meisterwerk von Kishiro-sensei nie aufgehört, Leser verschiedener Generationen zu erfreuen und zu inspirieren. Als 2019 der Live-Action-Film ALITA in die Kinos kam, war unser Box-Set der Perfect Edition ein großer Erfolg. Die deutschen Leser - und wir als hiesiger Verlag - sind große Fans und sehr dankbar für jeden neuen Band, der erscheint. Nach 25 Jahren rockt GUNNM immer noch die Show - Liebe und Respekt aus Deutschland!

BRAZIL

EDITORA JBC

MARCELO DEL GRECO SUPERFAN AND EDITOR OF BRAZILIAN EDITIONS OF *ALITA* AND *LAST ORDER!*

The *Battle Angel Alita* saga is a true sci-fi epic! Yukito Kishiro-sensei is a genius at envisioning a world and constructing a complex story within it. I'm so proud of JBC's Brazilian edition of the series. Not only have we produced bookmarks, postcards and posters, but we also organized special preview events for *Alita: Battle Angel.*

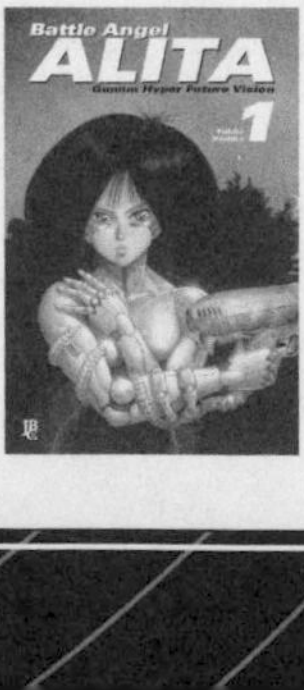
Battle Angel
ALITA
Gunnm Hyper Future Vision
1

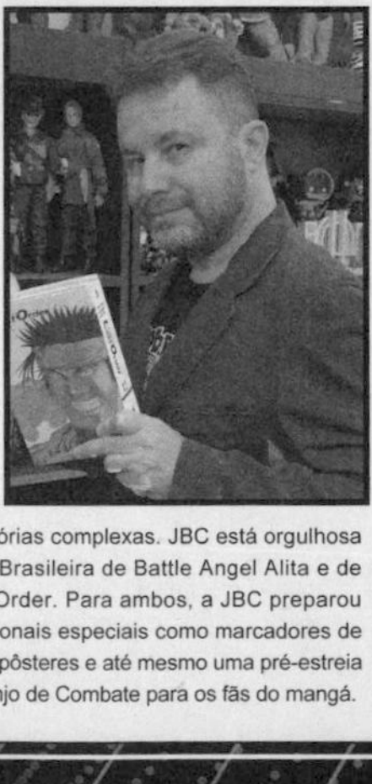

A Saga de Alita é absolutamente épica! Uma obra de arte dos quadrinhos de Ficção Científica. Yukito Kishiro-sensei é um mestre na criação de mundos fantásticos e histórias complexas. JBC está orgulhosa em ter lançado a edição Brasileira de Battle Angel Alita e de Battle Angel Alita - Last Order. Para ambos, a JBC preparou inúmeros brindes promocionais especiais como marcadores de páginas, cartões postais e pôsteres e até mesmo uma pré-estreia exclusiva do filme Alita - Anjo de Combate para os fãs do mangá.

FRANCE

ÉDITIONS GLÉNAT

SATOKO INABA MANGA EDITORIAL DIRECTOR

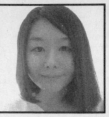

Alita has been a must-read for manga fans ever since it started, and Alita is the most recognized manga heroine around. Kishiro-sensei was a huge hit among comic readers, sci-fi enthusiasts, and other artists when his art was presented at the manga gallery at Angoulême in 2020!

Glénat
GUNNM
ÉDITION ORIGINALE
1

Last Order
1
Glénat

GUNNM
MARS CHRONICLE
1
Glénat

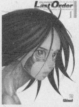

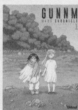

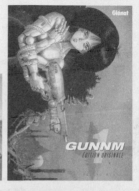

Gunnm fait partie des œuvres pionnières et incontournables du manga en France et Gally reste à ce jour la plus connue et la plus badass des héroïnes du genre. La venue de Yukito Kishiro à Angoulême en 2020, pour une exposition qui lui était consacrée, a montré que son œuvre était toujours aussi plébiscitée par un public très hétéroclite !

RUSSIA

XL MEDIA LTD.

KIRILL IVANOV EDITOR

1
ЮКИТО КИСИРО

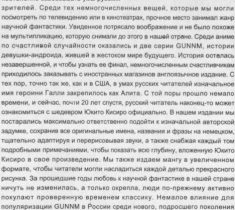

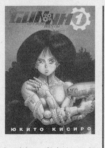

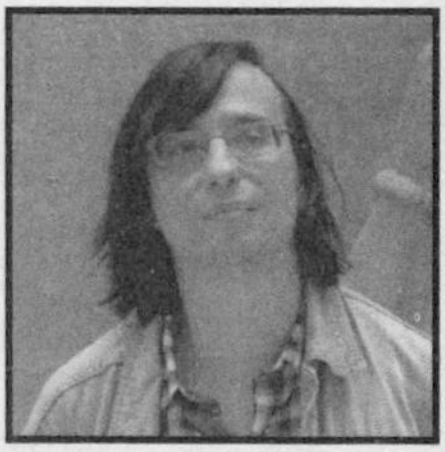

The series has been known in Russia since the anime was aired in the late '90s, but there was never a Russian release of the manga. Fans had to import the English edition, and that's how the name "Alita" became beloved here. At last, nearly twenty years later, we've released an official Russian edition of this masterpiece. It's printed in large format so you can soak in the incredible detail, and we worked hard to make the translation as true as possible to the original. There's no end of enthusiasm for science fiction in Russia, and with the release of the Hollywood movie, Alita's popularity is greater than ever.

С конца 1990-х аниме начало постепенно завоевывать умы русских зрителей. Среди тех немногочисленных вещей, которые мы могли посмотреть по телевидению или в кинотеатрах, прочное место занимал жанр научной фантастики. Увиденное потрясало воображение и не было похоже на мультипликацию, которую снимали до этого в нашей стране. Среди аниме по счастливой случайности оказались и две серии GUNNM, истории девушки-андроида, жившей в жестоком мире будущего. История осталась незавершенной, и чтобы узнать ее финал, немногочисленным счастливчикам приходилось заказывать с иностранных магазинов англоязычное издание. С тех пор, точно так же, как и в США, в умах русских читателей изначальное имя героини Галли закрепилось как Алита. С той поры прошло немало времени, и сейчас, почти 20 лет спустя, русский читатель наконец-то может ознакомиться с шедевром Юкито Кисиро официально. В нашем издании мы постарались максимально ответственно подойти к изначальной авторской задумке, сохранив все оригинальные имена, названия и фразы на немецком, тщательно адаптируя и перерисовывая звуки, а также снабжая каждый том подробными примечаниями, чтобы показать всю глубину, вложенную Юкито Кисиро в свое произведение. Мы также издаем мангу в увеличенном формате, чтобы читатели могли насладиться каждой деталью прекрасного рисунка. За прошедшие годы любовь к научной фантастике в нашей стране ничуть не изменилась, а только окрепла, люди по-прежнему активно покупают проверенную временем классику. Немалое влияние для популяризации GUNNM в России среди нового, подросшего поколения читателей, сыграла и недавняя американская экранизация, где главную героиню опять зовут не Галли, а Алита.

Young characters and steampunk setting, like *Howl's Moving Castle* and *Battle Angel Alita*

Beyond the Clouds © 2018 Nicke / Ki-oon

A boy with a talent for machines and a mysterious girl whose wings he's fixed will take you beyond the clouds! In the tradition of the high-flying, resonant adventure stories of Studio Ghibli comes a gorgeous tale about the longing of young hearts for adventure and friendship!

PERFECT WORLD

Rie Aruga

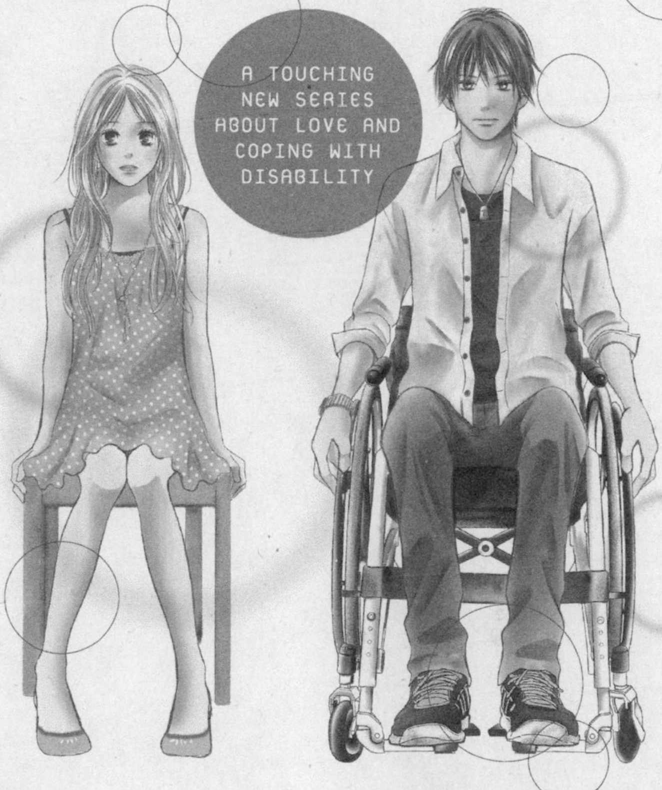

A TOUCHING
NEW SERIES
ABOUT LOVE AND
COPING WITH
DISABILITY

An office party reunites Tsugumi with her high school crush Itsuki. He's realized his dream of becoming an architect, but along the way, he experienced a spinal injury that put him in a wheelchair. Now Tsugumi's rekindled feelings will butt up against prejudices she never considered — and Itsuki will have to decide if he's ready to let someone into his heart...

"Depicts with great delicacy and courage the difficulties some with disabilities experience getting involved in romantic relationships... Rie Aruga refuses to romanticize, pushing her heroine to face the reality of disability. She invites her readers to the same tasks of empathy, knowledge and recognition."
—Slate.fr

"An important entry [in manga romance]... The emotional core of both plot and characters indicates thoughtfulness... [Aruga's] research is readily apparent in the text and artwork, making this feel like a real story."
—Anime News Network

The boys are back, in 400-page hardcovers that are as pretty and badass as they are!

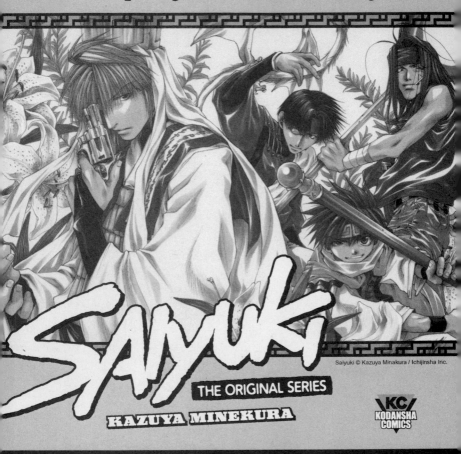

Saiyuki © Kazuya Minakura / Ichijinsha Inc.

SAIYUKI
THE ORIGINAL SERIES
KAZUYA MINEKURA

"AN EDGY COMIC LOOK AT AN ANCIENT CHINESE TALE." —YALSA

Genjo Sanzo is a Buddhist priest in the city of Togenkyo, which is being ravaged by yokai spirits that have fallen out of balance with the natural order. His superiors send him on a journey far to the west to discover why this is happening and how to stop it. His companions are three yokai with human souls. But this is no day trip — the four will encounter many discoveries and horrors on the way.

FEATURES NEW TRANSLATION, COLOR PAGES, AND BEAUTIFUL WRAPAROUND COVER ART!

A SMART, NEW ROMANTIC COMEDY FOR FANS OF *SHORTCAKE CAKE* AND *TERRACE HOUSE*!

A romance manga starring high school girl Meeko, who learns to live on her own in a boarding house whose living room is home to the odd (but handsome) Matsunaga-san. She begins to adjust to her new life away from her parents, but Meeko soon learns that no matter how far away from home she is, she's still a young girl at heart — especially when she finds herself falling for Matsunaga-san.

THE SWEET SCENT OF LOVE IS IN THE AIR! FOR FANS OF OFFBEAT ROMANCES LIKE *WOTAKOI*

Sweat and Soap © Kintetsu Yamada / Kodansha Ltd.

In an office romance, there's a fine line between sexy and awkward... and that line is where Asako — a woman who sweats copiously — meets Koutarou — a perfume developer who can't get enough of Asako's, er, scent. Don't miss a romcom manga like no other!

Something's Wrong With Us

NATSUMI
ANDO

The dark, psychological, sexy shojo series readers have been waiting for!

A spine-chilling and steamy romance between a Japanese sweets maker and the man who framed her mother for murder!

Following in her mother's footsteps, Nao became a traditional Japanese sweets maker, and with unparalleled artistry and a bright attitude, she gets an offer to work at a world-class confectionary company. But when she meets the young, handsome owner, she recognizes his cold stare...

KC KODANSHA COMICS

The adorable new odd-couple cat comedy manga from the creator of the beloved *Chi's Sweet Home*, in full color!

Praise for Chi's Sweet Home

"Nearly impossible to turn away... a true all-ages title that anyone, young or old, cat lover or not, will enjoy. The stories will bring a smile to your face and warm your heart."

~School Library Journal

Sue & Tai-chan

Konami Kanata

Sue is an aging housecat who's looking forward to living out her life in peace... but her plans change when the mischievous black tomcat Tai-chan enters the picture! Hey! Sue never signed up to be a catsitter! *Sue & Tai-chan* is the latest from the reigning meow-narch of cute kitty comics, Konami Kanata.

KC KODANSHA COMICS

Knight *of the* ICE

Yayoi Ogawa

Knight of the Ice ©Yayoi Ogawa

SKATING THRILLS AND ICY CHILLS WITH THIS NEW TINGLY ROMANCE SERIES!

A rom-com on ice, perfect for fans of *Princess Jellyfish* and *Wotakoi*. Kokoro is the talk of the figure-skating world, winning trophies and hearts. But little do they know... he's actually a huge nerd! From the beloved creator of *You're My Pet* (*Tramps Like Us*).

Chitose is a serious young woman, working for the health magazine *SASSO*. Or at least, she would be, if she wasn't constantly getting distracted by her childhood friend, international figure skating star Kokoro Kijinami! In the public eye and on the ice, Kokoro is a gallant, flawless knight, but behind his glittery costumes and breathtaking spins lies a secret: He's actually a hopelessly romantic otaku, who can only land his quad jumps when Chitose is on hand to recite a spell from his favorite magical girl anime!

KC
KODANSHA
COMICS

THE WORLD OF CLAMP!

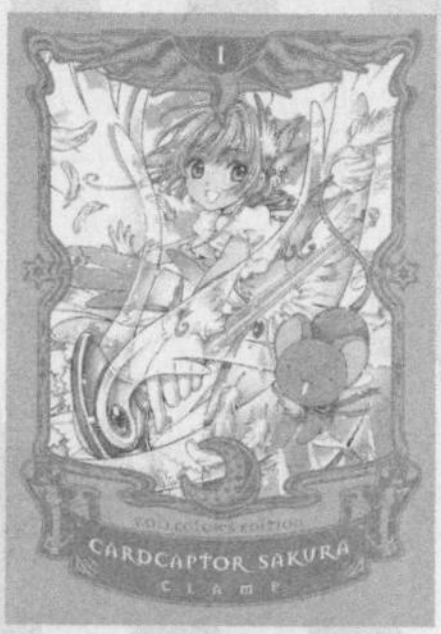
1
CARDCAPTOR SAKURA
CLAMP

Cardcaptor Sakura
Collector's Edition

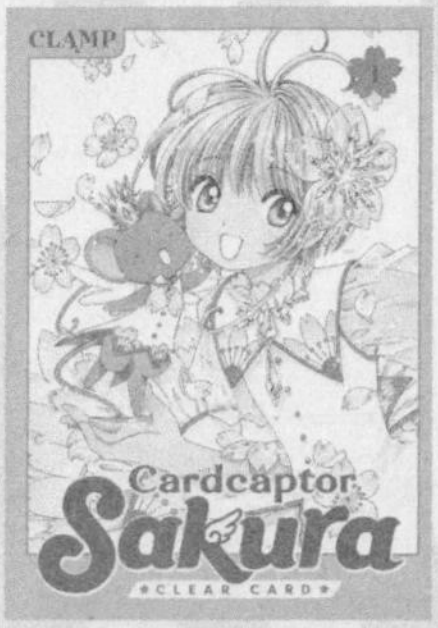
CLAMP
Cardcaptor
Sakura
CLEAR CARD

Cardcaptor Sakura:
Clear Card

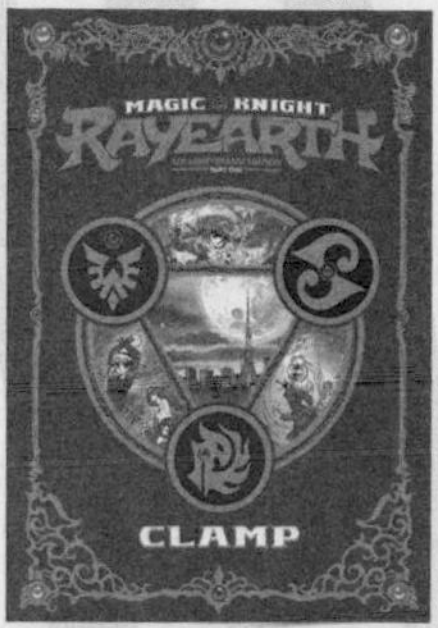
MAGIC KNIGHT
RAYEARTH
CLAMP

Magic Knight Rayearth
25th Anniversary Box Set

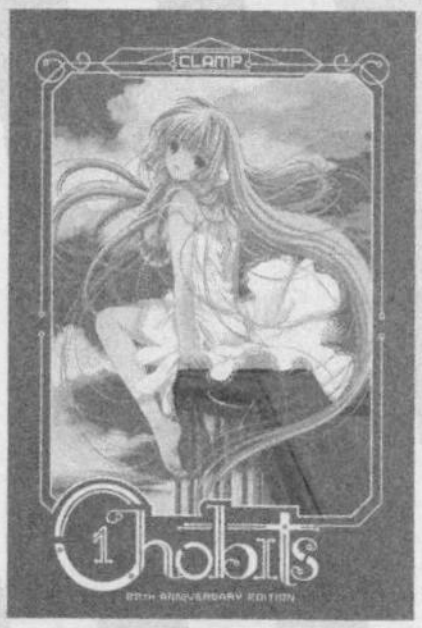
CLAMP
1
Chobits

Chobits

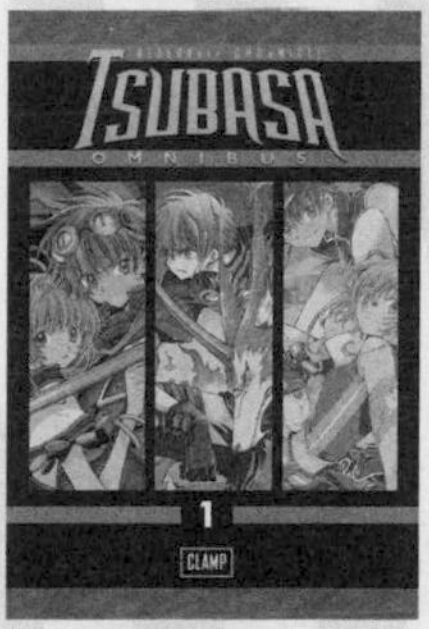
TSUBASA
OMNIBUS
1
CLAMP

TSUBASA Omnibus

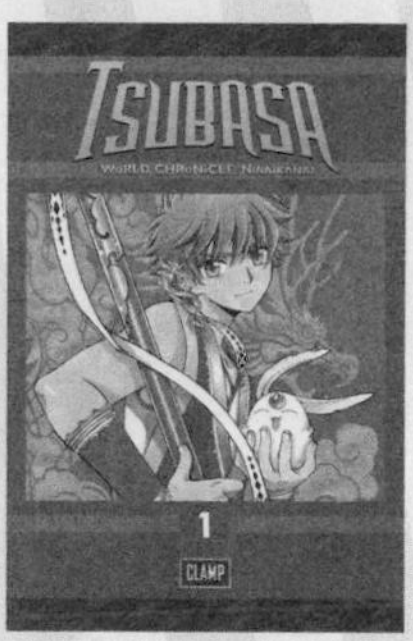
TSUBASA
1
CLAMP

TSUBASA WoRLD CHRoNiCLE

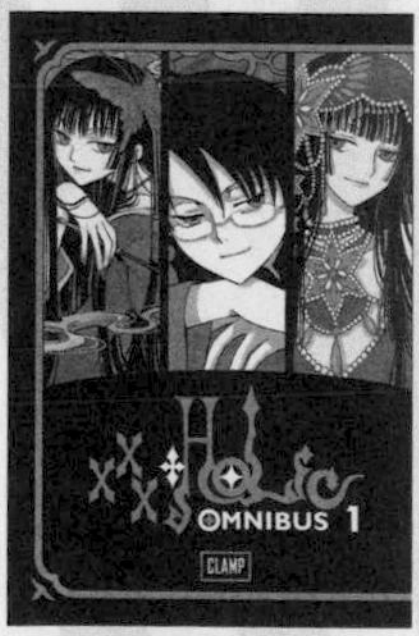
xxxHOLiC
OMNIBUS 1
CLAMP

xxxHOLiC Omnibus

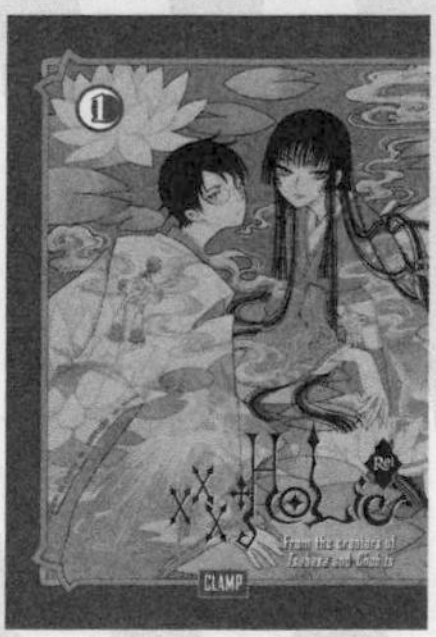
1
xxxHOLiC
CLAMP

xxxHOLiC Rei

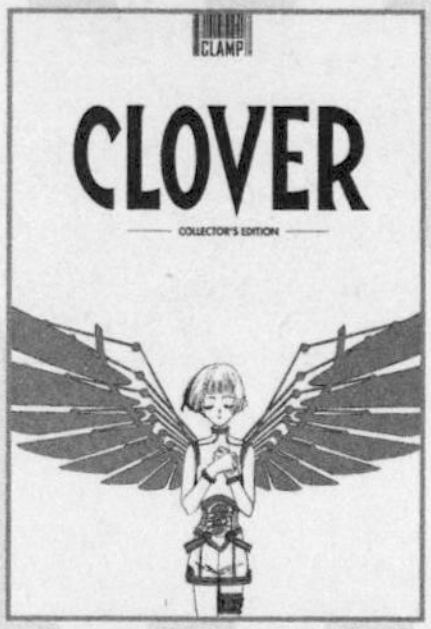
CLAMP
CLOVER
COLLECTOR'S EDITION

CLOVER Collector's Edition

Kodansha Comics welcomes you to explore the expansive world of CLAMP, the all-female artist collective that has produced some of the most acclaimed manga of the century. Our growing catalog includes icons like *Cardcaptor Sakura* and *Magic Knight Rayearth*, each crafted with CLAMP's one-of-a-kind style and characters!

Battle Angel Alita: Mars Chronicle volume 8 is a work of fiction. Names, characters, places, and incidents are the products of the author's imagination or are used fictitiously. Any resemblance to actual events, locales, or persons, living or dead, is entirely coincidental.

A Kodansha Comics Trade Paperback Original

Published in the United States by Kodansha Comics, an imprint of Kodansha USA Publishing, LLC, New York.

Publication rights for this English edition arranged through Kodansha Ltd., Tokyo.

First published in Japan in 2021 by Kodansha Ltd., Tokyo, as *Gunnm: Mars Chronicle*, volume 8.

ISBN 978-1-63236-903-1

Printed in the United States of America.

www.kodansha.us

9 8 7 6 5 4 3 2 1
Translation: Stephen Paul
Lettering: Evan Hayden
Editing: Vanessa Tenazas
Kodansha Comics edition cover design by Phil Balsman

Publisher: Kiichiro Sugawara

Director of publishing services: Ben Applegate
Director of publishing operations: Dave Barrett
Associate director of publishing operations: Stephen Pakula
Publishing services managing editors: Alanna Ruse, Madison Salters
Production managers: Emi Lotto, Angela Zurlo